DI

MOST HOLY VIRGIN

Being an Abridgment of
THE MYSTICAL CITY OF GOD

By
Ven. Mary of Agreda

Abridged by
Fr. Bonaventure Amedeo de Caesarea, M.C.
CONSULTOR OF THE SACRED CONGREGATION OF THE INDEX

Translated from the French of
The Abbé Joseph A. Boullan
DOCTOR IN THEOLOGY

TAN BOOKS AND PUBLISHERS, INC.
Rockford, Illinois 61105

Imprimatur: ✠ James Frederic Wood, D.D.
           Bishop of Philadelphia
           April 25, 1872

Previously published by P. J. Kenedy & Sons, New York, in approximately 1872, under the title *The Life of the Blessed Virgin Mary* or *The Divine Life of the Blessed Virgin Mary*. Retypeset by TAN Books and Publishers, Inc. The type in this book is the property of TAN Books and Publishers, Inc. and, except for brief selections, may not be reproduced without written permission of the publisher. (This restriction applies only to reproduction of this type, not to quotations from the book.) The footnotes herein are from the original 1872 edition, unless otherwise noted.

ISBN 0-89555-596-4

Library of Congress Catalog Card No.: 96-61303

Cover illustration by Heinrich Kaiser.

Printed and bound in the United States of America.

TAN BOOKS AND PUBLISHERS, INC.
P.O. Box 424
Rockford, Illinois 61105
1997

DEDICATION

TO THE DIVINE HEART OF JESUS, TO MARY
IMMACULATE, AND TO THE GLORIOUS ST. JOSEPH.

O Jesus! Only Son of the Eternal Father! Divine
Redeemer of our souls! By choosing the august Mary
from all eternity to be Thy Mother, Thou hast
exalted her far above the Angels, and she has thus
become the cause of our hope.

Word of God, Who hast loved men to excess, to
Whom, if not to Thy Divine Heart, can I worthily
present the offering of *The Divine Life of the Blessed
Virgin Mary?* This book has been the source of great
blessings to the humble translator; for this reason I
dare, although unworthy, supplicate Thee to bless it
anew, so that it may bear abundant fruits of benediction in the souls of its readers. Master of Eternal
Wisdom! make it, as it has already been, a source of
grace in the houses which it shall enter: by it may
the sinner be converted and the just become more
holy. Thus Thou wilt show how pleasing to Thee
are the perfect love and fidelity ever entertained by
the Queen of Heaven, for Thee her perfect Model.

O Mother of the Divine Jesus! Immaculate Virgin and Reparatrix! In thy merciful designs on men,
thou hast deigned to communicate to us, by means
of thy loving daughter and servant, Mary of Jesus of
Agreda, *The Mystical City,* of which I offer thee this

faithful abridgment; then, O Queen of Heaven, refuse
not to bless it. Thou knowest that, overwhelmed by
the infirmities and miseries of my soul, I have turned
towards thee by the impulse of grace. Obtain that
the trials which the publication of this book has
caused me may, by thy powerful intercession, be
changed into sources of great benedictions. In fine,
it is to this "Mystical Life" that I owe the grace of
being numbered among those who are dear to the
Heart of thy Divine Son.

Glorious St. Joseph, whom the august Mary has
permitted me to address as Father, thou knowest
that to thee I owe my life and honor; to thy intercession, also, I am indebted for remaining faithful
to God. Allow me then to place this work in thy
hands. O thou who hast so worthily appreciated the
Queen of Heaven, deign to obtain that the reading of her admirable life may serve as an instrument for the conversion of sinners and the
sanctification of the just.

St. Ann and St. Joachim, worthy parents of the
Queen of Heaven, deign to present to her the humble offering of this book. Obtain also that by your
efficacious intercession, I may receive the grace of
persevering until death in the vocation to which
the Divine Jesus, by the mediation of Mary, has so
gratuitously predestined and called me.

To Mary of Jesus of Agreda, to the seraph, M.
Olier, to St. Teresa, to St. Margaret of Cortona, to
St. Catherine of Siena and to St. Gertrude.

Live Jesus, Mary, Joseph.

—The Abbé J. A. Boullan

CONTENTS

APPROBATIONS

The volume which we offer to the public under the title of *The Divine Life of the Blessed Virgin Mary*, is a faithful abridgment, without change, alteration, or modification of the facts, taken entirely and literally from the celebrated work, *The Mystical City*, by Mary of Jesus of Agreda. Therefore, all the approbations granted to that admirable book may and ought to be applicable to this.

We append a summary of these divers approbations of which we can warrant the authenticity, having copied them from the acts of the process of the beatification and canonization of the above-mentioned servant of God, Mary of Agreda.

1st. Approbation of the Ordinary of the diocese wherein the servant of God died in the odor of sanctity, and also of the bishop of the place where the work was printed. The bishops are, as we all know, according to the canon law, the first judges of books published within their jurisdiction.

2nd. Approbation of the learned tribunal of the Inquisition in Spain, which, having examined the book word for word, authorized its publication and diffusion among the faithful.

3rd. Approbation of theologians of all religious bodies, Benedictines, Carmelites, Dominicans and

Jesuits, called upon to examine the work. They have eulogized it in the highest terms and recommended it as the fruit of the Spirit of God.

4th. Approbation of the most celebrated universities of foreign lands, Salamanca, Louvain, Toulouse, etc., which after the most minute examinations have declared that the book contains nothing against faith or morals; they have exalted it immeasurably, as Pope Benedict XIV expresses it in his decree of 1748. The University of Paris alone is an exception, because it was, at that time, tainted with Jansenism, to which this work is so adverse.

5th. In fine, Pope Innocent XI, after having placed this work on the Index, August 4th, 1681, *because,* said the postulator of the cause of canonization, *of the contests which it had raised,* withdrew it himself three months later, November 9, 1681. This last decree has the force of a universal law of the Church, for in 1713, a bishop having forbidden the reading of this work, the Holy Office declared his prohibition null and obliged him to retract it, as being contrary to the decree of November 9, 1681, *which decree,* said the Sacred Congregation, *has the power of a law throughout the universal Church.* We know it is the same in our days. Alexander VIII authorized the reading of this work *oraculo vivae vocis.* In 1704 Clement IX forbade it to be placed on the Index, and it would be vain to seek for it among the forbidden books.

And in fine, in 1729, with the approbation of Benedict XIII of happy memory, the Sacred Congregation of Rites published a decree which permits the faithful to read and retain it without any other examination. Therefore he who, whatever may be his title, honor, or dignity, presumes to forbid the reading of this work, authorized by the Holy See, would be obliged to retract, even publicly, if necessary.

Thus the cause is decided; pious Reader, accept the book and read it without fear, for Rome, which cannot fail in its examination of doctrine, has spoken.

INTRODUCTION
TO THE SECOND EDITION

Among the pious faithful of the present day there is a holy desire to know everything that may concern the Blessed Virgin Mary, whom God predestined to be the Mother of the Eternal Word, who was to become incarnate for the salvation of men. It seems to us that many souls having an ardent devotion to the august Queen of Heaven will rejoice to read a work which contains a faithful, minute and complete relation of her marvelous life. Therefore, we are well assured of the welcome which this Life will receive from pious Catholics, who justly glory in living in the age of Mary. What a sweet joy shall it be for children devoted to the august Mother to know that which constitutes the glory and grandeur of the incomparable Queen of Angels and men!

According to the designs of His divine providence, God did not manifest all the ineffable mysteries of the life of the august Mary during the first ages of the Church. In fact, it was but right that the law of grace should be established and the Gospel of Christ promulgated before the faithful should learn the grandeur, glory, titles and prerogatives of her who was raised above the Angels. The holy Evangelists themselves were compelled to be silent concerning many of these ineffable mysteries. The human mind is so weak and ignorant that the manifestation of those mysteries, at a time when the faith and doctrine of the Incarnation were not fully established, would have occasioned much trouble and difficulty. The august Queen of Heaven made this known to her beloved daughter, Mary of Jesus of Agreda, in order to explain to her why she had been chosen by God to make known to the faithful the secret mysteries communicated to her. We will quote the words addressed by the Blessed Virgin to the seraphic servant of God. It is important that they should be read with the utmost attention.

"I see, my daughter, that thou art astonished that the Evangelists have not written the wonderful things which the Most High operated in my regard. I answer (and desire that my words be engraven on the hearts of all men) that I myself ordered the Evangelists to write of me only that which was necessary to establish the articles of faith, and the precepts of the law of grace. As Mistress of the Church and from the inspirations of the Most High, I knew it was not proper to reveal more at the first foundation of the Church.

"All my prerogatives were included in my dignity of Mother of God, and in what had been said of me, that I was *'full of grace.'* But the manifestation of all that remained hidden was reserved by Divine Providence for a suitable time, when the faith would be more firmly established. It is true that, even from the beginning, the Church has announced some of the mysteries which concern me, but the revelation in its fullness has been made to thee, although a vile creature, because of the wants of the world in its present unhappy state. For this reason, the Divine Mercy has willed to give to men so efficacious a means *(as this work)* that they may seek their remedy and eternal salvation through my intercession." (*Mystical City*, II., p. 5-6, chap. 28).

Before His glorious Ascension, the Divine Jesus spoke to the one hundred and twenty persons assembled by Divine Providence to be witnesses of that sacred mystery. They were, in one sense, the entire Church, to whom the Divine Master left His last instructions regarding His Blessed Mother.

"My dear children," said He, "I return to My Father, from whom I came to save and redeem men. In My stead, I leave you My Mother, who will be your protectress, your advocate, your consoler and your mother.

"Listen to her counsels, and obey her. As I have already told you, whoever will see Me will also see My Father, and whoever will know Me will also know Him. In the same manner I assure you that he who will know My Mother will also know Me; he who will hear her will hear Me; he who will obey her will obey Me; he who will offend her will offend Me, and he that will honor her will honor Me. You and all those who will come after you shall acknowledge her for your Mother, and when you seek Me, you shall find Me in her." (Part II, book

6, chap. 18). As He thus spoke, He looked at His most holy Mother and revealed to her that He was about to command all those there assembled to honor her by the worship[1] due to her as Mother of God, and even to make it a precept of the Church. But the humble Queen begged her Divine Son to allow the sacred worship to be addressed to Himself alone, that it might serve for the propagation of the Gospel and the exaltation of His name.

Our Saviour granted her prudent prayer, but reserved to Himself the right of making her known at the proper time. Who among faithful Catholics can doubt that this is clearly the chosen time reserved by God for the manifestation of Mary's glory? It is of the greatest importance that we who live in this happy time should listen to the words of our Divine Saviour, addressed to the children of His Church. It is our duty to have recourse to the august Queen of Heaven and to glorify her, that we may fulfill the designs of the Most High and save our souls.

It seems to us incontestable and it is an opinion widely spread and universally admitted, that the epoch is near at hand when the Church will be extended over the entire earth. But all those who believe this are also convinced that it will be granted only through Mary. She is the Mediatrix near the Sovereign Mediator, and her powerful intercession shall be experienced by all the chil-

---

1. See explanation on page xxiii, paragraph 2.—*Publisher,* 1997.

dren of men. If this be true, who does not perceive the necessity of making known her titles, her grandeur, her perfections, in a word, all the hidden mysteries of the Queen of Heaven? *The Divine Life* is the only work calculated to effect this; hence it is important that it be read with attention, and diffused as widely as possible, in order to correspond to the designs of God and His Church. We take the liberty of speaking thus, because the book is not the fruit of our labor, but was communicated by the Blessed Virgin herself to her faithful daughter and servant, the Ven. Mary of Jesus of Agreda. Our eulogiums are then addressed to the true author of this *Divine Life*—to the august Mary herself, who has deigned to give it to her children.

The success which attended the first edition is to us a certain proof that this work has been appreciated and has been productive of good among souls.

Six thousand copies of any work could not have been sold in so short a space of time, unless it was valued, esteemed and truly sought after. In order to respond to the confidence reposed in us, we have scrupulously revised our first translation, so that our words might be the faithful expression of the authentic text.

We cannot cite the number of letters we have received, felicitating us on the happy idea communicated to us of publishing the Mystical Life. They have been the sources of great consolation to us, for, at the first appearance of the book, Hell found means to raise strong opposition against it, from persons little enlightened with regard to the designs of Satan, who sought to have this work discredited: *qui non cognoverunt altitudines satanae*—"who have not known the depths of Satan" (*Apoc.* 2:24). The publication of the documents and authentic decrees of the Holy See in favor of the work of Mary of Jesus of Agreda, which may be read in the notice preceding this work, will no doubt contribute to the dissipation of all doubts.

We must also say that if Satan has found accomplices so blind as to seek to bring discredit on this life, the Queen of Heaven has also raised devoted souls to defend and propagate it. We most cordially testify our gratitude to the Delegate of the Holy Apostolic See in France, who has encouraged us both by word and authority. How many pious servants of Mary have become ardent propagators of this *Divine Life*, being undeterred by any human consideration! They have merited a large share of the great blessings of which this book is the fruitful source. We entertain the sweet confidence that all those also, who glory in loving Mary, will zealously contribute to the propagation of this book, so useful for the good of souls.

Our age, which so justly glories in the name of the "Age of Mary," should be anxious to learn the hidden mysteries of the august Queen of Heaven, which God has been pleased to reveal to us, after having reserved them for our time. Let us then cease to occupy ourselves inordinately with the inventions of modern science, in order to lend an attentive ear to the marvels of grace which God has operated in Mary. In them we will find the way of salvation, and the means of escaping the cruel ravages which pride works among men.

This work, we must say, is better suited to persons of great piety and consecrated by the vows of religion than to persons of the world. Nevertheless, these last will not read it without fruit; its perusal always awakens in the soul a greater confidence and love towards Mary. This is the unanimous testimony of all those who have read it impartially and under the guidance of the Spirit of God.

We believe we may affirm that by the doctrine of the works of Mary of Agreda are to be formed the great Saints who are soon to appear in the Church. Thus, with good authority, the venerable Grignon De Montfort says: "The happy time and age of Mary will soon arrive, when souls, losing themselves in the abyss of the interior of the Queen of Heaven, will become living copies of Mary, in loving and glorifying Jesus Christ."

Then shall be verified the following words: *Ut adveniat regnum tuum, adveniat regnum Mariae*—May the reign of Mary arrive, that the reign of Jesus Christ may also arrive.

Here we must quote the words of the pious and learned M. Emery, with regard to the works of Mary of Agreda. Towards the end of his long life, speaking of the works of this seraphic servant of God, he said: "It was only after having read and meditated on them, that I understood the wise recommendation of our founder, M. Olier, 'Study the interior of Jesus in Mary.'"

The solemn definition of the Immaculate Con-

ception as a dogma of Faith, has, besides, answered
every pretext that could be alleged against the *Divine
Life*. If we were not confined within the circum-
scribed limits of a preface, we would demonstrate
to our readers how the Bull, *Ineffabilis Deus*, is but
the solemn and authentic echo of the doctrine contained in the incomparable works of Mary of Jesus
of Agreda. But the incontestable proof in favor of
those writings is the sanctity of their author. Therefore it is a great consolation to us to be able to
announce that the cause of the beatification and
canonization of the Venerable Mother Mary of
Agreda is to be resumed and continued. We shall
then, we fondly trust, have the happiness of venerating on our altars her whom the Church has
already declared Venerable.

Before concluding, we feel it our duty to make
known in a few words the pious author of this
abridgment of *The Mystical City* by Mary of Jesus
of Agreda, under the title of *The Divine Life of the
Blessed Virgin Mary*.

The Rev. P. Bartholomew of Caesarea was an eminent theologian, and his writings, so highly
esteemed by scientific men, are evident proofs of
his great learning. He was Consulter of the Sacred
Roman Congregation of the Index, which title is
granted only to men of profound learning and well-
tried faith in doctrine. *The Divine Life* is considered
in Rome to be a true masterpiece.[2]

---

2. Many abridgments of the *The Mystical City* have already been
published. We have before us that of the learned Francis-

Our readers are now acquainted with the motives which have led us to publish this work. Our wish is to aid as much as in our power, in making the august Mary, our divine Mother, known, loved, blessed and glorified. May this object be accomplished according to the desire of our hearts!

To prevent all objections, we declare, in conclusion, that the words *to adore, divine,* and similar expressions to be found in this work are to be taken in a relative sense, and not in that in which they are applied to God. St. Thomas teaches that we may use them in this sense, and after the "Angel of the Schools," we have not hesitated to employ them.

We submit our writings to the judgment of the Holy Apostolic See, for we are submissive children of the Holy Roman Church, to which we have vowed obedience and love.

---

can, Ximenes Samaniego, which is also a masterpiece. We have used it to establish the authenticity of the text which we have translated. That which we now give to the public seems the best of all; for this reason, we have chosen it.

NOTICE ON THE WORKS OF THE VENERABLE MARY OF JESUS OF AGREDA

By The Abbé J. A. Boullan, D.D.

Among the holy souls of past centuries who have been loaded with signal favors and privileges by the Queen of Heaven, we must, without doubt, place in the first rank Mary of Jesus, often styled of Agreda, from the name of the place in Spain where she passed her life. The celebrated J. Goerres, in his monumental work, *Mysticism,* fears not to cite as an example the life of Mary of Agreda, in a chapter entitled, "The Culminating Point of Christian Mysticism." Indeed, there could be found no more perfect model of the highest mystic ways. Her life is a striking example, in which it is important to study attentively the progress of a soul which, according to the words of the prophet, ascends by degrees to the height of perfection: *ibunt de virtute in virtutem*—goes from virtue to virtue.

A powerful motive makes it a duty for us to publish a rather lengthy notice on Mary of Agreda. We wish to call the attention of our readers to so important a work as *The Mystical City,* of which *The Divine Life,* which we publish, is a faithful abridgment.

We hesitate not to acknowledge that there is in France much prejudice against the venerable Mary of Agreda and her works. Men, swayed by the power of unfounded prejudice, have assailed this pure memoir and forbidden the reading of her works. For more than seven years we have pursued our researches on this subject and have been successful in finding irrefutable documents regarding it.

In one of the libraries of Paris we have discovered the acts of the process of canonization of this servant of God. It is on the authority of these incontestable writings that we will proceed; thus we hope to close the debate upon this question.

There are divine and supernatural gifts so marvelous that, were it not for the authority of the Church and the holy Doctors, we would be tempted to doubt them. But doubt can only be the effect of ignorance or bad faith, and neither the one nor the other can justify man at the tribunal of his conscience, any more than at that of God.

The God of mercy grants to some souls those privileges known under the name of "clear, distinct and precise words, or supernatural expressions"; that is, He deigns to speak to them either directly and immediately from Himself, or by the ministry of Angels, as is more generally the case.

Sometimes it is God the Father, at others Our Lord, or the august Mother of God, or, as more rarely happens, some of the Saints, who consent to speak to souls raised to a particular degree of contemplation. St. Teresa, whose authority on these matters is indisputable, because of the approbation with which the Church has stamped her writings, treats of this question in *The Interior Castle* (sixth mansion, chap. 3). "God," says she, "makes the soul feel His presence by various means. He causes her to hear words in different ways; sometimes they seem to come from the exterior, sometimes from the interior. Some seem to proceed from the superior part of the soul, while others are so exterior, that we hear them with our ears."

Alvarez de Paz adds that "they sometimes seem to come from the center of the heart"—*Interdum ex ipso penetrali cordis assurgere.* (Vol. 3, Book 5, chap. 6). The seraphic Saint explains the means for distinguishing the origin of these words, for they may proceed from the imagination, from the devil or from God.

"When God speaks to us," says she, "He suddenly hushes all other thoughts that we may be attentive to what He says, and it is less in our power to be deaf to His voice than for a person of very acute hearing not to hear what is uttered in a loud tone.

"When God speaks, it is impossible for the soul to close her ears or think of anything but of what she hears.

"May my explanations," continues she, "regarding the divine words, and the few admonitions which I have given, be useful to those souls whom the Divine Master may honor with these favors."

Suarez, in whom we hear all the Doctors, explains the manner in which this is operated.

Examining the manner in which the Angels communicate their thoughts to each other, he applies it to the souls to whom God grants this gift. (*Suarez,* Part 2d, Book 2, chap. 27).

Scaramelli, in his *Directorio Mystico*, treats of this sublime subject *ex professo* and, having for his basis the doctrine of the great Fathers, develops this matter under every point of view. (*Tract 4*, chap. 14-15).

We must add that all the servants of God who hear these supernatural and heavenly words sometimes behold under corporeal forms the heavenly personages who pronounce them; at other times, they hear without seeing. What we have said will suffice to draw the attention of clergymen and induce them to study these marvels of grace. In view of the phenomena of magnetism and neo-spiritualism which now inundate the world, they will be able the more readily to distinguish truth from error; they will clearly discern the snares which the enemy, the angel of darkness, has laid for men, even from the beginning of the world, by leading them to reject all that is supernatural or by plunging them in the gross deceits in which he involves the unfortunate adepts in his dark doctrines.

Let us examine first whether anyone, no matter with what authority he may be vested, is allowed to forbid the reading of the works of Mary of Agreda.

Secondly, whether it is true to say that the reading of them is permitted, and that we have nothing to fear from the doctrine taught in them.

Regarding the first point, our task is very easy. Eleven years after the appearance of this work, after it had been translated into Italian, discussions concerning it were immediately raised. The tribunal of the Holy Office, "on account of the state of the times," to quote the words of the postulator of the cause of the canonization of Mary of Agreda, passed a decree of prohibition on the 4th of August, 1681.

But God, who knows how to draw good from evil, allowed this prohibition to serve for the greater triumph of these works.

Three months afterwards, on November 9, 1681, the decree was revoked. Happily, we can give our readers the authentic text of the decree which declares the suspension of the first. It is extracted from the process of the cause for canonization.

INNOCENTIUS PAPA XII

In negotio librorum sanctimonialis Mariae a Jesus de Agreda supersedendum duximus, quamvis sacrae hujus inquisitionis ratio et stylus aliter suaderent. Datum Romae, sub annulo piscatoris, 9 Nov. 1681.

POPE INNOCENT XII

"With regard to the books of the holy nun, Mary of Jesus of Agreda, we have thought best to suspend our judgment, although the custom and manner of the sacred Inquisition would suggest otherwise.

"Given in Rome, under the ring of the Fisherman, this ninth day of November, 1681."

The reader will, no doubt, ask what is the power

of this last decree, and if it truly has the character of an obligatory law in the universal Church. In answer to this, we have only to refer to the general teachings of the Doctors. The sovereign authority has decided the question; on this matter the slightest doubt, the least discussion, is no longer allowed. In 1713 the Holy Office published a decree in which the Bishop of C—— is ordered to conform to the suspensive decree of Innocent XII, and not again to forbid to anyone the reading of the works of Mary of Agreda.

We subjoin it as follows:

DECREE OF THE HOLY OFFICE

"In the congregation held Sept. 19th, 1713, at which were present their Eminences Cardinals Acciaioli, Spada, Fabroni, and Ottoboni, it was resolved that the letter of the Inquisitor of C—— should be withdrawn, and that the suspensive decree has the power of law throughout the universal Church."

The original is preserved in the Convent of Ara Coeli in Rome.

1st. Thus it is true to say that no one is allowed to forbid the reading of these works.

2d. By permission of Divine Providence, the Holy See has done more than protect the works of Mary of Agreda against her adversaries; it has formally permitted the reading of them.

Pope Alexander VIII, of happy memory, was prevented by death from giving a decree, but he expressly authorized the reading of them, *oracula vivae vocis*. In fine, the Sacred Congregation of Rites, under Benedict XIII, passed a decree as follows:

"It is ordered that the cause of the said servant of God shall be continued without any re-examination of 'The Mystical City,' and her works may be kept and read. March 14th, 1729."

This decree is signed by Benedict XIII.

The tribunal of the Holy See having definitively judged the cause, the reader will no longer hesitate to edify himself by the doctrine of the works of this servant of God.

We may pass over the clamor raised against this book by the partisans of Satan, as our cause has been judged.

Having cited the authentic decrees of the court of Rome, we come now to the eulogiums given to these works. About a year ago, was found in the Imperial Library a collection of the correspondence of Mary of Agreda with Philip IV of Spain. These letters have been published in one volume by M. Vaton.

M. Germond de Lavigne, speaking of *The Mystical City*, says: "We have read this wonderful book, this treatise *ex professo* of the celebrated ascetic, and can only say with the Doctors who have edited it that the mysteries of the Christian religion, principles of the Catholic Church, the most abstruse texts of Holy Scripture, confused computations of evangelical history, the most hidden decrees of Divine Providence, of theology, sacred, dogmatic, expositive, scholastic, moral, deliberative, mystic, all are united in it."

We will now repeat briefly the words of the most competent judges of these matters. F. Anthony, surnamed the Very Celebrated Doctor, says: "This book has delighted me. Every word of it is clear and full of life; in a word, the reading of it raises the mind, inflames the heart and excites to great devotion."

F. Andreas Mendo, of the Society of Jesus, says: "The whole work is a continuous light which illumines the intellect and a flame which kindles the will; it banishes tepidity, and incites to the practice of virtue. He who reads it carefully cannot fail to be instructed and feel an ardent desire of becoming a saint."

F. Dydace de Sylva, a Benedictine, says: "The reading of this book is very profitable; it has an admirable and efficacious power to persuade. All that can be said of it falls far short of the truth. When we begin to read, we are filled with admiration. I feel with regret that it would require the wisdom of an Angel to adequately express my wishes, my thoughts and my veneration with regard to it."

F. John of the Mother of God says: "I have been so happy as to receive this book; it fills me with admiration. All in it causes me to think that the author has been illumined with light from above. It will bring great consolation to the faithful."

The most renowned and celebrated universities have extolled this admirable work. We will omit the testimonies of the universities of Madrid, Alcala, Salamanca and Toulouse, which leave nothing to be desired, and will only cite that of Louvain, which says: "The learned and the ignorant can gather admirable fruits from this book; the faithful may read it without fear of danger to faith or morals. There is nothing contained in it that tends to relaxation of virtue or to any indiscreet rigor. While reading it, we feel a special grace which is not experienced in reading others; the more we study it, the greater become our appreciation and pleasure."

The Ordinary of the place in which Mary of Agreda dwelt says in his approbation: "I conclude by saying that this work is truly good; that, without the least doubt, it contains a heavenly doctrine, which we find to be solid, strong, true and conformable to the Gospel, which leads to the true knowledge of God and the most pure Virgin Mary, Mother of God, and excites to the love of virtue and the horror of sin."

In his beautiful introduction, Father Laurent speaks of Mary of Agreda as follows: "At thirty-five years of age, in one of her ecstatic visions, she receives from Heaven the order to write the history of the Mother of God. Through humility she declines the honor, thinking herself unworthy; she seeks to avoid that mission which she judges herself incapable of accomplishing, but the will of the Lord being clearly manifested, she obeys as a sub-

xxxiv   The Divine Life of the Most Holy Virgin

missive daughter, and writes that admirable book *The Mystical City*. Divine inspiration is impressed on every page. Reading it we become convinced that it was only in the heavenly regions into which she was ravished, that she could have acquired the knowledge of the most sublime mysteries, the revelation of the most adorable and ineffable designs of the Most High on the august Mary.

"It is under the direction of Mary that she retraces the history of the mortal life of the Queen of Heaven, so that this work, written by a poor girl, destitute of human or acquired science and living in the obscurity of the cloister, is, perhaps, the most extraordinary and astonishing which has ever come from the hand of a human creature. The author unhesitatingly touches on the highest mysteries of religion, and explains them with rare clearness. She develops without embarrassment, and with wonderful facility, Catholic dogma and the most difficult passages of the Scriptures; sacred chronology is as familiar to her as to the most eminent doctors; she reveals the most hidden ways of Providence; sacred theology, sublime philosophy, knowledge of natural sciences, persuasive eloquence, all are found there, even to neatness, correctness, sublimity, strength and elegance of style." (*Introduction to the Life of the Ven. M. Mary of Agreda*, p. 16, 17).

We dwell purposely on the works of this servant of God. In our opinion, *The Mystical City* is, not only as F. Laurent says, "the most extraordinary and astonishing book which has ever been written by a human creature," but it appears to us to be manifestly designed, in the views of Divine Providence, to produce great fruits for the sanctification and high perfection of souls in these latter times. But the servant of God, or rather God Himself and the august Queen of Heaven, by her organ, will reveal the designs of God with regard to this book and will manifest to us why it has been given to the world. It is in particular the priest, devoted to Mary, whom we ask to meditate on the following.

The Most High, addressing the servant of God, said to her:

"My daughter, when I sent My only Son into the world, men, except the small number who served Me, were in the most deplorable state they had ever been. And as in time of deepest misery I show My greatest mercy, so I will now grant to men a new favor, because the proper time has arrived. In order the more to confound them, this is the time when My mercy shall shine, and in which I desire that My love may not be idle, notwithstanding that this is the most unhappy age of the world since the Incarnation of the Word. I desire to give to men a sovereign remedy, by which, if they wish to use it, they may receive My grace; those who find it shall be happy, those who will know its value shall not be less so. I will that men should know the worth of the intercession of her who brought the remedy to their sins, when in her virginal womb she gave mortality to the Immortal. I will discover to them many of the marvels which My power has operated on Mary in her quality of Mother in My Incarnate

Son; marvels which, by My secret judgment, have been hidden until now.

"I did not manifest them to the primitive Church, because they contain mysteries so high and sublime that the faithful would have paused to search and admire them, when it was necessary to establish the law of grace, and to publish the Gospel. And although this would not have been incompatible, nevertheless, men, so blind and ignorant, might have been perplexed at a time when faith in the Incarnation was yet feeble, and the precepts of the New Law as yet in their infancy.

"I present to them this Mystical City of refuge (the Mother of Mercy); describe and explain it as well as thy weakness will allow.

"I do not wish this to be considered as merely an opinion, or a simple vision, but as a constant and certain truth."

In order to avoid unnecessary discussion, we will explain these last words.

We know and acknowledge with all the Doctors that the Church never gives absolute authority to the particular revelations vouchsafed to some privileged souls. By her *approbation* she merely permits us to believe that, probably, they have been inspired by God. If, however, the faithful have sufficient motives to believe that they come from God, there is nothing to prevent them from admitting them, and giving in their adhesion. Those who have reason to doubt are not required to believe, on condition, however, that they neither blame nor condemn those who believe them according to the approbation of the Church, which is the supreme judge in these matters.

"One day, the feast of the Immaculate Conception, being in the choir for Matins, I heard a voice which demanded of me renewed attention for heavenly things. I was then raised from that state to another more sublime, wherein I beheld the throne of the Divinity radiant with immense glory and majesty. From it proceeded a voice, which, it seemed to me, could be heard throughout the entire universe, saying: 'Poor, abandoned, ignorant sinners, great and small, sick and weak, and all the children of Adam, of whatever state, condition, or sex you may be; prelates, princes, and subjects, all over the entire world, come and seek a remedy from My liberality and infinite providence, through the intercession of her who gave humanity to the Word.'

"After having heard this voice from the throne, I saw four globes coming forth from the Divine Being, which diffused a brilliant light over the four quarters of the world.[1] It was revealed to me that in these latter ages, the same Lord wished to exalt and spread the glory of His most holy Mother, and manifest to the world hidden miracles and mysteries reserved by Divine Providence for the time of greatest necessity, so that we may all avail ourselves of the help, the protection and the powerful inter-

----

1. We believe that by these symbols were designated four religious bodies which are to appear in the "Age of Mary."

cession of our august Queen. I then saw, coming out of the abyss, a formidable dragon which had seven heads; accompanied by many others, it traveled over all the earth, seeking and perverting persons, by whose means it might oppose the intentions of the Lord and prevent the glory of Mary and the benefits which, by her means, were to be conferred on the world.

"This vision of the infernal dragons caused in me the greatest sorrow. I understood that the victory would be strongly contested, but as reason, justice, and power are on the side of our Queen, there is nothing to fear. Nevertheless, men, by their malice, may hinder the great designs of God." (*Mystical City*, vol. 8, p. 377. Brussel's edition).

The servant of God continues: "Let holy priests, who are devoted to the glory of the august Mary, deign to pay great attention to the following:

"On another occasion, I found myself in great affliction, as was but just, on account of my not knowing if I had written well this sacred history, the sublimity of which surpasses all comprehension, angelic as well as human. Whilst thinking thus, I was drawn into a higher state, in which I beheld the throne of the Most Holy Trinity, the three Divine Persons, and the Blessed Virgin at the right hand of her Divine Son; all were vested with immense glory.

"There was profound silence in Heaven. The Angels and Saints seemed attentive to what was transpiring at the throne of Supreme Majesty. I beheld the Person of the Father, taking as if from the bosom of His infinite and immutable Being, a book, beautiful and enriched beyond human imagination, but it was closed. Giving it to the Incarnate Word, He said: 'This book and its contents are Mine; it is very agreeable to Me.' Our Lord received it with great complaisance; and the Divine Word and the Holy Ghost, having touched Their breasts with it, confirmed the same words and placed it in the hands of the most pure Mary, who received it with incomparable joy.

"Then this great Queen called me and said, 'Do you wish to know what this book is? Be attentive and look.' The kind Mother opened and presented it to me, that I might read. I did so, and found it was the history of her most holy life, written in the same order, and with the same chapters as mine, under the title of 'The Mystical City.'"

During the past six years we have had the joy and consolation of perusing and re-perusing this work, always with new increase of faith and edification to our soul. We know that some religious bodies make use of it for their spiritual reading. A Carmelite prioress, who had read it during twenty years, told us that, at the commencement of her religious life, she had not understood the doctrine contained in it, but it soon became as a heavenly manna, with which she could not be satiated. A superioress of the Ladies of the Sacred Heart has said that the book was really her treasure; she could not cease to read it, such abundant fruit had she drawn from it for the salvation of her soul. In fine, our readers will permit us to relate a fact which happened a short time ago. A sick man had received the last Sacraments with a fervor that edified all present. After the ceremony, raising himself in the bed, he called the priest and presented to him this book, saying, "Keep this: it has edified me during life; I do not wish it to be lost. Give it to someone, that it may prove for him the same source of benediction."

We know the clergyman, the place, and the time of this occurrence, and to us it seems a most perfect eulogy on a book.

In order to remove all that might embarrass the reader, we will say that the *Historical Dictionary* of Moreri, speaking of this book, says that it is filled with visions, fables and reveries which the author gives as revelations. This appreciation has been based on the censure of Paris in 1696, a censure which is declared by Amort, the greatest adversary of Mary of Agreda, to be without foundation. From the edition of this dictionary printed in 1712, this falsehood has passed into many other books, among the number, that of Feller, in which we pointed it out to the editors. Everyone knows that dictionaries are often copied from preceding ones. J. Goerres in his *Mysticism* does not value this work as it deserves, but as he was no theologian, his authority is of little account.

We give below a succinct summary of the acts for the cause of the beatification and canonization in favor of Mary of Jesus of Agreda. The reader can see that God has been pleased to manifest the glory and sanctity of His servant, declared by the Church "Venerable," and who will be, we hope, placed on our altars before many years.

She died on the 24th of May, 1665, on the day of Pentecost. Shortly afterwards, the process of the Ordinary was drawn up on the virtues and miracles in general of the *fama sanctitatis*. The petition for her canonization was offered November 21, 1671. Clement X introduced the cause on the 24th of August, 1672. The commission of introduction was signed January 28, 1673. The decree of *non-culte* was carried on June 27, 1674. The apostolic process on the sanctity, the virtues and miracles in general was begun on September 2, 1679. The process was opened, the servant of God declared Venerable, and, in fine, on the 16th of December, 1689, a committee of consulters was named by Innocent XI for the examination of the works. In fine, Clement XIV declared that the book, *The Mystical City,* really was written by Mary of Agreda. At this time steps are being taken to reopen the cause, and we trust that in the "Age of Mary" the servant of God will receive the supreme honors of beatification and canonization, which will fill up the measure of her glory in this world.

THE
DIVINE LIFE
OF THE
MOST HOLY VIRGIN

Chapter 1

THE MOST HOLY VIRGIN IN THE
DIVINE COUNSELS—HER HOLY PARENTS.

Before we begin to write the admirable life of the Mother of God, it is necessary to make known the sublime rank which, from all eternity, she held in the divine counsels.

Although the Divine Intelligence, one, indivisible and very simple, conceives and decides on an act in an infinitely simple manner, without relation to time, either past or future, nevertheless, according to our manner of understanding, we distinguish different moments.

1. From all eternity God knew His attributes and perfections, with an infinite inclination to communicate Himself exteriorly, as the infinite, sovereign Good.

2. He decreed to make this exterior communication of Himself by the participation and manifestation of His grandeurs.

3. He determined the order, manner and disposition of this communication, decreeing that the Divine Word should become visible in His Sacred Humanity.

4. He decreed the gifts and graces to be con-

ferred on the Divine Humanity of Christ, the Chief of all creatures. Then, regulating the perfect economy of the Incarnation, He included the Virgin Mother, before all other decrees relating to the creation of all other creatures. God also determined to create a place where the Incarnate Word could dwell with His Mother, and first, for them alone, He willed to create Heaven and earth, with the stars, the elements, and all that they contain; and, secondly, for men, who were to be the vassals of this great King and Queen.

5. He decreed the creation of the Angels, who were to dwell in the presence of the Divine Majesty, to honor and to love Him; they were also to serve the Eternal Word, made man, and His most holy Mother, their Queen. To this moment belongs the creation of the empyreal Heaven, where the glory of God is unveiled and the good are rewarded; as also the predestination of the good Angels, and the reprobation of the bad; the creation of the earth for other creatures, and Hell in its center, for the chastisement of the rebellious angels.

6. He decreed to create a people and a society of men like unto Christ, who were to be His brethren. God determined on the favors and graces He would grant to this people, through the merits of Christ, and on giving original justice to man, if he would persevere in it. He foresaw the prevarication and fall of Adam and, through him, that of all his posterity, excepting only the Blessed Mother, who was not included in this posterior decree. He decreed that this misfortune should be repaired, and

that the humanity of Christ should be passible.

For the execution of His designs, in time God created Heaven and earth, and the light, not only material, but also intellectual light, that is to say, the Angels. At the division of light from darkness occurred also the separation of the good Angels from the bad.

The Angels remained for some time in a state of trial, which may be divided into three moments. In the first, they were created and endowed with gifts of nature and grace; in the second, the will of their Creator was proposed for them to follow, and obtain the end for which they had been created. He gave them abundant lights with regard to good and evil, and eternal rewards and chastisements. Some were obedient, others rebellious; the good were confirmed in grace, and rewarded with eternal glory; the obstinate were chastised and precipitated into Hell, there to be tormented for all eternity. The cause of this rebellion and disgrace was that the Angels, having a very clear knowledge of the Divine Being with the Unity of Essence and Trinity of Persons, received the command to adore God as their Creator. All obeyed this precept, yet with some difference. Lucifer submitted because he thought it would be impossible to do otherwise, yet he did not obey with perfect charity. Although this baseness in this first act did not deprive him of grace, nevertheless it was the cause of his evil disposition, for it weakened his virtues and his mind. God made known to the Angels that He would create human nature, and that the Second Person of the Blessed Trinity would become incarnate, and the human nature be thus raised to the Hypostatic Union. They received the command to adore the God-man, and acknowledge Him as the Chief of all creatures. Lucifer resisted this mandate, and urged his adherents to do the same, persuading them that he would be their chief, and would found a kingdom independent of Christ. But his evil dispositions were increased when he was ordered to acknowledge as his queen and sovereign, a Virgin, the Mother of Christ, who was to be enriched with such gifts of grace and glory that she would surpass all other creatures, angelic as well as human. He resisted with horrible blasphemies, and condemned these divine decrees as unjust and injurious to his greatness. This extreme presumption irritated Our Lord in such a manner that He told the serpent, as He did later in the terrestrial Paradise, that she (Mary) should crush his head—*Ipsa conteret caput tuum.* After having precipitated from Heaven the rebellious angels, with Lucifer their chief, God created other creatures, modeled after Christ and His Blessed Mother as their divine exemplars, but He formed Adam and Eve, alike, above all and in all things to these divine originals. He gave them the power of motion and an entire perfection, and blessed them in consideration of their perfect resemblance to their Models. The Lord concealed from Lucifer the creation of Adam and Eve, during a part of the time that they lived together. He did so, that the demon might be in doubt whether Eve were she who was to crush his head, or whether Adam were the Incarnate Word. The implacable enemy of mankind, filled with rage, began to lay his snares. Having succeeded in causing the fall of the woman, and, through her, of the man, he with his demons proudly rejoiced over his triumph. But his satisfaction was of short duration. He saw how merciful God was with the two criminals, and that He would restore them to His grace and friendship by means of penance, and it was an additional torment to him to hear again that a woman should crush his head.

By the divine benediction, mankind multiplied. God chose for Himself an elect people, and from out of this people an illustrious and holy line to which He was to belong, according to the flesh. He granted signal favors to this people, and revealed to it profound mysteries; He raised up holy patriarchs and prophets who were to point out figuratively the Incarnate Word, and foretell His coming, so much desired.

In fine, the appointed time approaching, God sent into the world two brilliant flambeaux, to announce the coming dawn of the Sun of Justice, Jesus, our Saviour. These were St. Joachim and St. Ann, whom the Divine Will had prepared and created to be the parents of the Blessed Virgin, the Mother of God. Joachim, with his parents and friends, lived in Nazareth, a small town of Galilee. He was a just and holy man, enlightened in a special manner with regard to the mysteries of the Holy Scriptures and the meaning of the prophecies. St. Ann dwelt in Bethlehem; she was humble, chaste and beautiful, and had also received great infused lights as to the meaning of the prophecies.

The Archangel Gabriel was sent in corporeal form to bid her accept Joachim for her spouse. A short time afterwards, he was sent to Joachim, to command him in a dream to choose St. Ann for his wife. The marriage was solemnized without their having revealed this command to each other. The holy spouses dwelt in Nazareth, following the ways of the Lord, and performing their actions with all possible perfection. Every year they divided their revenue into three parts: the first, they offered to the Temple; the second, they distributed among the poor; the third, they reserved for the moderate support of the family.

The holy spouses lived together for twenty years without having any children. This drew upon them the contempt of their neighbors, for it was a belief among the Jews that those who had no children would have no share in the future Messias. Even the priests rebuked them, and once, when Joachim had entered the Temple to pray, a priest named Issachar sent him away, reproaching him as being sterile, and therefore unworthy to offer sacrifice. Much afflicted, the holy man retired to his house and prayed with tears that the Lord would give him a child, which, at the same time, he vowed to consecrate to the Temple.

The Angel of the Lord appeared to St. Ann and declared to her the will of the Lord that she should ask for offspring. She obeyed, and promised that the fruit of her womb should be consecrated to the service of the Most High.

The prayers of these holy spouses ascended before the throne of the Divine Majesty, and the Archangel Gabriel was sent to St. Joachim. "The Most High," said he, "has heard thy prayer. Ann, thy wife, shall conceive and bring forth a daughter, who shall be blessed among women, and whom all nations shall acknowledge to be blessed. The Lord wills that she shall be consecrated to Him in the Temple, even from her infancy."

At the same time, St. Ann, being raised into sublime contemplation and absorbed in the mystery of the Incarnation, prayed most fervently that she might be permitted to behold and serve the holy woman destined to be the Mother of the promised Messias. Then it was that the Archangel Gabriel announced to her that she herself was to be the Mother of the most holy Mother of the Divine Word.

Filled with inexpressible joy and surprise, she hastened to the Temple to offer her thanksgiving to the Lord. She met St. Joachim and told him of the Angel's promise; both entered the Temple to renew their vows and give thanks to the Author of all these wonders. They returned to their house, conversing on the signal favors they had received from the Most High, and they communicated to each other the first visit of the Angel, as also the order they had received to espouse each other, which they had hitherto concealed.

The prudent Ann did not discover to her husband that the promised child was destined to be the Mother of the Messias, because the Archangel had forbidden her to reveal it.

The fullness of the time being arrived, the three Divine Persons, according to our manner of thinking, spoke thus among Themselves: "It is time that We commence the accomplishment of Our good pleasure, and create that pure creature who is dearer to Us than all others; she must be exempt from the ordinary laws of the generation of mortals, so that the seed of the infernal serpent shall have no part in her. It is fitting that the Divinity should clothe her in very pure matter, never sullied by sin; Our justice and providence demand that which is most fit, most perfect, and most holy; all this shall be accomplished, because nothing can resist Our will. The Word, who is to become man and the Master of all creatures, will teach them more effectually to honor her whom He has chosen for His Mother; among the dignities which He will confer on her, the first shall be that of never being subdued by her enemies. As He is to be the Redeemer of mankind, it is fit that He should exercise that office first in regard of His own Mother. She must have a particular redemption, and by this, be preserved beforehand from all sin; thus she shall be always pure and immaculate, and the Son of God will rejoice at beholding between His terrestrial Mother and His Heavenly Father, the closest resemblance possible between God and His creature." Such was the decree manifested to the blessed spirits by the three Divine Persons. Prostrate before the divine throne, with great humility, they praised God, and rendered most fervent thanks because He was pleased to grant the prayer they had made before the great battle with Lucifer, when they had begged for the accomplishment of the mystery of the Incarnation, which had been revealed to them. With a holy emulation, each desired to be employed in the court of the Son of God and His most pure and holy Mother.

Twenty years had passed by since the marriage of St. Joachim and St. Ann: Joachim was then sixty years old, and Ann forty-four.

According to the divine promise, they engendered, in a manner truly wonderful, a child who was to be the Mother of God. Everything happened as in other conceptions; nevertheless, the virtue of the Most High removed everything imperfect or inordinate, in order that, according to the laws of nature, the most perfect body ever created should be formed free from the least imperfection. The divine virtue is revealed principally in the miraculous operations which removed from St. Ann her natural sterility, yet it was still more marvelous in removing from her holy parents all trace of sin, that the sting of Original Sin should have no share in her. The wisdom and power of the Most High were particularly exercised in the formation of the most pure body of Mary, so that by its perfect and just proportions it might aid the operations of the holy soul which was to animate it. It was endowed with a temperament so equal, and faculties so perfect, that it would be impossible for nature to have formed anything equal to it.

According to our manner of expression, we may

say that God took more care in the formation of this most pure body than in the creation of the heavens and the entire universe.

Chapter 2

THE IMMACULATE CONCEPTION OF MARY—HER HOLY EXERCISES IN HER MOTHER'S WOMB.

The Holy Ghost has ordained that the Church should consecrate Saturday to the most holy Virgin, it being the day on which her most holy soul was created and united to her body, free from any stain or effect of Original Sin. At the moment of its infusion, the most holy Trinity repeated the words spoken at the creation of man: *Faciamus hominem ad imaginem et similitudinem nostram*—"Let Us make man to Our image and likeness." By virtue of these divine words the most blessed soul of Mary was replenished with graces, gifts, privileges and favors far exceeding those of the highest seraph, together with the most perfect use of reason, proportionate to the gifts of grace which she had received. Then the Most High repeated the words which He had pronounced at the creation: *et erant valde bona*—"and they were very good," thus testifying the great complacency He took in so glorious a work. At the time of the infusion of the soul into the body, God willed that St. Ann should feel and know the presence of the Divinity, and being filled with the Holy Ghost, she fell into a sublime ecstasy, in which she received an exalted knowledge of the most hidden mysteries. This cheerfulness and spiritual joy were not momentary; they lasted until her death, although they were more frequent while she bore the treasure of Heaven within her womb.

Although the holy soul of Mary was endowed with all perfections and the infused habit of every virtue in a degree greater than any and all the Saints together, nevertheless it was not necessary that she should practice all immediately, but only those suitable to the state in which she then was. She practiced then, in the first place, the theological virtues of faith, hope and charity, but particularly the virtue of charity, contemplating God as the sovereign Good with such attention and love that it would be impossible for the Seraphim ever to attain to so eminent a degree. She also practiced those other virtues which adorn and perfect the reasonable part.

She received infused science, the moral virtues and the fruits and gifts of the Holy Ghost in a degree corresponding to the theological virtues; thus, from the first instant of her conception, she was wiser, more prudent, and more enlightened with regard to God and His works than all creatures united. This great perfection of Mary consists not only in the habits which were infused into her, but also in the acts which, by the Divine power, she exercised at the very first instant. In a word, she knew God such as He is in Himself, as Creator and Glorifier; she honored, praised and thanked Him; by heroic acts she loved, feared, adored and offered sacrifices of praise and glory to His immutable Being. She understood the gifts she had received and returned most humble thanksgivings to God, accompanied with profound bodily inclinations made in the womb of her mother; and by these acts, merited more in that state than all the Saints in their highest degrees of perfection and sanctity. Besides the acts of infused faith, she possessed a clear knowledge of the Divinity and most Holy Trinity, and, although at that time she did not see it intuitively, nevertheless she beheld it abstractively, and this kind of knowledge was the most perfect by which God could communicate Himself to the human understanding in this world. At this time she knew of the creation, the fall of the Angels, that of Adam and its consequences; Purgatory, Limbo, Hell and everything enclosed in these abodes; she knew all men, all Angels, with their divers orders, dignities and operations, and all other creatures, with their different instincts and qualities. She also knew her genealogy; the chosen people of God; the patriarchs and prophets, and how admirable was the Divine Majesty in the gifts, graces and favors He had conferred on them.

But what is most worthy of our admiration is that, by the divine power, her knowledge of Adam's fall and her sorrow for it caused her to shed tears; thus she began, even in the womb of her mother, to exercise her office of co-redemptrix of the human race. She offered her tears in union with the desires of the patriarchs, and this offering was more agreeable to God than the united prayers of all Angels, Saints and men. She prayed in particular for her holy parents, whom she knew in God before she beheld them in the flesh, and towards whom she exercised the virtues of the love, the gratitude and the respect of a daughter. During the time which this holy child passed in her mother's womb, her visions were continual and uninterrupted, and she was raised three times to very sublime, although abstractive contemplation of the Most Holy Trinity. The first took place at the moment when her soul was infused into her body; the second, within the nine months, and the third, on the day previous to her birth. She occupied herself in heroic acts of adoration and love of God, continual prayers in favor of mankind, and holy communications with the Angels. She felt not the enclosure of her prison, the inconvenience of her natural state, nor the suspension of the use of the exterior senses. She begged of God, with true fervor, never to permit her to see the light of day if she were ever to fail in His love or service; this was in her third abstractive vision of the Most Holy Trinity, which immediately preceded her birth. After this prayer the Most High bestowed on her His benediction, and commanded her to come forth from the maternal womb into the material light of the visible sun.

In order to augment the glory and virtue of St. Ann, God willed that, during the time of her pregnancy, she should suffer many afflictions. Lucifer, discovering in her such great sanctity, suspected that the child which she bore might be the illustrious woman destined to trample him under her feet and crush his head. Actuated by rage, he tried in every way to compass her death. Desirous of weakening the Saint's faith, he tempted her with many false persuasions and doubts regarding her condition, but in this he failed. He then tried to overthrow the house, hoping that the shock and terror would cause the death of the child, but the Angels who guarded her frustrated the evil design. Finally, at his suggestion, some foolish women, being angry at our Saint, loaded her with injuries and sensible affronts with regard to her condition, but this artifice of Lucifer was also unsuccessful.

Chapter 3

THE HAPPY BIRTH OF MARY—
FIRST FRUITS OF HER MARVELOUS LIFE.

When the nine months were accomplished, the Almighty made known to St. Ann, by an interior communication, that the time of her happy delivery had come.

Prostrating herself in presence of the Divine Majesty, she humbly besought Him to grant her the aid of His grace. Suddenly she felt a gentle motion, from which she understood that she was about to bring forth her child. Her blessed infant was born on the 8th of September, at midnight, and in order that she might neither see nor feel her birth, she was ravished in sublime ecstasy.

The saintly mother received her in her arms and enveloped her in swaddling clothes, allowing no one but herself to touch the cherished infant; this loving office she was able to fulfill, not having experienced the pains of childbirth. Holding the holy child in her arms, St. Ann addressed to God the following prayer: "O Lord, Whose wisdom is infinite, Creator of all beings, I humbly offer Thee the fruit of my womb, which I have received from Thy infinite goodness; I thank Thee from the bottom of my heart. Do with the daughter and the mother according to Thy most holy Will, and from Thy throne look down upon our lowliness. I felicitate the holy fathers in Limbo, and all mankind, on the certain pledge of speedy redemption which Thou hast given them. But how shall I behave properly towards her whom Thou hast given me as my daughter, I who am not worthy to serve her? How shall I dare touch the Ark of the Covenant? Give me, O Lord, the lights necessary to know Thy Will, and to execute it according to Thy good pleasure, in the services I shall have to render to my dear daughter."

The Lord gave her to understand that she should treat her child exteriorly as a mother treats her daughter, but that she should preserve interiorly the respect due to her dignity. The Angels venerated her as their Queen, in the arms of her mother, and those who were appointed as her guardians rendered themselves visible to her eyes; this was the first time in which she beheld them under corporeal forms. One thousand were commissioned by God to defend her, from the very instant of her conception. After they had rendered their homage, God sent the Archangel Gabriel to announce the good tidings to the holy patriarchs in Limbo.

At the same time He ordered an innumerable multitude of Angels to transport into Heaven the body and soul of her who was to become the Mother of the Eternal Word. At her entrance into Heaven, the little Mary prostrated herself with love before the royal throne of the Most High. She was received by God Himself upon His throne, and the titles of Mother of God and Queen of all creatures were given to her, although she remained still ignorant of the designs of this profound mystery, God concealing them from her for His greater glory.[1] It was determined to bestow a name on this well-beloved child, and a voice, proceeding from the throne of God, said: "Our chosen one must be called Mary. This name shall be marvelous and magnificent. Those who will invoke it with devout affection shall receive abundant graces; it shall be terrible against Hell, and shall crush the head of the serpent."

The Almighty commanded the angelic spirits to announce the blessed name to St. Ann, so that what had been decreed in Heaven might be accomplished on earth. The Angels appeared to St. Ann, bearing luminous bucklers, on which was inscribed the name of Mary, and announced to her that this was the name to be bestowed upon her child. Mary was reposited in the arms of her mother, who had not perceived her absence because she herself had been rapt in sublime ecstasy, and also because an Angel

---

1. We must not be surprised when it is said that the august Mary was transported into Heaven by the ministry of Angels. The greatest theologians teach that there is nothing repugnant to faith in this, because the Blessed Virgin was *Immaculate*. This privilege, which has been declared a dogma of faith, is the foundation of all the marvels which occurred during the infancy of Mary. She was endowed with the highest gifts, prerogatives and privileges that could be granted to a pure creature. After the Immaculate Conception, we can wonder at nothing in Mary.

had assumed a body like to Mary's and had occupied her place.

It is well for us to consider what were the daily occupations of the holy child. At the commencement of each day she interiorly prostrated herself in the presence of the Most High, praised Him for His infinite perfections, and acknowledging herself to be the work of His hands, returned most humble thanks to God for having drawn her forth from nothing. She blessed, exalted and adored Him as the Sovereign Lord and Creator of all things, and surrendered her mind and entire being into His hands. Animated with profound humility and perfect resignation, she begged Him to dispose of her for that day and all the days of her life according to His holy Will, and to teach her what was most agreeable to Him, that she might accomplish it perfectly. In this habit, begun at her birth, she persevered throughout the whole course of her life, never omitting it, whatever might be her occupations, and she even repeated it frequently during the course of the day.

The sixty-six days of purification being ended, St. Ann went to the Temple carrying her most pure child in her arms. She presented herself at the door of the tabernacle with the offering required by the law. The holy priest Simeon felt extraordinary joy, and St. Ann heard a voice bidding her renew the vow she had made to offer her daughter in the Temple when she should be three years old. When this amiable child was carried into the Temple, she felt great joy at beholding so much magnificence consecrated to the worship of God, and as she could not prostrate herself to adore the Divinity, she supplied for this action in spirit. She humbly prayed the Lord to receive her in His holy Temple at the time appointed by His holy Will. In testimony of His acceptance of her prayer, a bright light from Heaven descended in a sensible manner upon the mother and the child. Having finished her prayers and presented her offering, St. Ann returned to her house in Nazareth. The holy child was treated in all things as is usual with those of her age. She partook of the same nourishment, but in a very small quantity; her sleep was short, although she allowed herself to be put to bed at her mother's pleasure.

She was not troublesome, never wept for the petty troubles common with children, but was very mild and quiet; nevertheless, she concealed this wonder by weeping for the sins of men, that she might obtain pardon for them and hasten the coming of the Messias. Her countenance was ordinarily joyful, yet serene and full of majesty, and there never was seen anything light in her actions. Occasionally she would receive the caresses lavished on her, but with regard to those not given by her mother, she moderated them by her reserve. The Lord had inspired St. Joachim and St. Ann with great respect and modesty, so that they were extremely prudent and reserved in the sensible demonstrations of their affection. When alone, or when placed in her crib to sleep, she never interrupted the interior actions of holy love, and she conversed with the Angels on the mysteries of the Most High.

She was subject to hunger, thirst and bodily suffering, that thus she might be the imitator of Jesus; these sufferings were felt by her even more keenly than by other children, and the privation of food was the more dangerous, on account of the perfection of her constitution; yet if nourishment was not given to her at the proper time, she waited patiently for the opportunity of making her wants known by signs.

She felt no pain at being wrapped in swaddling bands, for she knew that the Incarnate Word would, in after times, be ignominiously bound. When alone, she placed herself in the form of a cross, knowing that in such a manner the Redeemer of the world would expire. She very frequently returned thanks for the food that nourished her, for the influence of the planets, the stars and the heavens, acknowledging them all to be the benefits of Divine goodness; yet if she was in want of anything she was not troubled, for in everything she recognized a grace and favor from God.

We have said that, when alone, her principal occupation was to converse with the Angels. To make this the more easily understood, we will give an exact idea of the manner in which they rendered themselves visible to her, and say who those angelic spirits were.

Out of each of the nine choirs were chosen one hundred of those who had particularly distinguished themselves in the combat against Lucifer, by their love for the Incarnate Word and His most holy Mother. They appeared to her under the forms of young men, of marvelous beauty and of noble and majestic appearance, whose bodies participated but little of terrestrial matter, seeming like pure crystal, brilliant with the light of Heaven. Their garments were like pure gold, enameled and embellished with the richest colors, which, however, were apparent only to the sight, and could not be touched any more than can the light of the sun. On their heads were beautiful crowns of rich and varied flowers, which exhaled a celestial perfume. In their hands they bore interwoven palms, signifying the virtues which Mary was to practice and the glory she was to obtain. On their breasts were devices resembling the decorations of military orders, each bearing a cipher signifying *Mary, Mother of God.* This was one of their most brilliant and beautiful ornaments; nevertheless, the Blessed Virgin did not understand it until she had conceived the Incarnate Word. Human language cannot describe the effects which these heavenly spirits operated in Mary's soul.

Besides the nine hundred Angels already spoken of, seventy of the Seraphs nearest to the throne were chosen from among those most devoted to the Hypostatic Union of the divine and human natures, to attend upon their young Queen. When they rendered themselves visible to her, it was under the same form as those seen by Isaias, having six wings, two of which veiled their faces, two covered their feet, and two were used in their flight, thus signifying the hidden mystery of the Incarnation and the ardent flight of their love towards God. Their manner of communicating with the Blessed Virgin was the same as amongst themselves; that is, the superior enlightened the inferior; for, although the Queen of Heaven was their superior in grace and dignity, nevertheless, the nature of man, as says the prophet David, has been made inferior to that of the Angels.

There were also twelve Angels whom St. John has mentioned (*Apoc.* 21:12) who were distinguished by their desire for the redemption of man. They were chosen to cooperate with Mary in her privilege as Mother of Mercy and Mediatrix for the salvation of the world. These twelve Angels, like the others, appeared in corporeal forms and carried many palms and crowns, reserved for those devoted to this august Queen. They were particularly deputed to make known the charity of Our Lord towards mankind. The eighteen Angels who completed the thousand of her guard were those most distinguished for their affection to the sufferings of the Incarnate Word.

These Angels appeared to Mary in wondrous beauty, bearing the emblems of the Passion and other mysterious symbols of our redemption. On their breasts and arms were emblazoned crosses of singular beauty and extraordinary splendor. These Angels were frequently employed by Mary as ambassadors to her Divine Son for the good of souls.

These angelic spirits continually and faithfully watched over their blessed Queen, as we shall frequently have occasion to notice in this Life, on which account they now in Heaven experience a particular delight in her holy company.

Although Mary was not like other infants, incapable of speech, nevertheless, she did not pronounce a word during the first eighteen months of her existence, as well to conceal the science and capacity of which she was possessed as to avoid astonishing others by the knowledge of this miraculous gift.

She dispensed herself from this law of silence only when she prayed to the Lord in solitude or conversed with the Angels of her guard. At length arrived the time in which Mary was to break her holy silence, and the Lord commanded her to speak with creatures.

Before obeying this command, she humbly and fervently supplicated the Lord to assist her in the dangerous and difficult act of speaking, that she might commit no fault therein. The Lord having promised her the divine assistance, she, for the first time, loosened her tongue, and her first words were to ask the blessing of her parents.

During the eighteen months which intervened between this and her entrance into the Temple, at the age of three years, she seldom spoke except to her mother, who conversed with her of God and His mysteries, principally that of the Incarnation of the Divine Word. It was admirable to see the care which she took at so tender an age to perform humble and menial works such as sweeping and cleaning the house, and in these acts the holy Angels aided her to gather the fruits of humility. St. Joachim belonged neither to the very rich nor to the very poor class; therefore St. Ann clothed her daughter the best possible, within the bounds of honesty and modesty. As soon as she began to speak, she entreated her parents to dress her like the poorer class of children, in a coarse dress of an ash color. St. Ann did not judge proper to acquiesce in her desire; however, she satisfied her as to the color and form of her garments. Without answering a word, she submitted to her mother, and by her obedience supplied for the act of humility she was not allowed to practice.

Chapter 4

HER HOLY OCCUPATIONS—HER PRESENTATION IN THE TEMPLE.

One of Mary's occupations was to retire into solitude, there to enjoy God with greater liberty and to weep secretly over the sins of men. Her affection for sinners and the poor was very great. After completing her second year, she began to beg alms from her mother for those in want and frequently retrenched a part of her meal in order to give it to the poor. She did not give alms as if she were conferring a favor, but rather as if paying a just debt. She gave a singular evidence of her humility by allowing herself to be taught to read by others, she, the Mother of the Divine Wisdom, who knew all things by infused science, even from the first moment of her conception.

When the time arrived for the accomplishment of the vow which her parents had made, of consecrating her to the service of the Temple, she herself was the first to beg them, with all humility, to fulfill their promise without delay, and she most fervently entreated God to inspire them to do it promptly. The Lord granted the humble prayer of His beloved, and her parents, obedient to the heavenly inspiration, parted with their amiable child, though not without the deepest sorrow.

The grief of St. Ann, in particular, exceeded even that of Abraham when commanded to sacrifice his son Isaac. At the expiration of the three years St. Joachim and St. Ann, accompanied by many of their relations and by a great number of angelic spirits, who, during the journey, sang hymns of praise to the Most High, left Nazareth and journeyed to Jerusalem, bearing in their arms their young and happy child.

Having arrived at the Temple, St. Ann heard a voice which said: "Come, My spouse, My beloved, come into My Temple, where it is My will that thou shalt offer Me a sacrifice of praise and thanksgiving."

They conducted her to the apartments of the virgins, who were young girls brought up together in holy retreat until they arrived at the age for entering the married state. They belonged principally to the royal tribe of Juda and the sacerdotal tribe of Levi. The staircase which led to this apartment had fifteen steps, and the priest who came to receive Mary placed her on the first. Having asked his permission, Mary turned to her parents, and kneeling, humbly asked their blessing, kissed their hands and begged them to recommend her to God. They blessed her tenderly and with many tears. Then she ascended the staircase alone, and with admirable fervor and modesty. The holy priest appointed as her mistress the prophetess Anna, who had received from God particular graces to fit her for this office.

The holy child knelt before her, begged her blessing and entreated her to teach her everything necessary, after which she visited the young virgins, to thank them for having admitted her, although unworthy to be their companion; she offered her services to them and saluted and embraced each in particular. Prostrating herself upon the ground, she kissed it as being the pavement of the house of God, and returned thanks for His great benefits. Then calling the twelve Angels of whom we have already spoken, she entreated them to console her parents in their sorrow.

After they had departed, the Most High commanded the sixty Seraphs who assisted her to transport her into the highest Heaven. This was immediately executed, and there she beheld the Divine Essence by an intuitive vision. Humbly prostrate before the throne of God, she earnestly prayed for two particular graces; one, that she might suffer much for His love; the other, that she might be allowed to take in His presence four vows, viz: poverty, chastity, obedience and perpetual enclosure in the Temple. The Most High granted her request; yet, with regard to the vows, accepted only that of chastity, and He regulated the manner in which she was to conduct herself towards others, and act as if she had taken solemn vows.

After this clear vision of God, she remained in Heaven by an ecstasy of the imagination, during which she was most magnificently adorned by the Angels. They enlightened all her senses with a light and clearness which filled her with grace and beauty;

they clothed her in a gorgeous robe, with a cincture of precious stones of various colors, most transparent and resplendent; this cincture was the emblem of the purity and heroic virtues of her holy soul. Around her neck they placed a necklace of inestimable value, from which three large precious stones, symbolizing the theological virtues of faith, hope and charity, hung upon her breast, as if to show that these virtues dwelt therein. On her fingers they placed seven rings of extraordinary beauty, the emblems of the seven gifts of the Holy Ghost. The Most Holy Trinity crowned her as Queen of the World with an imperial diadem of incomparable splendor, and she was vested in a magnificent robe adorned with ciphers of the finest gold, which signified, Mary, Daughter of the Eternal Father, Spouse of the Holy Ghost and Mother of the true Light, but these titles were understood only by the blessed spirits.

Thus adorned, Mary was so pleasing to Almighty God that He bade her ask for whatever she desired, assuring her that it should be granted. She begged that He would deign to send His only Son into the world for the redemption of men; that He would augment His holy love in the hearts of her parents, and load them with gifts of His bountiful hand; that He would console the poor and afflicted, and assist them in their labors and pains. For herself she only asked that the Divine Will might be accomplished in her. After this wonderful vision, the Angels reconducted her to the Temple, where, more humble than ever, she began to practice all that she had promised to God.

Going to her mistress, she surrendered into her hands all that her mother had given her, either for her necessities or pleasures, retaining only one poor garment and a manuscript of prayers, and she begged her to distribute those things among the poor.

Her acts and practices of sublime virtue were so perfect that her merits exceeded those of all the Seraphim. But let us enter into detail. Having thus disposed of all her possessions, she begged her mistress and the high-priest to prescribe for her all that she was to perform. Kneeling most humbly, with crossed hands and bowed head, she received Simeon's orders. "My daughter," said he, "thou shalt assist with the greatest respect and devotion at the praises of the Lord, and pray to the Most High for the necessities of His Holy Temple and people, and also for the coming of the Messias. At the third hour, thou shalt retire to rest, and at dawn of day shalt arise and pray to the Lord until the hour of tierce, after which thou shalt employ thyself in manual labor. Observe temperance at thy meals, which thou shalt take after work; after which, go to receive the instructions of thy mistress. The remainder of the day thou shalt spend in reading the Holy Scripture. Be in all things humble, affable and obedient." The holy child listened to these words with the utmost attention; she begged the priest's blessing, kissed his hand and resolved to observe faithfully the rules he had prescribed for her. From her mistress she obtained permission to serve the other young virgins and perform for them the most menial offices, in which she usually contrived to anticipate others.

Every morning and evening she went to beg the blessing of her mistress; sometimes she kissed her hand, and sometimes her feet, if permitted to do so. Much of her time was employed in reading the Holy Scripture, particularly Isaias, Jeremias and the Psalms, because they spoke in a forcible and expressive manner of the mysteries of the future Messias and of the law of grace.

Chapter 5

HAPPY DEATH OF HER HOLY PARENTS—
PERSECUTIONS TO WHICH
SHE WAS SUBJECTED.

Six months after Mary's entrance into the Temple, her father, St. Joachim, fell ill. God revealed it to the holy child, and in answer to her prayer, sent twelve Angels to assist and console him. Having learned the day and the hour in which his death was to occur, she sent to his aid all the Angels of her guard, who were immediately recognized by the Saint as those who attended on his beloved daughter.

The blessed spirits conversed with him on divine mysteries, and, by the order of God, revealed to him that Mary had been chosen by the Most High to become the Mother of the Messias, and this happy tidings he was commissioned to bear to the holy patriarchs in Limbo. By the divine permission, St. Ann was not only present at, but also heard those sublime communications. When they were ended, St. Joachim fell into his agony, his heart divided between the joy he felt at the glorious tidings and the sufferings of death. He expired peacefully, at the age of sixty-nine and a half years.

He had espoused St. Ann in his forty-sixth year; twenty years after this marriage the most pure Mary was born; thus she was three and a half years old at the time of her father's death.

Although the Angels on their return communicated to their heavenly mistress all that had occurred, yet she, in her great prudence, did not reveal her knowledge, even after the news had been made known to her by her mother in a letter to the prophetess Anna. This was the first affliction which befell Mary in her childhood.

A short time before this event, the Most High had spoken to her in a vision, saying: "Thou art My beloved. I love thee with an infinite love, and therefore will not deprive thee of the rich treasures which I reserve for those whom I love. These treasures are the Cross and affliction." With a courage far surpassing that of the Saints and martyrs, she answered that were she allowed to make any choice, it would be to suffer even unto death for His love. God was pleased with her desire and, after the exterior affliction of her father's death, began to exercise her by interior trials. He deprived her of the sensible communications with the Angels and of the continual vision of the Lord. Her trials were more acute than those of all the Saints, because she loved God with a love incomparably greater than that of the Seraphim.

Fearing that she had been deprived of the sensible demonstrations of His love in punishment for some neglect or ingratitude, she was overwhelmed with grief and would have died a thousand times, had she not been upheld by God's miraculous power.

To these trials were now added the assaults of Hell, for Lucifer, seeing the great sanctity of the child, began to fear that it was she who was destined to crush his head. He communicated this suspicion to his demons, and bade them attack her with the most violent temptations; he set all his engines at work, and redoubled his infernal suggestions, but Mary repulsed him with the invincible buckler of prayer and the powerful arms of the Holy Scripture. Finding all his artifices and interior assaults to be useless against a heart so full of love, Lucifer tried another means. He excited against her the envy of her companions by suggesting to them that they would be looked upon as inferior to Mary; that she alone would be loved and esteemed by the priests and her mistress. Influenced by these evil suggestions, they began to hate and despise their holy companion and to treat her as a hypocrite. They held council with one another, and resolved to rob her of the good opinion of her superiors and cause her to be expelled from the Temple. They loaded her with insults and injuries, to which Mary only returned the meek answer that she would endeavor to do better. Far from softening those hardened hearts, her meekness provoked them to still greater fury, and they sought every opportunity of ill-treating her.

On one occasion they led her into a distant room, where they treated her most injuriously, going even so far as to inflict blows upon her. They raised their voices to so high a pitch that they were overheard by the priests in the Temple, who hastened to learn the cause of the tumult. The young girls answered indignantly that it was impossible to dwell with Mary in peace, that her temper was violent and her manners haughty and hypocritical. Leading her into another apartment, the priests and her mistress reproved her severely and threatened to expel her from the Temple. The humble maiden thanked them for the correction and asked their pardon, promising to do better. Then she went to rejoin her companions, and prostrate at their feet, begged their forgiveness. They received her among them, because they thought that this act had been imposed upon her by the priest as a punishment.

The infernal dragon continued to increase the fury of these girls, who incessantly calumniated her, inventing new lies with great effrontery; nevertheless, the Almighty did not permit that they should lay to her charge anything considerable or indecent, but only foolish trifles. All this gave Mary occasion for exercising virtues, principally humility, by never excusing herself or endeavoring to refute their false imputations.

At length God was pleased to put an end to the trials of His immaculate spouse. He appeared to Simeon and Anna in a dream, and made known to them that Mary was very agreeable in His sight and that she was innocent of all that had been alleged against her. After hearing these commendations from the Lord, they called the holy child and begged pardon for having believed the inventions of her companions, but she replied to them with still greater humility.

The priests being thus disabused, the persecution ceased, and Our Lord changed the hearts of those who had caused her so much suffering.

Nevertheless, her interior trials continued for ten years, during which she suffered inexpressibly. The Almighty, it is true, discovered Himself to her at times that she might receive some consolation, but this happened very rarely. This privation, although painful, was very necessary, as by it Mary was to be prepared by the exercise of every virtue for the sub-lime dignity of Mother of God, to which the Most High had destined her from all eternity.[1]

In the twelfth year of her age, the Angels revealed to her that the life of her saintly mother, Ann, was drawing to a close. God commanded the blessed spirits to carry the holy child to the bed of her dying mother; He also bade an Angel assume a body like hers and fill her place in the Temple. These royal commands were punctually executed, and Mary comforted and consoled her dear mother. She begged her blessing, strengthened her by holy con-versation, and gave her a last embrace.

The prudent mother did not reveal to Mary that

---

1. Persons who lead a spiritual life should not be surprised when God permits trials in order to purify them and prepare them for signal favors and graces, seeing that even the august Mary was not exempt from them. It reminds us of the words addressed to St. Bridget by the Queen of Heaven: "I obtained no virtue without pain and effort." Let us then not seek to be more privileged than Mary; let us know how to suffer for the love of God.

she was chosen to be the Mother of the expected Messias.

She exhorted her not to quit the Temple until she should have embraced a state of life, which she was to do only by the consent of the priests; she also begged that if it should be the Will of God for her to marry, that she would choose a spouse of the family of David and the tribe of Juda. She advised her to share her property with the poor, and to pray unceasingly for the coming of the Messias.

St. Ann had a noble and magnanimous heart and an elevated intellect. She was of medium height, somewhat less in stature than her beloved daughter; her complexion was fresh and ruddy, and her manner always even. At the time of her death she was fifty-six years old; she had married at the age of twenty-four, and having passed twenty years without children, was forty-four at the time of Mary's birth. Of the remaining twelve years, she passed three in Mary's company, and nine whilst she dwelt in the Temple. She was forty-eight years old when St. Joachim died. Some authors have written that she married three times, and each time became the mother of one of the three Marys.[2] But the Lord has only revealed to me her marriage with St. Joachim, and He has not made known to me that she had any other children but the Most Holy Virgin, the Mother of God.

––––––––

2. The opinion which holds that St. Ann was married three times seems to be destitute of proof or serious authority. See Trombelli: *Viti di S. Anna et di S. Joachino.*

Chapter 6

HER MARRIAGE WITH THE
CHASTE ST. JOSEPH.

When the august child had been brought back
to the Temple by the Angels, she entreated them
sweetly and earnestly to make known to her the
faults by which she had lost the presence of her
divine Spouse.

The Lord heard these earnest entreaties, and
deigned at length to manifest Himself to His spouse
in an abstractive vision of the Divinity. He dispelled
the darkness of her soul and filled her with heavenly consolation and most pure joy. At the age of
thirteen years and a half there happened to Mary
an incident like that which the Scripture records
of Abraham, when he was commanded to sacrifice
his son Isaac. She had made a vow of perpetual virginity in the presence of God and His holy Angels,
and had nothing more at heart than to preserve
ever untarnished the lily of her purity. But the Most
High commanded her to embrace the married state,
without, however, discovering to her that she was
chosen to be the Mother of God. Hearing this unex-
pected order, she became greatly afflicted; nevertheless she suspended her judgment, and with a faith

even stronger than Abraham's, hoped against hope and resigned herself to the Divine Will. In a dream, God bade Simeon seek a husband for the daughter of Joachim. He ordered him to assemble the priests and doctors and tell them that the child was an orphan, who had no desire to enter the married state, but as it was the custom that no young girl should leave the Temple until provided for, it was necessary for them to choose a husband for her. In obedience to the divine command, Simeon spoke of the matter to the priests, who resolved to beg the Lord to make known him whom He had chosen to be the spouse of the child.

They agreed that all the young men of the family of David who lived in Jerusalem should meet together in the Temple on the day which would complete Mary's fourteenth year. Simeon acquainted the holy child with the decision of the priests, and advised her to recommend the affair to God. So great was the grief which this announcement caused her, that she would have expired had she not been supported by the Divine power.

This occurred nine days before that appointed for the assembly, and during this time Mary prayed most earnestly that the Will of God might be accomplished in her regard.

In answer to her prayer the Almighty appeared to her and said:

"My spouse and My dove, console thy afflicted heart; I am attentive to thy desires and prayers. I will guide the priests by My light, and will give thee a spouse who will oppose no obstacle to thy desires. I will aid thee by My grace, and will choose a man perfect and according to My heart. My power is infinite, and it shall be exercised for thy protection."

These words gave consolation to the heart of the Holy Virgin, and she again most fervently supplicated the Most High to preserve her purity inviolate. She also had recourse to the Angels, who strengthened her by speaking of the power of God and His infinite love for her.

The appointed day having arrived, all the young men of the family of David assembled together, and Joseph, whose birthplace was Nazareth, yet who at that time dwelt in Jerusalem, was among the number. He was thirty-three years old, of comely figure and pleasing countenance, very modest and incomparably graceful in appearance. At the age of twelve years he had made a vow of chastity. He was related to the Blessed Virgin in the third degree. In order to obtain the divine assistance in what they were about to do, the priests began to pray. The Lord inspired Simeon to place a dry rod in the hand of each of the young men, telling them at the same time to pray for the manifestation of the Divine Will. While all were engaged in prayer, they beheld the rod of Joseph blossom, and at the same moment a white dove, most pure and brilliant, hovered above his head. St. Joseph heard an interior voice which said, "Joseph, My servant, Mary is to be thy spouse. Receive her with all care and respect, for she is agreeable in My sight; she is just and pure in mind and body. Thou must perform all that she shall ask."

Beholding this manifestation of the Will of God, the priests gave the most holy Virgin to be the spouse of St. Joseph.

Mary kissed the hands of Simeon and Anna and departed from the Temple, accompanied by her spouse and some servants from that holy place. They traveled together to Nazareth, where, having visited their friends and relations, as was customary on such occasions, they took up their abode in their own house. Then the most pure Mary prayed the Angels to assist her, now that, for the first time, she was to be alone with a person of the other sex. The thousand blessed spirits of her guard appeared under visible forms; by their inspirations they gave great power to her words, and inflamed St. Joseph's heart with the fire of ardent charity. Mary then made known to him that she had taken a vow of chastity and begged him to aid her in keeping it faithfully, upon which St. Joseph discovered to her that he also had made the like vow at the age of twelve years.

Filled with joy at the conformity of sentiment and will with which God had inspired them, they renewed their vows and promised to mutually aid each other in the path of perfection. The inheritance which Mary had received from St. Joachim and St. Ann they divided into three parts; the first they gave to the Temple, the second to the poor, and the third they reserved for their support.

As in his youth St. Joseph had learned the trade of a carpenter, he asked his spouse if it was agreeable to her that he should work at it. The Blessed

Virgin consented, saying it was the Will of God that they should be poor and should also aid the poor, and begged his permission to give alms, which he readily granted.

In order to inspire St. Joseph with the veneration and respect due to Mary, God willed that the presence and sight of her should fill him with a reverential fear, impossible to describe. This was caused by the refulgence and splendor of a divine light, united to the ineffable majesty of her appearance.

This holy marriage was celebrated on the 8th of September, the holy Mary being fourteen years complete, and St. Joseph thirty-three.

Chapter 7

HOW THE MOST HIGH PREPARED THE BLESSED VIRGIN AND FILLED HER WITH GRACE, SO AS TO RENDER HER WORTHY OF BEING THE MOTHER OF GOD.

During the six months which elapsed between the marriage of the Blessed Virgin and the Incarnation of the Eternal Word, she occupied herself in acts of profound humility and heroic virtue. In order to accomplish this mystery in a becoming manner, God prepared His spouse by a most extraordinary way during the last few days which preceded the descent of the Word into her womb.

On the first day of this preparation, when Mary, according to custom, rose at midnight to praise the Lord, the Angel spoke thus to her: "Spouse of our Divine Master, arise; His Divine Majesty calls thee." She answered: "The Lord bids the dust arise from the dust." And to the Lord she said: "My Divine Master, what wilt Thou have me to do?" At these words her soul was raised to more intimate union with the Lord, and the Divinity was manifested to her in an abstractive vision. She beheld and understood with great clearness the works operated on the first day of the Creation, and the Lord discovered to her that she should pray most urgently for the accomplishment of the mystery of the Incarnation. In this vision she saw in particular how she had been formed from vile, contemptible, earthly matter, and acquired so clear a knowledge of her own terrestrial being that she humbled herself profoundly and abased herself lower than all other children of Adam, although they are so full of miseries. By this knowledge was established in her heart a foundation of humility, proportionate to the edifice which God wished to raise in her; for the dignity of Mother of God being, in a manner, infinite, it was necessary that her humility should be unlimited.

On the second day she learned all that had occurred on the second day of the Creation. God gave her full power over the ethereal regions and all the elements, and this for two principal reasons: the first, because the Holy Virgin being exempt from Original Sin, should therefore be exempt from all its consequent miseries entailed upon the children of Adam, against whom, on account of sin, God had given creatures the power to avenge the outrage offered to their Creator; the second, because it was but just that all creatures should obey her to whom the Creator was to be subject. Nevertheless she never employed her power over the wind, the sea, cold, heat, or the seasons except when the glory of God seemed to demand it.

On the third day she received infused science with regard to all that had been created on the third day. She understood very clearly the different properties of water, herbs, fruits, plants, stones, metals and minerals, with a knowledge surpassing that of Adam, Solomon and all men. She received a power so great that no creature could harm her without her permission, yet this science or power she never employed to save herself from suffering; she sometimes exerted it in favor of the poor. God also gave her knowledge of the infinite love of God for man, and this inspired her with so vehement a desire to save us, and repair our evils that we might become pleasing to God, that she would have died had not God sustained her by His almighty power. This great charity and ardent desire for the salvation of sinners fitted her still more to become the Mother of the Saviour.

On the fourth day she was raised to more sublime knowledge of the Divine greatness; she saw all that had been created on that day, and learned the arrangement, the number and properties of the planets, the stars, and all heavenly bodies, over which she received absolute power. This she sometimes exerted in favor of her Son whilst in Egypt, where the heat was very great, by commanding the sun to temper his rays, but never for herself, because she did not wish to avoid suffering. The Lord, by a particular light, revealed to her the new law of grace which was to be instituted by our Saviour, the Sacraments it was to contain, and the abundant gifts and graces prepared for those who would profit by the grace of Redemption. But knowing the corruption of the world, which, by innumerable sins, would oppose obstacles to the accomplishment of the loving Will of God for the eternal salvation of all, she suffered a kind of martyrdom, caused by her grief for the eternal loss of men. She offered up most fervent prayers to God that no one might be damned in the future and that all might attain eternal glory. Her heart overflowed with bitter sorrow for the folly and insensibility of sinners in resisting the merciful designs of God for their eternal salvation, and this sorrow lasted throughout the whole course of her mortal life.

On the fifth day the Lord revealed to her how men retarded, by their sins, the accomplishment of the mystery of the Incarnation, and also the small number of those who would profit by so great a grace and correspond to it. In this vision she beheld every creature, present, past and future, their actions, whether good or evil, and all that they would possess. God also imparted to her the knowledge of all that had been created on the fifth day, and gave her power over all. He then asked her name, to which she answered, "I am a daughter of Adam, formed by Thy hands out of vile matter." The Most High replied: "Henceforth thou shalt be called the Elected One, chosen to be the Mother of My only Son." These last words were heard only by the blessed spirits, Mary understood but the word *elect*. With a heart burning with love, she again prayed for the accomplishment of the Incarnation, which the Most Holy Trinity promised should speedily be granted; then, filled with joy, she asked and received the Divine benediction.

On the sixth day, after Mary had persevered for nine hours in prayer, the works of the same day of the creation were displayed before her. She was given the knowledge of all species of animals, with their different qualities and functions, and also received absolute power over them; at the same time they were commanded to render obedience to her, which they afterwards did on several occasions, as when the ox and the ass prostrated themselves before the Lord on the day of His birth. Besides this, she understood the manner in which the first man had been created, the perfect harmony of the human body, its faculties and constitution, the nature and perfection of the soul, and its union with the body. She knew also of the state of original justice, and in what manner Adam had lost it by his fall; also how he had been tempted and vanquished; what were the effects of his fault; and how great was the rage of the demons against mankind. Through this knowledge she mourned and wept for the first sin, and those which were the consequences of it, as if she herself had been the guilty one.

We may then call Adam's fault, in some sort, a happy one, in having caused such precious tears.

Acknowledging herself a child of parents so ungrateful to God, she abased herself in her own nothingness, not because she had any share in the sin of Adam, but that she was of the same nature, and also his daughter.

On the seventh day she was transported by her Angels into the empyreal heavens, where God celebrated with her the new espousals. For this end

He commanded two Seraphs to assist her, in visible forms, and adorn her person exteriorly, in a manner suited to the interior beauty of her soul. They vested her in a robe, like a long tunic, which was so resplendent that had a ray from it fallen upon the earth, it would have given more light than the sun, and even more than if each star had been a separate sun. They girded this robe with a rich cincture, the symbol of her fear of God, as the robe was an emblem of her incomparable purity. They adorned her with beautiful golden hair, bound with a precious band, to give her to understand that all her thoughts were to be animated with the most ardent charity, of which gold is the type. On her feet they put magnificent slippers, to signify that all her steps and motions were to be directed to the highest ends for the glory of God. Rich bracelets were bound around her arms to signify the magnanimity of soul with which she was endowed, and her fingers were covered with precious rings, the emblems of the gifts of the Holy Ghost. She also received a necklace of marvelous brilliancy, from which hung three precious stones, representing the three divine Persons, or the three theological virtues. Her ears were adorned with magnificent earrings, to signify that her ears were to be prepared for the message of the Archangel, which she was to receive so soon. Monograms were placed around the edge of her robe, some of which signified Mary, Mother of God, and others, Mary, Virgin and Mother.

On the eighth day she was again transported both

in body and soul into Paradise, where her incomparable beauty ravished the heavenly hosts, and in her even the Most High took complacency. In order to give her the highest honor, He proclaimed to the Angels that she was their Queen; by them she was acknowledged and joyfully accepted; they sang hymns of thanksgiving to the Lord with inexpressible harmony, for that day was the greatest in joy and happiness that they had enjoyed since their creation. The Most High then addressed the Holy Virgin, saying:

"My spouse and My chosen one, since thou hast found favor in My sight, ask without fear for whatever thou desirest, for God is an omnipotent King, ever faithful to His promises. I assure thee I will refuse thee nothing, even shouldst thou ask for a part of My kingdom." The august Virgin, humbled in the depth of her own nothingness, replied: "O my King and Master! I do not ask a part of Thy kingdom for myself, but I humbly beg that mankind may have a share in it. I supplicate Thee, O powerful King, by Thine infinite mercy, to send Thine only Son to be our Redeemer."

The Lord answered: "Thy supplications are pleasing to Me, and thy prayers most agreeable. It shall be done according to thy will, and My Son shall soon descend upon the earth."

On the ninth and last day she was again ravished both in body and soul into the highest Heaven. In an abstractive vision of God, she beheld anew all the wonders of the Creation, and understood their mutual harmony, connection, order and

dependence, and also the end for which each creature was destined.

Then to signify that she was queen over all the
works of Divine Omnipotence, a diadem of gold
bearing a character or mark which signified Mother
of God, yet which Mary could not understand, was
placed on her head, and as a final preparation for
this eminent and incomparable dignity, she received
incomprehensible gifts.

What we should most admire in all this, is that
although these amazing privileges were conferred on
the Blessed Virgin, yet so profound was her humility that she never once conceived the thought that
she was chosen to be the Mother of the Messias.

Chapter 8

ANNUNCIATION OF THE BLESSED VIRGIN —THE INCARNATION OF THE WORD.

The fullness of time in which the only Son of God was to become incarnate having arrived, God made known His Will to the Archangel Gabriel, not in the ordinary way, by enlightening the inferior by the superior, but He revealed immediately to himself the order, and even the words of his embassy. Gabriel, having received this commission, assumed a corporeal form and descended from Heaven, accompanied by thousands of blessed spirits. His face was of radiant beauty and his garments of resplendent brightness; on his breast was a beautiful cross, emblematic of the mystery of the Incarnation.

At this time Mary was fourteen years, six months and seventeen days old. In height she exceeded other girls of her age; she was perfect in form and extremely beautiful; her complexion, manner and deportment were so admirable that no creature shall ever be like to her; her dress was poor and modest, yet very clean; it was of ash color, and arranged most faultlessly.

When the Archangel appeared, she was rapt in

sublime contemplation of the mysteries which she had learned during the preceding days, and she felt an ardent wish to be the servant of that blessed woman destined to be the Mother of the Messias. The heavenly ambassador, accompanied by a multitude of blessed spirits, entered the chamber of the humble Virgin, and, not allowing her to salute him as had been her wont, bowed before her with most profound respect and saluted her with the words, *Ave Maria! gratia plena!*—"Hail Mary! full of grace!" At this Mary was troubled, because, through her profound humility, she believed herself the least of all creatures, and again she could not understand how she was to become a mother, yet, at the same time, preserve her vow of chastity. The Archangel having explained the difficulties and dissipated her doubts, the Blessed Virgin humbly bowed her head and gave her consent to the ineffable mystery of the Incarnation of the Word. Absorbed in the thought that God wished her to become His Mother, she offered ardent acts of love and conformity to the Divine Will. Her chaste heart, generally compressed by the ardor of its motions and of her affection, distilled three drops of blood, which fell into her virginal womb. Of these the Holy Ghost formed the little body of our Saviour, so that, by the force of divine love, the most pure heart of Mary alone furnished that from which was formed the divine body of the Son of God. The Incarnation was really effected at the moment in which Mary, bowing her head, pronounced the words: *Ecce ancilla Domini; fiát mihi secundum verbum tuum*—"Behold the handmaid of the Lord, be it done unto me according to thy word." At the same instant the most holy soul of our Saviour was created and infused into His body, and His Divinity was united to His humanity by the Hypostatic Union. This was operated on Friday, the 25th of March, at dawn of day, the same hour in which Adam had been created. At the moment of the Incarnation of the Eternal Word, the heavens, earth and all creatures rendered homage to their Creator. They gave evident signs of the interior renovation and change produced by the living presence of the Redeemer of the universe.

Men remained ignorant of this marvelous change, for God was pleased to reveal it to the Angels alone; nevertheless, He diffused in the hearts of many of the just an extraordinary joy, for which they could assign no cause, although many suspected that it might be an effect of the coming of the promised Messias. The Archangel Michael was deputed to bear the glad tidings to the holy patriarchs in Limbo, who were filled with unutterable joy. Hell also experienced the effects of the coming of the Redeemer; the demons were oppressed with sadness and intolerable anxiety, for by the impetuous force of the divine power they were precipitated like the waves of the raging sea into the lowest caverns of the abyss, yet they remained ignorant of the cause. From the moment in which, by the operation of the Holy Ghost, the Word became incarnate in the womb of the Blessed Virgin, she was raised to an intuitive vision of God, in which she learned the deepest mysteries and understood the signification of those ciphers and numbers which, until then, had been hidden from her. The Divine Child grew by the aid of His Mother's substance in the same way as other children, yet in a wonderful manner.

To make this the more clearly understood, it is necessary to explain that acts of fervor and love cause the blood and the humors of the body to circulate more freely. Therefore Mary's heroic acts of virtue and love of God, causing the blood and humors to flow more freely through her virginal body, furnished the substance necessary to the Divine Infant. Thus the Humanity of the Word was nourished according to the order of nature, while the Divinity at the same time took complacency in the heroic acts exercised by Mary, who gave the natural aliment by the force of divine love. At the thought that her food was to nourish the Infant God, she took it with such great love and such sublime acts of virtue that the Angels were ravished with admiration to see actions, so common in themselves, rendered so agreeable to God and so meritorious for herself. As soon as the body of the Divine Infant was formed and His most holy and august soul united to it, He began to practice virtues in a most heroic degree.

I. By His knowledge of the Divinity as it is in itself, and as it is when united to the holy Humanity.

II. By acknowledging Himself to be, in His human nature, inferior to God, and on this account humbling Himself profoundly.

III. By loving God with a beatific love.

IV. By offering Himself in sacrifice for our salvation and by accepting His suffering humanity for the redemption of the world.

V. In taking possession of the virginal womb of Mary, and therein finding His complacency.

VI. By thanking the Eternal Father for having endowed Him in His creation with such great gifts and graces, and having preserved Him from Original Sin.

VII. By praying for His holy Mother and St. Joseph, and asking for their eternal salvation.

These acts were of such great merit that they would have sufficed to redeem an infinity of worlds, and the act of obedience alone, performed in submitting to suffering, and of preventing the glory of His soul from reflecting on His body, far exceeded the price of our Redemption. The Blessed Mother practiced these same acts in union with her Son. She abased herself profoundly before the Divine Majesty, and adored Our Lord in His infinite being and in His union with the humanity. She glorified God in the name of all men, and, in particular, for having chosen her to be the Mother of His Son; she most humbly offered herself to nurse Him, to serve and accompany Him, and to cooperate as far as in her power in the work of the Redemption: at the same time she prayed fervently for grace to perform zealously her duties in this great work.

To these interior acts, which she began to practice after the conception of the Word, she joined exterior acts of prostration and adoration, which she continued to the end of her life. From mid-

night to midnight she made three hundred genuflections, and even this number she often exceeded
when not traveling or busily occupied; these and
all other actions were performed in honor of the
Divine Child.

On the day of the Incarnation, her attendant
Angels rendered themselves visible to her. Filled
with joy, they adored their God incarnate in her
womb; they offered to serve her as their Queen, to
aid her in her employments, to do all things according to her desires; and in the absence of her holy
spouse, St. Joseph, they waited upon her at table.
Whilst she bore the Infant God within her womb,
she ordinarily enjoyed His presence in divers ways,
but her greatest consolation was to behold, as
through pure crystal, the holy humanity receiving
light from the Divinity.

Frequently the little birds would gather around
her to adore their Creator and praise Him with their
joyous and melodious harmonies, God ordering this
for the consolation of His dear Mother. Sometimes
they would bring most beautiful flowers, which they
dropped into her hands, while they seemed to await
her permission to chant their joyous melodies.
Sometimes, in order to be secure from the rigor of
the seasons, they would take refuge near her, and
our sweet Lady not only received them, but frequently fed them with her most pure hands.

Chapter 9

HER VISIT TO ST. ELIZABETH—
BIRTH OF ST. JOHN THE BAPTIST.

In one of the visions which followed the Incarnation, it was revealed to Mary that the Lord willed her to visit St. Elizabeth, in order that, by the presence of her Divine Son, His precursor might be sanctified. She spoke to St. Joseph regarding this journey; and he, with great respect, offered to accompany her. The day appointed for their departure was the fourth after the Incarnation of the Word. They prepared all that was necessary; that is to say, they borrowed an ass from one of their neighbors, and took with them some fruit, bread and a few fishes, and set out from Nazareth for the dwelling of Zachary, distant four days' journey, along a rough and toilsome road. In obedience to her spouse, the Holy Virgin sometimes rode, but more frequently walked, endeavoring at the same time to persuade St. Joseph to mount in his turn, which he most strenuously refused.

The holy patriarch passed many hours in silence, conversing with God alone in prayer, while the Blessed Virgin sang canticles of praise with the holy Angels, who were visible to her alone. Sometimes also they conversed together, and St. Joseph felt himself inflamed with extraordinary devotion. Being ignorant of the cause of this emotion, he wished to learn it from the Holy Virgin, but his modesty and reverence prevented him; neither would the prudent Virgin resolve his doubt, although she had an entire knowledge of all that was passing in his interior.

During the four days of their journey, the Queen of the Universe wrought many miracles; on one occasion she cured a poor, sick girl.

At length the holy pilgrims arrived at Juda, the city in which St. Elizabeth dwelt; it was afterwards destroyed, and no house remained but that of St. Elizabeth, which, in course of time, was used as a church.

Zachary did not always reside in Juda, but also in Hebron, where he had another house, in which he died. Being arrived at Juda, St. Joseph wished to prevent Zachary, but St. Elizabeth, enlightened by the Holy Ghost, came to meet the Holy Virgin, accompanied by some members of her family.

The most pure Virgin saluted St. Elizabeth first with the words: "May the Lord be with thee, my cousin." To which Elizabeth replied: "The Mother of the Most High comes to visit me! May the Lord reward thee for giving me so great a consolation." They retired together, and the Mother of Grace again saluted her cousin with the words: "May God protect thee, my dear cousin, and may His divine light communicate life and grace to thee!" At these words Elizabeth was filled with the Holy Ghost, and, in that moment, being interiorly enlightened, she comprehended the most sublime mysteries. Whilst Mary was speaking, Our Lord looked on St. John and granted him the perfect use of reason, purified him from Original Sin, and filled him with the Holy Ghost. At the same time St. John beheld the Incarnate Word; prostrating himself, he adored the Redeemer of the world, and leaped for joy in his mother's womb. Ravished out of herself at this wonder, St. Elizabeth fixed her eyes on Mary and spoke the words recorded by St. Luke: "Blessed art thou amongst women," etc. The little Baptist comprehended clearly the sense of these words. In a sweet and modest voice the Holy Virgin answered in the words of the Canticle: *Magnificat anima mea Dominum*—"My soul doth magnify the Lord."

Elizabeth offered herself and all her household to serve Mary; she begged her to accept for her own use the best apartment in her house, which hitherto she had used as an oratory. Mary accepted the offer with sincere thanks, and after her departure this room was never entered by anyone except St. Elizabeth. Before she retired for the night, Mary begged Zachary, as a priest of the Lord, to bestow on her his benediction. She did not try to cure his dumbness, yet she prayed for and compassionated him in his affliction.

After three days St. Joseph begged permission of his holy spouse to return to Nazareth, offering to return for her at whatever time she might appoint.

After his departure, Mary regulated her time as she had done at Nazareth, and also began to make the clothes for the Divine Babe who was so soon to appear in the world.

In an humble contest with her cousin, she obtained that she might obey and St. Elizabeth command. She diligently performed the work given her by her holy relative, and this work was never afterwards used by the Saint, but preserved with the greatest care.

In the society of the blessed Mother of God, Elizabeth attained to a high degree of sanctity; she frequently beheld the Holy Virgin resplendent with light and raised from the ground, completely absorbed in God, and on those occasions she was accustomed to prostrate herself before her and adore the Incarnate Word. This hidden mystery she never revealed, except to Zachary and her son, and not to the latter until after the birth of the Divine Infant.

Elizabeth had a servant of exceedingly violent temper, addicted to anger, detraction and swearing; in punishment for her sins she had been possessed by many devils for fourteen years. Knowing the miserable state of the unfortunate girl and the causes which had led to it, the Blessed Virgin, by her prayers, obtained for her contrition and the pardon of her sins and commanded the infernal spirits to torment her no longer, but to depart far from her.

There was in the neighborhood another woman in the same unhappy condition, who, hearing of the arrival of a young stranger, remarkable for her modesty and humility, expressed an ardent desire to see her, and for this purpose visited St. Elizabeth's house. No sooner did she behold the most pure Mary than her depraved heart was changed, and she wept bitterly over her past sins, yet without knowing that this great miracle had been operated by Mary. In this manner the Mother of God drew many souls out of the state of sin, yet as she worked in secret, they knew not that their conversion was due to the efficacy of her prayers.

Two months had passed away since Mary's arrival at the house of her cousin, during which time she had sanctified the whole family by her acts and examples of humility. Elizabeth dreaded the approaching separation, and endeavored to persuade Mary to leave Nazareth and take up her abode in Juda, saying that she would send for St. Joseph, and that her house, her family and even herself, should be devoted to their service. The humble Virgin, having listened to this proposition, answered that she would not decide upon it until she had learned the Will of God and the pleasure of her spouse. Elizabeth was satisfied with this answer, but entreated her to remain with her until after the birth of her child. Mary retired into her oratory to consult God in prayer. She immediately fell into ecstasy, in which state the Lord revealed to her that she should remain with her cousin until the birth of the child, but should return to Nazareth after its circumcision.

When the time was accomplished, the Lord made known to John the Baptist the hour at which he was to come into the world. At the news the holy child was at a loss what to do. On one side the laws of nature obliged him to be born, and on the other, he seriously considered the dangers of the perilous voyage of life.

Surrendering himself to the Lord with entire obedience and great confidence in His goodness, he said: "Lord, that Thy Divine Will be accomplished, grant that I may employ my life in Thy service, and give me Thy benediction at my coming into the light of the world." By this prayer the holy child merited the additional grace and benediction which the Most High bestowed upon him.

Soon after the birth of her child, St. Elizabeth sent a messenger to Mary [who was in another room] to apprise her of it. The Blessed Virgin sent her some swaddling clothes made by her own hands, and, shortly afterwards, by divine inspiration, visited her. Taking the babe in her arms, she offered him to the Eternal Father. The child testified great joy at finding himself in the arms of the Mother of God; he bowed his head in respect and gave other tokens of his affection towards her; nevertheless, being mindful of her dignity, she did not kiss and caress him, as is usually done to children of his age. Wholly absorbed in the contemplation of his great and wonderful soul, she did not look at him, and would not have recognized him again with the eyes of the body.

On the eighth day he was circumcised and called John, with all the circumstances related at large by St. Luke. Zachary recovered his speech through Mary, who, making use of her power over creatures, untied his tongue, that he might praise the Lord on this occasion, which he did to the admiration of all the assistants, who were ignorant of the manner in which the miracle had been operated. After the circumcision, St. Joseph came from Nazareth to reconduct his spouse thither. She received him with great joy and respect; kneeling, she asked his blessing and immediately began her preparations for departure. Profiting by the presence of the Mother of Wisdom, St. Elizabeth begged her to give her some instructions which might serve to regulate her life, and by her urgent entreaties she obtained this consolation from the Holy Virgin.

"Always," said Mary, "raise thy heart and mind to God, and with the light of grace which thou dost possess, never lose sight of the immutable being of the infinite and eternal God, or of His incomprehensible goodness which has led Him to draw man out of nothing, to raise him to His glory and enrich him with precious gifts. Endeavor most earnestly to disengage thy heart from the things of this world, that being entirely free and detached, it may attain to its true end.

"Purify thy heart from everything earthly, that being freed from the trammels of this life, thou mayest correspond to the designs of God, and be prepared to follow the Lord, not only without pain, but even with joy, when thou shalt be called to leave this body and its affections. Now is the time to suffer and to gain a crown; learn to render thyself worthy, and walk diligently, that thou mayest attain to an intimate union with thy true and sovereign good. Be particularly careful to obey, serve and love Zachary, thy spouse and head. Offer thy son to God his Creator, in whom and for whom thou mayest love as a mother. Employ thy zeal in causing God to be feared and honored in thy family; be kind to those in want and in distress; aid them liberally out of the abundance which God has plentifully bestowed on thee. We are all children of the same heavenly Father, to whom all created things belong; therefore, it is not just that one of His children should live in plenty, and another in poverty and destitution. Continue what thou art engaged in, and execute what thou hast planned; as Zachary places all at thy disposal, thou mayest be liberal with his permission.

"Place thy entire confidence in God in the midst of the trials which He may be pleased to send thee. Be good, mild, humble, benevolent and patient with everyone; although some may cause thee trouble, look on them as instruments for thy greater merit. Bless the Lord eternally for having revealed to thee His grand and sublime mysteries, and pray with great zeal and charity for the salvation of souls. Beg the Lord that He would govern and direct me, that I may act worthily and according to His Will in the mystery which His infinite goodness has confided to me, His vile and unworthy servant."

Such were the words addressed by the Blessed Virgin to her cousin at the moment of separation.

When taking her leave, Mary humbly knelt to receive the blessing of Elizabeth and Zachary, which he gave in words drawn almost entirely from the Holy Scripture.

"May the Almighty," said he, "ever assist thee and deliver thee from all evil. May His protection defend thee, and fill thee with the dew of Heaven and the fat of the land. May the people serve, and the tribes venerate thee, because thou art the Tabernacle of the Lord. Thou shalt be the mistress of thy brethren, and the sons of thy mother shall bend the knee before thee.

"He that will exalt and bless thee shall be blessed, but he that will not praise thee shall be cursed. May every creature know God in thee, and by thee may the name of the Most High be glorified."

Having received this benediction, she kissed the hand of the holy priest, who was deeply affected. He ever preserved most faithfully the secret of these great mysteries; yet, on one occasion, being in the Temple in the midst of the assembly, he was inspired by the Holy Ghost and exclaimed in a loud voice: "I firmly believe that the Most High has visited us, by sending into the world the Messias, who is to redeem His people."

At these words, Simeon, deeply moved, cried out: "O God of Israel! Allow not Thy servant to depart from this vale of tears until he has seen our salvation and the Redeemer of his people."

The Blessed Virgin, having bade adieu to the two holy spouses, wished also to see John the Baptist before her departure. She received him in her arms and bestowed upon him many mysterious benedictions.

By the permission of God, the holy child spoke to the Blessed Virgin in a low tone and begged her intercession and her blessing; he kissed her hand three times and adored the Incarnate Word within her womb; the Divine Child in return looked on him with infinite love and tenderness, knowing which, Mary was filled with great joy.

Chapter 10

THE BLESSED VIRGIN'S RETURN
TO NAZARETH.

The holy guests set out for their poor home in Nazareth, which they reached in four days. They did not exercise the power which they possessed over creatures, although in their journey they suffered much from heat, and from stones and briars; nevertheless they wrought many miracles, and secretly delivered many of the sick and poor from their infirmities. As soon as they arrived in Nazareth, Mary began to cleanse the house and put all things in order, in which lowly offices she was aided by the Angels. She regulated the acts of virtue which she intended to practice with the greatest exactitude. Seeing the heroic virtues of Mary, the devil began to suspect that He who was to conquer him would be born of her. Therefore he called in Hell a council of his demons, to whom he made known his doubts and suspicions. The members of this accursed assembly resolved to employ every kind of temptation, and to set every engine at work to oppress and conquer the Holy Virgin.

But the Incarnate Word knowing of Lucifer's designs, and desiring to give additional strength to the fortitude of our invincible Queen, stood erect in His virginal tabernacle, as if preparing Himself for her defense. In this posture He prayed His Eternal Father to renew His favors to His dear Mother.

Lucifer arranged his forces for the combat and led on the seven legions whom he employs to tempt men to the seven capital sins. The Blessed Virgin was engaged in meditation at the time in which, by the permission of God, she was assaulted by the demons, who exerted against her every means suggested by their malice, rage and desire of obeying the prince of darkness.

The prudent Virgin understood all their artifices and repelled them by her superior wisdom and incomparable watchfulness. These numerous enemies, with all their stratagems and suggestions, could not distract her in the least or prevent her performing even the most trivial action with all possible perfection. The infernal powers were completely vanquished. Lucifer, enraged at his failure, wished to renew the combat and placed himself at the head of those legions by whose agency he has introduced into the world so many errors and sinful disorders. All his efforts were vain; neither did he succeed by the malice of many persons, neighbors to Mary and Joseph, whom he incited to annoy and disquiet them. All the result which he obtained was to cause the holy spouses to practice acts of sublime virtue, and thus increase their merit before God. But a still greater trial was allowed by God to afflict these holy souls and render their sanctity still greater.

Mary was in the fifth month of her pregnancy when St. Joseph began to perceive it, for, being most perfect in the proportions of her body, the slightest change was the more apparent. This knowledge filled the heart of St. Joseph with inexpressible grief, caused by the sincere love which he felt for his spouse and the danger to which he saw her exposed of being put to death according to the law. He had recourse to God in prayer, for although he suspected some hidden mystery, he had no certainty of it and was in most agonizing doubt, God willing it so, that he might have occasion to practice acts of heroic virtue. The sorrow which oppressed his heart began to manifest itself by great exterior sadness, yet the Blessed Virgin needed not such evidence of the state of her spouse; she saw clearly all that was passing within his heart, nevertheless she did not discover to him the wonderful mystery, but abandoned herself and the anguish of St. Joseph into the hands of Divine Providence, although she felt a tender love for her spouse and deep compassion for the sorrowful martyrdom which he was undergoing.

As his suspicions became more and more confirmed, the Saint became more thoughtful and melancholy, and sometimes when overwhelmed with grief, he spoke to her with more severity than formerly. The most Holy Virgin never complained, but preserved the same unalterable sweetness, serving him at table and attending to all his wants; seeing which, St. Joseph was rendered still more uneasy, not knowing whether to credit the evidence of his senses, which became more and more certain, or the incomparable purity and sanctity which he perceived in her. In this perplexity, he came to the resolution of leaving his spouse before the child should be born.

Knowing of this resolution, the Blessed Virgin addressed herself to the Angels and begged them to prevent its execution. In obedience to their Queen, they inspired St. Joseph with many holy thoughts regarding the incomparable purity of Mary, and thus caused him to defer the accomplishment of his design. Yet, as his suspicions became fully confirmed and his anguish increased, he resolved to depart, after having passed two months in cruel uncertainty. For this end he prepared a bundle of clothing and a small sum of money which he had received in payment for work. Before taking his departure, he had recourse to God in prayer, begging His assistance and protesting that he was not leaving Mary through fear of her having committed sin, but, because that, seeing her condition, he was ignorant of the cause and the manner.[1] He made a vow to visit the Temple at Jerusalem, and there offer a part of his money, that his chaste spouse might be preserved from the calumnies of men.

_____

1. The greater number of the authors who speak of the conduct of St. Joseph in this delicate circumstance are either more or less in error. They teach in general, and without hesitation, that the incomparable Saint suspected the sanctity of his spouse. But this cannot even be supposed of two souls of such sublime sanctity. The entire truth is given in the revelations of Mary of Agreda, and Christian piety is fully satisfied with this admirable explanation.

After this he retired to take a little rest, intending to rise at midnight and begin his journey. Meanwhile the Blessed Virgin was in her oratory, and by divine light knew what St. Joseph was doing and saw his preparations. Touched with compassion, she prayed most earnestly for him, and her powerful prayer was granted. While the Saint slept, the Archangel Gabriel, sent by God, announced to him the fruitful virginity of his spouse. Although the Saint did not see the Angel, yet he heard his interior voice and comprehended the sublime mystery. He awoke and, prostrating himself before the Lord with profound humility, adored Him, rendered thanks for having been chosen by Him to be the spouse of His Mother, and begged pardon for the suspicions and sadness to which he had given way.

He dared not disturb his holy spouse, who, retired in her oratory, was in a state of sublime contemplation. Meanwhile he untied his parcel and practiced many acts of virtue. When the proper time arrived he entered Mary's chamber, and casting himself at her feet implored her pardon, offered himself to be her servant and promised that henceforward he would acknowledge her as his Queen.

The Blessed Virgin entreated her spouse to rise; then kneeling at his feet, she gave him her reasons for concealing the mystery. She begged him not to change his conduct towards her, for her duty was to obey and his to command. On this occasion St. Joseph was interiorly enlightened and filled with the Holy Spirit. He intoned a canticle of thanksgiving to which Mary responded by the *Magnifi-cat*—"My soul doth magnify the Lord," singing which, she was rapt into sublime ecstasy, and surrounded, as it were, with a globe of heavenly light, to the great admiration of the Saint, who had never before seen her in a state so glorious.

He then clearly understood the mystery of the Incarnation and beheld the Son of God in the virginal womb of His holy Mother. He learned also that his holy spouse had been the instrument of the sanctification of John the Baptist and Elizabeth, and that she was also the cause of the plenitude of grace which he himself had received from God, with even greater abundance than St. John the Baptist.[2] Being thus enlightened, he resolved to treat the Blessed Virgin with great respect, and in order to testify his great veneration, whenever she spoke to him or passed near him, he respectfully bent his knee; neither would he allow her to serve him or employ herself in menial household labors, determining to attend to them himself in order that she might not derogate from the dignity due to her as the Mother of God. The most humble Virgin earnestly opposed this manner of acting; she begged him not to bend the knee before her, because no one could distinguish whether this honor was offered to her or to the Divine Child. The Saint acqui-

---

2. The most illustrious Doctors of the Church have not hesitated to place St. Joseph above all other Saints. According to their opinion, he fills the place of Lucifer, the first-born among the Angels, and possesses gifts and graces even far greater than those of the apostate Angel.

esced in her desire, but continued to genuflect when unperceived by her.

The contest was still greater with regard to humble and lowly employments, because St. Joseph, not wishing our august Queen to occupy herself with them, tried to prevent her by doing many things himself, whilst she was engaged in prayer.

But the Blessed Virgin, addressing herself to the Lord, prayed Him to forbid her spouse to perform such lowly offices. Then the Most High bade the Guardian Angel of the Saint to make him understand, by interior inspirations, that although he should always entertain for Mary the utmost respect and veneration, yet he should allow her to exercise those humble employments, because the Mother, as well as her Divine Son, came into this world to serve and not to be served. To this order the Saint humbly submitted. The house wherein they dwelt was divided into three small rooms or apartments. This number was sufficient for their wants, as they kept no servant, it not being convenient that others should be witnesses of the wonderful miracles wrought in that holy dwelling. In one of these rooms St. Joseph slept, another he used as a workshop, and the third was reserved for the use of the Virgin Mother.

Mary never quitted her house without urgent necessity; when anything was needed, she employed a pious neighbor to attend to it, who, in recompense for her services, received great graces for herself and family. It frequently happened that the holy spouses were subjected to want because St. Joseph did not receive payment for his services, but only accepted of what was given as an alms. Yet, after having sufficiently tried their patience, the Lord always provided for their necessities. This He did in many ways, sometimes by means of birds who brought them bread, fruit and even fish, again by the ministry of Angels.

On one occasion when they had nothing to eat, they retired to pray, after which they found their table spread with fruit, bread, fish and another dish of rare delicacy and delightful flavor. The most ordinary way in which their wants were supplied was by the agency of Elizabeth, who, from the time of her cousin's visit, was accustomed to send them gifts.

The Holy Virgin took her rest on a small bed of boards made for her by St. Joseph; it had two coverings, which she wrapped around her over her clothes when she sought the repose necessary to sustain life. St. Joseph never saw her asleep, nay, he did not even know from experience that she ever slept. Under her garments she wore a long cotton tunic,[3] which she never changed after leaving the Temple, for it did not become soiled or worn out. Hence it was never seen by anyone, not even by St. Joseph.

Her outer garment was of ash color; this, as also her veil, she sometimes changed, in order to con-

---

3. This holy tunic is preserved in the Church of Our Lady at Chartres, as an object of the highest veneration. We have visited this holy relic, and thereby received many precious graces.

ceal the wonderful miracle by which nothing that touched her virginal body became soiled, for she was exempt from all the weaknesses and infirmities of our sinful nature. In all things she was perfectly pure, and every piece of work executed by her was perfect and most beautiful. Although she ate but sparingly, yet she took her meals regularly with St. Joseph. She never partook of flesh meat, although she prepared it for her holy spouse. Her ordinary diet was bread, fruit, boiled herbs and fish, of which she took only what was necessary to sustain life, and being the Mother of Wisdom, she knew the exact quantity required by her constitution; the same rule she observed with regard to drink. This moderation she continued throughout her life, yet she varied the quality of her food when occasion seemed to require it.

As the time of her happy delivery was approaching, the Blessed Virgin began to prepare the swaddling clothes for her Babe. In return for several articles of furniture made by St. Joseph, he had received two pieces of woolen material, the best that could be procured, one white, the other of a dark color. From these the august Mother made the clothes for the Divine Infant. For His undergarments she used linen which she herself, after the mystery of the Annunciation, had woven on her knees and watered with tears of devotion. All that remained of these materials she gave for the use of the Temple. These clothes she placed in a small casket, which they afterwards carried with them to Bethlehem. She had first perfumed them with delicious aromatic water, which she had made from flowers and herbs gathered by St. Joseph.

But the interior preparation of the divine Virgin was incomparably greater; by acts of heroic virtue and ardent love she endeavored to render herself more worthy of receiving the Infant God in her arms. Within herself she prepared for the Lord a temple of which Solomon's was but a figure. She united all her actions to those of her Divine Son, and when she beheld Him kneeling to pray to the Eternal Father, or extending His body in the form of a cross, thus prefiguring what He was to suffer, she imitated Him most perfectly.

Chapter 11

THE JOURNEY TO BETHLEHEM—
THE BIRTH OF JESUS.

During this time of holy preparation, an edict was published by Augustus Caesar, as St. Luke relates.

At this news St. Joseph was greatly afflicted because of the condition of his holy spouse, whom he did not wish to leave alone, yet whom he feared to take with him on so long and tedious a journey. He begged her to pray the Lord to reveal His Will. She obeyed, although she already knew that, according to the designs of God, she also was to go to Bethlehem. They prepared everything for the journey and committed the care of the house to a pious neighbor. St. Joseph had great difficulty in procuring a beast of burden, on account of the immense number of persons who were seeking them. The Blessed Virgin carried with her the small chest containing the swaddling clothes. Kneeling, she asked the blessing of St. Joseph, after which they set out from Nazareth for Bethlehem.

On this occasion, besides her usual guard of Angels, Mary was attended by nine thousand others, commanded by God to accompany her; they were also employed in bearing messages from God

to her, and all were distinctly visible to her. The
journey occupied four days, because they traveled
by short stages. They experienced great annoyance
from the immense numbers traveling towards
Jerusalem, and at night could find a lodging place
only in some obscure corner or vestibule, their
poverty causing them to be refused, while the rich
were welcomed. To these privations were joined the
rigors of the season—cold, rain, snow and wind—
all the more severely felt, as they were often compelled to rest on the bare ground or in stables among
the beasts, who, more grateful than men to their
Creator, honored Him in the womb of His holy
Mother.

Yet the greatest affliction of the holy pilgrims
was to hear indecent expressions from their fellow
travelers and to see the unhappy state of some souls
whose interior was clearly visible to the Queen of
Heaven. This horrible sight often caused her to
swoon away, on which occasions the holy Angels
assisted her; the Archangel St. Michael never left
her, and frequently upheld her when she was about
to fall. When the holy spouses were obliged to stop
at inns, the Angels were accustomed to range themselves around them as an impregnable defense; frequently they sang holy canticles to assuage their
sorrows and lighten their fatigue, and at night they
illumined their path with a refulgence brighter than
that of the planets and stars.

In the midst of these trials and consolations they
arrived at Bethlehem on Saturday, about the time
of sunset. They sought for a lodging among the rela-

tions and friends of St. Joseph, but no one would receive them; they were refused with insults and injuries. Although our Blessed Lady knew that they would not receive admittance, yet, in order to practice humility and patience, she followed her spouse from house to house, from door to door, through the streets. Whilst wandering about, they found the house in which they were to register their names; they inscribed them and paid the tribute, that they might not be compelled to return. They continued to seek for shelter, yet always in vain, although they applied at over fifty houses and inns.

It was almost nine o'clock at night when St. Joseph, oppressed with sadness, turned to his spouse and said: "I remember having seen, outside the walls, a grotto used by shepherds. Let us go there, and if we find it unoccupied, take up our lodgings in it, as it is impossible to procure one here."

The Blessed Virgin consoled him by kind words, and they proceeded to the spot, accompanied by many Angels, who by their brightness dispelled the gloom of the night. This grotto was so miserable that, notwithstanding the multitudes of people of every condition who were then in Bethlehem, no one had thought of using it. The holy spouses entered the stable, and, by the light diffused by the Angels, discovered how poor and humble was the place. They knelt and returned thanks to God for having given it to them, and our Blessed Lady prayed Him to reward liberally the inhabitants of Bethlehem, who, by refusing them shelter, had procured for them so great a good.

The grotto was hewn out of a rock and was used as a lodging place for animals. The Angels thronged around it in visible forms, and were clearly perceived by St. Joseph. The Blessed Virgin, knowing the wonderful mystery about to be operated that night, began at once to clean the place, in order to practice humility, and also to adorn, as well as possible, that abandoned spot, so soon to become the temple of a God. The Angels came to her aid; the work was quickly completed, and the dismal grotto filled with a heavenly perfume. As the night was cold, St. Joseph kindled a fire, after which they took some slight nourishment, and with great interior devotion passed some time in holy conversation. Then the Blessed Virgin begged St. Joseph to take a little repose, while he, on his part, asked her to do the same. He prepared and arranged a place for her by covering with some clothes the manger which was in the grotto; then he retired into an obscure corner and began to pray. Almost immediately he was rapt in sublime ecstasy, during which he beheld all the wonderful events which happened on this night.

In the meantime the Holy Virgin was raised to a state of high contemplation, in which she intuitively beheld the Divinity in a manner so ineffable that human tongue cannot express it. This ecstasy continued during the hour immediately preceding the birth of Our Lord. Coming to herself, she felt that the Divine Child began to move in her womb; this motion caused her no pain, but, on the contrary, such inexpressible joy, with effects so

supernatural and sublime that the human understanding is incapable of comprehending them. Her
body became so beautiful and her face so resplendent that she seemed no longer like a creature of
earth. She was on her knees, her eyes raised towards
Heaven, and her hands crossed upon her breast.

In this humble and pious posture, returning to
herself out of her ecstasy, she gave birth to the only
Son of the Eternal Father, who was also her own
Son—Jesus Christ, our Saviour, both God and Man.
This glorious event happened at midnight, and on
Sunday, according to the teaching of the Roman
Church.

The Divine Child came into the world most beautiful and resplendent, without detriment to the
holy virginity of Mary, for He passed through her
virginal womb like a ray of the sun.

His body was glorious and transfigured, for the
glory of His soul was reflected on it. Immediately
after His birth, the Archangels Michael and Gabriel
[in corporeal form], taking Him in their arms,
showed Him to the Holy Mother in the same manner as the priest exposes the Sacred Host to the
adoration of the faithful; the Infant God at that
moment spoke to His Mother, saying: "Mother, in
exchange for the human life which thou hast given
Me, I wish to give thee a life of grace far more elevated, so that from being merely a creature, thou
shalt become like to Me, who am both God and
man." Mary humbly answered: *Trahe me post te, cur-
remus in odorem unguentorum tuorum*—"Draw me
after Thee; we will run in the odor of Thy oint-

ments." She also heard the voice of the Eternal Father saying: "This is My beloved Son, in whom I am well pleased."

After this divine conversation, so replete with heavenly mysteries, the Divine Child ceased to be transfigured; by a no less wonderful mystery, He suspended the glorious gifts of His sacred body and manifested Himself only in His natural and passive state. The Blessed Mother again adored Him and, kneeling, she received Him from the hands of the holy Angels. Filled with sentiments of burning love, she offered Him up to the Eternal Father as His only begotten Son, who was to be the Saviour of men. While the most holy Mary thus held Him in her arms, first the ten thousand Angels of her guard adored Him, then all those blessed spirits who had descended into the grotto, chanting in His honor the new canticle, *Gloria in excelsis Deo, etc.* It was now time to recall St. Joseph from his ecstasy, that he might behold and adore the God whom he had known only by revelation. Returning to himself, he beheld the Divine Child in the arms of His Mother; he adored Him with profound humility, and kissed His feet with respectful tenderness.

Then the Blessed Mother asked of her Divine Son permission to seat herself; St. Joseph presented to her the swaddling clothes that she had prepared for Him, and she wrapped Him in them with inconceivable respect and devotion. She laid Him in the manger, in which she placed some hay and straw; this was the first bed whereon reposed the Incarnate Word.

At this moment, by the permission of God, an ox from the field entered the grotto, where was also the ass which Joseph and Mary had brought with them from Nazareth. The Blessed Mother commanded them to adore, after their own manner, their Creator lying in the manger. They immediately obeyed, and warmed the Divine Child with their breath, thus literally verifying the prophecy of Isaias: *Cognovit bos possessorem suum, et asinus praesepe Domini sui*—"The ox knoweth his owner, and the ass his master's crib." The Angels not only thronged around the stable and the manger, but many of them carried the glad tidings to divers places. St. Michael was sent to Limbo, to announce the glorious news to the patriarchs therein detained. Hearing it, St. Joachim and St. Ann begged the Archangel to entreat their daughter Mary to adore and venerate in their name the Infant God, which she immediately did.

Another Archangel was commissioned to bear the news to Elizabeth and St. John the Baptist; others announced it to Simeon, Zachary and Anna the prophetess; others to the three Magi, who were also warned by the star which was formed on this night and appeared to their eyes.

St. Luke relates in detail the embassy sent to the shepherds, who came to adore the Divine Child. They were interiorly enlightened, and many of them merited to have their children numbered among the Holy Innocents. St. Elizabeth did not visit Bethlehem, God not permitting it, that the mystery of the Incarnation might not be made more public, but she sent a messenger to congratulate the Holy Virgin and offer her presents, of which the Blessed Virgin retained a part and gave the rest to the poor. At the moment of our Divine Redeemer's birth, all the just experienced its salutary effects and felt an extraordinary supernatural joy, the cause of which was unknown to them. Many, however, were inspired with the thought that it was occasioned by the birth of the Messias.

Many other wonderful miracles were wrought during this night; the influence of the planets was renewed and the sun advanced in its course; many trees bloomed, and some bore fruit; several temples of idols were overthrown, and some entirely demolished, while the demons who dwelt in them were expelled. These marvelous events were attributed by mankind to various causes. The demons knew nothing whatever of the adoration of the shepherds, the embassy of the Angels, the coming of the Magi, or the appearance of the star. God concealed all from them, that they might be ignorant of the coming of the Messias. Regarding this, they were in uncertainty, for seeing this Child so poor and abandoned and also submitting to the rite of circumcision, Lucifer concluded that He was not the Messias; his proud and haughty spirit could not understand this sublime poverty and humility.

The shepherds remained in the grotto from dawn to midday; during this time the Blessed Virgin spoke to them and exhorted them to persevere in the service of God, after which she gave them food and dismissed them, full of holy joy and consolation.

They afterwards returned many times and brought such humble presents as their poverty allowed. When the Holy Family had departed from Bethlehem, these pious shepherds related to others all that they had seen and heard, but being simple and illiterate, they were not believed by all. Herod believed their relation, not through faith and devotion, but because he feared to lose his crown.

The Blessed Virgin ceased not to pray for those who had rendered themselves unworthy of knowing the true light of the world, and in this petition she occupied the greater part of the time that they dwelt in the grotto. When it was necessary for the Divine Infant to receive His natural nourishment, His holy Mother asked His permission to give it to Him.

She sometimes committed Him to the care of St. Joseph, who always genuflected three times and kissed the ground before receiving Him, and the Virgin Mother did the same when taking Him from her holy spouse. She also confided Him to the care of St. Michael or St. Gabriel, who had begged her to do them this honor, whilst she was at meals or taking her repose. God rendered her sleep miraculous, for during it she did not lose her strength, but could hold the Divine Babe in her arms as firmly as when awake; she also continued to contemplate Him interiorly as if she beheld Him with her eyes, and she knew all His interior and exterior actions.

Chapter 12

THE CIRCUMCISION OF OUR LORD.

The time of circumcision, according to the law, being arrived, the divine Mother fervently begged of God that He would inspire her with His Divine Will, and the Lord revealed to her that He wished to be circumcised. She then spoke of it to St. Joseph and humbly asked his advice, without acquainting him with the revelation of the Lord. The Saint was of the opinion that He should be circumcised, as He had taken upon Himself our humanity. The holy parents then prepared remedies to be applied to the wound, and also a crystal phial in which to preserve the precious relics, and linen to receive the first drops of that adorable Blood which was to be shed for the Redemption of man.

Speaking of the name which should be given to the Divine Infant, they agreed to give Him the name of Jesus, which had been revealed to them by the Angel. While they thus conversed, legions of Angels, descending from Heaven, surrounded the sacred grotto; and the Archangels Michael and Gabriel again revealed to them that this sacred name was to be given to the Divine Child.

There was in Bethlehem a synagogue, not for the

offering of sacrifice, for this could be done only at Jerusalem, but that there a priest might read the law to the people. Mothers were accustomed to carry their children to be circumcised by the priest, not that his ministry was really necessary, but because they felt that with him there would be less danger. On account of the dignity of her Divine Son, the Blessed Virgin wished the priest to perform the rite of circumcision. Therefore St. Joseph brought him to the grotto, and at the sight of the holy Babe, he felt his heart replenished with ardent love and devotion, yet remained ignorant of the cause.

The priest begged the Blessed Mother to consign her Babe to the care of His father and retire for awhile, that she might not be the witness of the painful sacrifice. Although the Holy Virgin desired to obey the priest, yet, at the same time, she ardently wished to remain and hold her Divine Son in her arms; therefore she begged to be permitted to stay, assuring the priest that he need not fear for her courage. The favor being granted, she removed the swaddling clothes and wrapped her Infant in linen, to preserve Him from the cold, and also to receive the precious Blood.

The priest performed his office and circumcised the sacred Infant, who wept a little, not so much from the sense of pain as from sorrow for the insensibility and hardness of men's hearts. His tender Mother most feelingly compassionated His suffering; she gathered the sacred relics and precious Blood and confided them to the care of St. Joseph. Then she dressed the wound of her beloved Infant, who, on His part, testified His love and compassion for His holy Mother. The priest inquired what name was to be given to the Child; out of humility each of the holy spouses kept silent, that the other might answer; at length, both, by the same inspiration, answered—"*Jesus* is His name." The priest inscribed it on the register, and whilst doing so, feeling himself moved by extraordinary emotion, said to the holy parents: "This Child shall be a great prophet of the Lord; therefore, take particular care of Him. If I can be of any assistance to you in your poverty, let me know, for it will give me the greatest pleasure."

After the priest had departed, the holy spouses conversed together on the mystery of the circumcision and composed canticles in praise of the sacred Name of Jesus, which the Angels sang with them, at their invitation.

Chapter 13

ARRIVAL OF THE MAGI—ADORATION
OF THE DIVINE INFANT.

After the rite of circumcision had been performed, St. Joseph spoke to the Virgin Mother of
the inconvenience of the place in which they were
staying. Our Blessed Lady felt great affection for
the holy grotto, so poor and humble; besides, she
knew by revelation that the holy Kings were coming to adore her Divine Son. However, without discovering to St. Joseph either her desire of remaining,
or the revelation which she had received, she
expressed her ready acquiescence in all that he
would command. St. Joseph, desiring to know the
will of his pure spouse more clearly, earnestly prayed
God to reveal it to him. The Archangel Michael
made known to him that they should remain there
to await the arrival of the Three Kings, who had
been ten days on their journey, yet were still at
some distance from Bethlehem. They determined
therefore to remain, and arranged the grotto in the
best manner they were able, considering the rigor
of the season. The Holy Virgin frequently exercised
the absolute power which she possessed over creatures by commanding the wind, rain and cold to

abstain from giving pain to their Creator, but to exercise all their severity against her alone. Thus it often happened that, whilst the Divine Child was sheltered in the arms of His Mother and felt neither wind nor cold, she herself suffered severely from their effects.

She gave nourishment to her Babe three times a day, always with profound respect and veneration; with the deepest humility she asked His permission to seat herself, although she generally remained on her knees during the greater part of the time that she held Him in her arms. Sometimes she would respectfully kiss His sacred feet, yet never His cheek without His permission. Jesus was accustomed to return the caresses of His Mother, sometimes by looking at her affectionately, or leaning on her breast, and at other times by lovingly clasping His tender arms around her neck, as other children are wont to do with their mothers.

In the midst of these sweet occupations, the Magi arrived; they had learned of the Saviour's birth from the Angels as well as by the star. They ruled over three adjacent countries, of small extent. They were mutually acquainted and had frequently conversed together on points of government and morality. They set out from their dominions at the same time, although each was ignorant of the other's design; they prepared gold, incense and myrrh, each being led by the Spirit of God in the choice of his mysterious gift.

The Angel who had announced the mystery to the Magi had, at the same time, formed a star and placed it at such a height and in such a position that it could be seen by all three, although they came from different directions. By following this guide, they met together, and having communicated their revelation to each other, continued their journey with their servants and camels. The star was in the region of the air, and its light was different from that of the sun or other stars. By night it gave light by its rays like that of a brilliant torch, and by day it could be distinguished from the sun by its extraordinary activity. When the Kings met together, it descended several degrees in the air and seemed to draw nearer them, which sign gave them great consolation. At their arrival in Jerusalem all things happened as is related by the Evangelists. Leaving the city, they journeyed to Bethlehem, and when they arrived at the place, the star decreased in size and entered into the holy grotto, where it placed itself on the head of the Divine Infant. When the holy Kings entered, they beheld the Blessed Virgin holding the Infant Jesus in her arms; she appeared with incomparable beauty and modesty.

A heavenly splendor shone on her countenance, but the face of the Child was incomparably more brilliant, and the dazzling rays which proceeded from it illumined the humble grotto. Struck with admiration, they prostrated themselves upon the ground, and with most lively faith, adored the Child; in this adoration they received extraordinary light on the mysteries which regarded the person of Jesus Christ, of His holy Mother, and the Angels who assisted her. Rising from the ground, they congratulated

Mary on her happiness and testified their veneration by bending the knee before her. They begged,
according to the custom of their country, to be
allowed to kiss her hand; the prudent Mother mod-
estly withdrew hers, but presented to them that of
her Divine Son. From the Blessed Virgin they
extended their congratulations to St. Joseph, who
was always present, and extolled his happiness in
having been chosen to be the spouse of the Mother
of God. Finally they requested permission to seek
for lodgings in Bethlehem.

There they rented a house and, when alone
together, entertained themselves by pious conversation on what they had seen and heard. They dispatched their servants to the grotto with presents
to relieve the poverty of the Holy Family. These
presents consisted of articles which they had brought
with them from their own country, as well as of
others purchased in Bethlehem. The Blessed Virgin
accepted their gifts, but distributed them among the
poor, who, attracted by her benevolence, came to
her for relief.

On the following day the Magi again presented
themselves at the sacred grotto, bearing the mystical offerings which they had prepared by the special inspiration of God and which are mentioned
in the Gospel, viz., gold, frankincense and myrrh.
Prostrating themselves upon the ground in adoration, they offered them to the Divine Infant. They
conversed with His holy Mother and received from
her sublime instructions on the mysteries of faith
and on the best manner of governing their respec-

tive countries. Mary received the mysterious gifts which they offered to Jesus, who testified His acceptance of them by a sweet and gracious air, and also by imparting to them His benediction. They offered to the Blessed Virgin many of the precious stones so much used in their countries, but this admirable lover of holy poverty sweetly refused them, showing that she was satisfied with their affection and generosity, in return for which she bestowed on them some of the garments which had been worn by the Divine Infant: these exhaled a delicious perfume, and, in the hands of the holy Kings, became the instruments of wonderful miracles. They were very desirous of building a house for the Holy Family and of furnishing it with everything necessary, but the most Holy Virgin would accept of nothing. So great was the consolation which the Magi experienced in listening to the holy and sublime discourses of the Blessed Virgin that they found it almost impossible to depart, but an Angel of the Lord, appearing to them, bade them return to their own countries. They received the benedictions of Jesus, Mary and Joseph, and having been warned to return home by a different route, they set out and were again guided by the miraculous star. These Kings were from Persia, Arabia and Saba, to the east of Palestine.

After their departure, a holy contest arose between the Blessed Virgin and St. Joseph with regard to the presents of the Magi. Mary was desirous that St. Joseph should distribute them according to his inclinations, while St. Joseph was equally anxious that Mary should be the dispenser of them. Finally, they agreed to offer for the use of the Temple the myrrh, incense and part of the gold; another part was given to the priest who had performed the circumcision, and the remainder distributed among the poor.

At a little distance from the grotto was a poor house inhabited by a humble and pious woman. Having witnessed the inconveniences suffered by the Holy Family in the grotto, she offered them her dwelling, miserable and poor without doubt, but preferable to the grotto. She spoke with such kindness and charity that the Holy Virgin, having conferred with St. Joseph, determined to accept her amiable invitation.

They quitted the holy grotto and went to dwell in this poor abode, outside the walls of Bethlehem.

All the Angels accompanied them in human forms; this they did every time that the holy spouses left their habitation to visit the holy grotto. At its entrance God placed an Angel with a fiery sword to prevent any animal from entering it, and even to the present day the Angel continues to guard the sacred spot.

Chapter 14

THE PRESENTATION IN THE TEMPLE.

The most Holy Virgin and St. Joseph remained with the Divine Child in the poor house of Bethlehem until the time prescribed by the law for the presentation in the Temple, which was forty days. Then they resolved to go to Jerusalem, to offer, according to the Law, the only Son of the Eternal Father, for they knew the desire He had to conform to the Law and be offered to His Divine Father.

On the day of their departure, they took leave of their pious hostess, whom they loaded with heavenly benedictions. Their first visit was to the grotto, where, prostrate on the ground, they venerated with deepest devotion that spot consecrated by the birth of the Infant God. Actuated by profound humility, the Blessed Virgin begged her holy spouse to allow her to perform the journey to Jerusalem barefoot and carrying her Infant in her arms. The latter part of her request he granted, but, from the fear that it would cause her too much suffering, he refused the first. Mary humbly acquiesced in his decision, and both having knelt to receive the blessing of the Divine Son, who gave it to them in a visible manner, they set out upon their journey. Mary was attended not only by the thousand Angels who had assisted her from the time of the Incarnation, but also by many other legions of blessed spirits.

The cold was very intense, and spared not its Creator, so that the Divine Infant wept several times in the arms of His Mother, to show that He was truly man. Touched by His sufferings, she exercised her authority over creatures and caused the weather to become very agreeable in favor of her Divine Son, but not for herself.

These holy travelers were approaching near Jerusalem, when God, by His interior lights, made known to Simeon and Anna the prophetess that the Messias was about to be presented in the Temple, in a state of humility and poverty. Simeon and Anna, having communicated their holy inspiration to each other, resolved to send one of their servants—without, however, discovering to him the quality of the persons he was sent to escort—to meet them on the road from Bethlehem and conduct them to his house. The servant carefully executed these orders; he met the three poor pilgrims, conducted them to the house and went to give the news to the holy priest. During this time the Holy Virgin and St. Joseph deliberated what they should do, and decided that St. Joseph should go that same evening to the Temple to offer the presents of the three Magi, in secret, and that on his return he should purchase the doves that were to be offered publicly on the following day, all which he punctually executed. The next morning the holy Mother, after having prepared everything necessary, wrapped the Divine Infant in swaddling clothes and set out for the

Temple, accompanied by St. Joseph and legions of Angels, who were distinctly visible to her.

Having arrived at the Temple, she prostrated herself upon the ground in humble adoration of the Most High. In the same moment she beheld the Most Holy Trinity by an intellectual vision and heard a voice saying: *Hic est Filius meus dilectus, in quo mihi bene complacui*—"This is My beloved Son, in whom I am well pleased." Conducted by the Spirit of God, Simeon now entered the Temple, and approaching the place where Mary stood, holding her Infant in her arms, he beheld them surrounded by a heavenly radiance. Anna, also by divine inspiration, entered and was witness of the same prodigy. Simeon received the Divine Infant in his arms, and offered Him to the Eternal Father; then he intoned his sublime canticle: *Nunc dimittis servum tuum, Domine, secundum verbum tuum in pace*— "Now thou dost dismiss Thy servant, O Lord, according to Thy word, in peace." He afterwards prophesied to the Mother the cruel martyrdom which she was to suffer interiorly at the sight of the sufferings of her Divine Son.

When the holy priest alluded to the Passion, the Infant Saviour inclined His head to testify His willingness to accomplish it. The Blessed Virgin then took leave of the priest, after having asked his blessing and kissed his hand; she also turned to Anna, her mistress, and begged her benediction.

Leaving the Temple, they returned to the house prepared for them by Simeon, where they remained for several days. They went each day to the Temple to renew their offering, and there, in the most humble and retired spot, remained in prayer from the hour of tierce until evening.

Chapter 15

THE FLIGHT INTO EGYPT.

The fifth day after the Presentation, the most Holy Virgin had an abstractive vision of the Divinity, in which she was warned to fly into Egypt, because Herod sought to kill the newborn Messias, and she was encouraged not to fear the inconveniences or fatigues of the journey because God would assist her in all things. With sentiments of profound humility she replied: *Ecce ancilla Domini, fiat mihi secundum verbum tuum*—"Behold the handmaid of the Lord, be it done unto me according to thy word." Then she prayed the Most High that she alone might be the sufferer. Nevertheless, considering the pains that so young an infant would have to endure in the execution of this order, she was touched with compassion and could not contain her tears. Seeing this sadness, St. Joseph, being ignorant of the cause, was somewhat afflicted, but would not question her. He did not remain long in uncertainty, for that same night an Angel of the Lord appeared and bade him fly into Egypt with the Child and His Mother, as is related by St. Matthew. The Saint arose and announced to the Blessed Virgin the order he had received. She instantly prepared to depart with her afflicted spouse, without saying that she also had received the same order.

Approaching the crib in which the Divine Infant slept, she knelt and raised Him in her arms most tenderly, but He awoke and shed many tears; then He gave His benediction to His holy parents, who had asked it. The Holy Mother having wrapped up her Child, they departed without further delay, it being a little after midnight. In their journey they made use of the same beast that they had brought from Nazareth to Bethlehem. The Holy Mother wished to visit the holy grotto once more, but the thousand Angels of her guard represented that it would be dangerous on account of Herod. Without reply she submitted to the will of the Lord, and was satisfied with saluting the venerable sanctuary from a distance. She was consoled by the sight of the Guardian Angel of the grotto, who came from Bethlehem to adore the Incarnate God in the arms of His Mother. She was also anxious to pass through Hebron, where her cousin Elizabeth at that time resided, in order that she might warn her of the danger impending over John the Baptist, but St. Joseph did not approve of this, because he feared Herod. His humble spouse then requested permission to send at least one of her attendant Angels to warn Elizabeth to remove her child to a place of safety. The Angel delivered his message to Elizabeth, who on hearing it expressed a desire to visit and adore the Divine Infant, but was prevented by the heavenly messenger, in order that she might not retard their journey. However, she dispatched one of her servants to carry provisions to the Holy Family, linen for the use of the Child, and also money; a part of which Mary, in her poverty, made use of to satisfy the pressing necessities of her Infant and her spouse; the remainder she distributed among the poor.

They remained for two days at Gaza, a town about fifteen leagues distant from Jerusalem, in which lodging had been procured for them by Elizabeth's servant, after which, aside from the inhabited portions of Judea, they advanced towards Egypt, through the desert of Bersabee. In the depth of winter they traversed this desert, one hundred miles in length, before they reached Heliopolis, now Cairo, in Egypt. During this journey they were compelled to pass the nights in the open air without any shelter. They spent the first night at the foot of a hill, the Queen of Heaven seated on the earth with her Divine Child in her arms. She took a little of the nourishment they had brought from Gaza, and St. Joseph with his mantle made a little tent to shelter the Holy Virgin and the Divine Babe.

The next day they continued their journey, but as their provisions failed, they suffered much, not only from the fatigues of travel, but also from want of food, which afterwards happened on another occasion. The Holy Virgin frequently inquired of her Divine Son if He did not suffer from the cold and severity of the season; the holy Child replied: "My Mother, it is sweet and agreeable to Me to suffer for the love of My Eternal Father, and for men, for whom I have come to serve as their Model;

besides, I am in thy company." The holy Child often shed tears, but they were tears of love and compassion for men. His merciful Mother imitated His example.

In order to console St. Joseph in this painful journey, the Holy Virgin frequently placed the Babe in his arms; then he would sometimes press Him to his bosom, sometimes kiss His feet, or humbly beg His benediction. One of the most cruel sufferings which they had to undergo in this journey was a violent storm of wind, accompanied by rain and frost, so that, notwithstanding all the Blessed Virgin's efforts to protect her beloved Infant, then only fifty days old, He was often so pierced with cold as to shed tears. It then became necessary for her to exercise her power over creatures; she commanded, and the rain and wind immediately ceased. To recompense the loving care of His holy Mother, the divine Jesus bade the Angels assist their Queen and preserve her from the rigor of the season. They formed a luminous globe in which they enveloped not only the divine Mother of the Creator, but St. Joseph also. This was not the only benefit which the Infant God operated in their favor; He also preserved them from hunger when they had nothing to eat. He bade the blessed spirits provide them with the necessities of life, and they brought to them white bread, exquisite fruits, and an agreeable liquor.

The Lord again took care to recreate them in an agreeable manner; for when they stopped to rest awhile, there came from the neighboring mountains a great number of birds, some of which sang melodious songs; others perched on their hands and shoulders, seeming by their manner to render homage to their Creator and the divine Mother. The Angels also added their celestial harmonies to cheer the hearts of the weary pilgrims.

The desert of Bersabee is that in which Elias received from the Angel the mysterious bread baked under ashes, when he was flying from the persecution of Jezabel.

After a long circuit of sixty miles, made by the order of God, with indescribable suffering, they at length arrived in Egypt. The Divine Child raised His eyes to Heaven and prayed to the Eternal Father in behalf of those miserable people, groaning under the dominion of the demons, whom they adored in their numberless idols. Exercising His supreme power over Hell, on His first entrance into that vast kingdom He cast the demons into the abyss, overthrew the idols and destroyed their temples. The merciful Mother, by her fervent prayers, cooperated with Him.

This wonderful event caused great anxiety among the Egyptians, who were ignorant of its cause; nevertheless, some of the wise men knew from the traditions of the ancients that a king of the Jews was to enter into their country, at whose arrival their idols were to be broken and their temples demolished.

In this trouble, many came to the Holy Virgin and St. Joseph to ask them, as they were strangers, if they knew the cause of the wonderful occurrence.

The Mother of Divine Wisdom took advantage of this favorable occasion to instruct them, to open their eyes to the falsity of their worship and teach them the truths of faith. Amidst these prodigies they continued their journey, expelling the demons from the possessed, until they reached Heliopolis. As they entered the city, a tree which stood near the gate bowed its branches even to the earth as if to render homage to its Creator and thank Him for having delivered it from a demon who had for a long time been venerated by the Egyptians. A great number of persons witnessed this prodigy, and many writers have preserved the remembrance of it to succeeding ages (see *Nic. Sozomen, Brochus*), as also that of the well at which the Blessed Virgin and St. Joseph drank, the water of which still operates many miracles.

Lucifer was confounded at these events and, seeing all his companions precipitated into Hell, inflamed with fury, he came forth from the abyss to discover the cause. He overran Egypt, but discovering nothing, began to judge that the Holy Virgin was the cause of all the evil; he did not suspect her Son, whom he believed to have been born like other children. Returning to Hell, he revealed his suspicions to his companions and led them out to wage a new war against this woman so terrible to them. But the Most High would not permit it, and they were compelled to remain at two miles distance from her.

While Lucifer was thus preparing to attack our Queen, God, by an act of His power, precipitated

him and his infernal battalions to the bottom of
the abyss, whence for some time they were not
allowed to come forth.

The holy travelers took up their abode in Heliopolis, where they found a house suited to the desires
of the Blessed Virgin, as it was poor and at some
distance from the city. Entering into it, she knelt
and kissed the ground, offering to God all the sufferings she might have to endure before returning
to her own country; then she cleansed the house
and arranged the articles in it, for she was always
a lover of neatness and order. Although they had
now found a lodging, yet they were destitute of even
the necessities of life, for since their arrival God
had ceased to provide miraculously for their wants,
as He had done during their journey in the desert.
Therefore they were obliged to turn to the last
resource of the poor—that of alms, and the holy
St. Joseph went from door to door, soliciting the
charitable aid of others.[1]

During the first three days they had no other
food than the pieces of bread which St. Joseph thus
received. The Blessed Mother and the Divine Babe
dwelt in this house destitute of every convenience,
and in a state of extreme want, without even a board
for their bed. In a short time St. Joseph, having

---

1. Is it not impossible for us to restrain our tears when we consider that the glorious Patriarch St. Joseph was obliged to
   beg from door to door the food which was necessary to support the King and Queen of Heaven? Oh, how much is
   poverty ennobled when we look upon it from this Christian point of view!

earned a little money by his labor, procured a bed for his holy spouse and a crib for the Child; as for himself, he lay only on the bare ground. The house remained entirely bare of furniture and utensils until he earned the price of them by the sweat of his brow. It contained three small rooms, one of which served as the oratory of the Blessed Virgin; there she retired to pray, and there also she kept the Holy Infant. The second was used by St. Joseph as a place of prayer and repose; and the third served as a shop wherein he followed his trade. The Blessed Mother, seeing that St. Joseph was compelled to redouble his labors in order to provide for the sustenance of the Holy Family, resolved to aid him by her own endeavors. She procured work from some of the neighboring women, and as all that she did was perfect, she was never in want of employment. In order to do this she devoted the day to work and the night to spiritual exercises.

Yet during the hours of labor, this great Queen never lost sight of her Son and her God; she never ceased her divine contemplations, but merely deferred until night the exercises of piety she had been accustomed to perform in the day. The Infant God was delighted with the prudence of His Mother; He regulated the distribution of her time and apportioned to each hour its particular duty. This manner of life she followed during all the time of their stay in Egypt. She always knelt by the crib in which the Child reposed: sometimes she conversed with Him, at other times, sang in His praise hymns and canticles, which, had they been written, would exceed in number those now chanted in our churches.

The fame of the sanctity of the Holy Family soon spread throughout the city, and persons of every condition flocked to visit them. The concourse of people became so great that the Blessed Virgin consulted God as to how she was to act with regard to them. Our Lord answered that she should instruct them in the truths of faith and the knowledge of the true God. The obedient Queen faithfully executed this order; the fruit which she produced in those souls was so great that it would be impossible to relate all the wonders and miraculous conversions which she operated. She devoted herself particularly to the care of the poor and infirm, in whose favor she exercised not only her charity, but also her wisdom and power.

The great and excessive heats of Egypt produced a pestilence in Heliopolis, during which she underwent incredible labors and fatigues in attending the sick. So great was the number that flocked to her that she asked Our Lord to permit St. Joseph to aid her in the work. He then instructed and cured the men, whilst she performed the like offices for the women, so that the love borne towards them by the inhabitants of that country was very great. Frequently, in evidence of their gratitude, they brought gifts and presents, yet the Queen of Heaven never accepted anything for herself; that which she could not possibly refuse she distributed among the poor.

Chapter 16

MASSACRE OF THE INNOCENTS.

The Holy Family had been six months in Egypt when Herod, furious at the news of the wonderful things that had occurred whilst the Magi were in Bethlehem, and again when the Child Jesus was in Jerusalem, determined on and commanded the massacre of the Innocents. Our great Queen understood at that time that her Son was praying to His Eternal Father for the afflicted parents and offering up those infant victims as the first fruits of His redemption of men. She knew also that, in order that they might be sacrificed in the name of their Redeemer, He would grant to the Holy Innocents the use of reason, that thus they might merit the crown and glory of martyrdom. The Blessed Virgin understood that the Eternal Father granted all the petitions of the Incarnate Word.

Although she was anxious to inquire respecting the fate of St. Elizabeth and St. John the Baptist, yet she hesitated to do so, on account of the reverence and prudence which she felt with regard to matters of revelation. At length with great humility she spoke of her fears to her Divine Son, who was pleased to let her know that Zachary had died four months after the birth of the Infant Jesus, that Elizabeth and her son had retired into the desert to escape the persecution of Herod, and that she there dwelt in a grotto and spent her life in the practice of the greatest mortification. In this revelation she also learned that Elizabeth would live only three years longer, and that after her death, St. John the Baptist would remain in the desert. From this time the Blessed Virgin frequently sent her Angels to visit her cousin and carry provisions to her, and those were the best meals which Elizabeth had in the desert. When the time of her holy cousin's death drew nigh, Mary sent many of her Angels to assist her, and after her happy departure, they buried her in her pious solitude.

During the seven years which followed, Mary supplied the young Baptist with the food necessary for his support, such as bread and other things, but after that time she ceased to do so, because he was then able to procure for himself the food which he required, such as herbs, locusts and wild honey.

The massacre of the Innocents was beheld by Mary as vividly as if she were present at it; she knew the exact number of the children, and also that they had received the use of reason, by which they were enabled to render their sacrifice voluntarily. Some of the infants were only eight days old, others two or six months, none over two years. They received a profound knowledge of the Divine Essence, and also the infused virtues of perfect charity, faith, hope and religion, and exercised heroic acts of these virtues as well as of the love of God and worship of the Divinity. She beheld a multitude of Angels who assisted them at their martyrdom, accompanied them to Limbo, and after Our Lord's Ascension, into Paradise also. At this sight, the holy Queen, inflamed with love and full of joy, intoned the canticle, *Laudate pueri, Dominum*, which the Angels continued with her.

One day, as the Blessed Virgin and St. Joseph were conversing together on the mystery of the Incarnation, the Divine Infant consoled His foster father by speaking to him for the first time. He addressed him by the sweet name of "Father," and so great was the impression made upon St. Joseph by this word that it was a miracle that he did not expire of love. This happened one year after their arrival in Egypt. During this period the Blessed Mother had kept her Son in swaddling clothes, but now she asked His permission to change them for other garments. The Divine Infant answered her thus:

"My Mother, the swathing bands of My infancy have been very pleasing to Me, because of the love I bear to the souls whom I have created, and whom I am come to redeem. In My more mature years I shall be bound, dragged to My enemies, and by them be put to death. And if even the thought of this is pleasing to Me, because I love the will of My Father, all other things will be easy. I wish to have only one garment in this world, for I desire only what is necessary to cover Me. Although all created things are Mine, yet I wish to teach men by My example to reject all that is superfluous. Clothe

Me then, My dear Mother, in a long, dark tunic; it will grow with Me, and for it they will cast lots at My death, so that, even of this, I will not have the disposal, in order that men may know that I was born, lived and died in poverty."

The Blessed Virgin replied: "Allow me to put shoes on Thy feet, that they may not be bruised at so tender an age. I also desire that Thou wouldst wear this linen under Thy tunic, to protect Thy flesh from the roughness of the wool." The Lord replied:

"My Mother, I consent that, for the present, thou mayest put poor sandals upon My feet: I will wear them until the time of My public life, when I will begin to go barefoot. The linen I will not use, that I may teach the world, and those who in future times will follow Me in great numbers, to practice poverty in their attire."

The Virgin Mother, having learned the will of her dear Son, made His sandals herself, as also His woolen tunic, which she wove without seam. This tunic grew with His growth, and never became old or soiled during the thirty-two years that He wore it, nor did it, in the least, lose its first color and lustre. When the Divine Infant began to walk, the consolation of the Blessed Mother and St. Joseph was indescribable. In their presence He walked without being held, but before strangers He concealed this wonder. The Holy Virgin continued to nurse Our Lord three times a day for six months longer, after which she began to give Him light food at morning, noon and evening, but this He never asked for. When He became a little older He took His meals with His holy parents, and it was He who gave the blessing before and after meals. As soon as Jesus began to walk, He frequently retired into His Mother's oratory to pray. Mary was in doubt whether she should follow Him thither, but Jesus Himself invited her to accompany and remain with Him. Thus, by the will of the Lord, she became the disciple of her Divine Son, and from that moment there were operated between them mysteries so hidden, yet so great, that human tongue cannot relate them.

Here we must not omit to relate that in the spiritual exercises which they performed, our Saviour often wept and had bloody sweats.[1] His dear Mother wiped away those holy tears and precious drops of Blood, occasioned (as she discovered by her knowledge of her Son's interior life) by the loss of the reprobates and the ingratitude of men towards their Creator and Redeemer.

When the Child Jesus attained the age of six years, He began to pay visits to the sick and infirm in order to console and strengthen them in their afflictions. A great number of children flocked to Him; to these He taught the practice of virtues and the way to eternal life. When engaged in conver-

---

1. It is important here to remark that the divine Jesus often shed tears, from His tender infancy even to His death. Both He and Mary wept for sins and faults committed by men against His Eternal Father. Let us, then, enrich ourselves with the infinite merits of the precious tears of Jesus and His Mother.

sation in His parents' house He assumed a more serious air and discontinued the caresses which He had sometimes bestowed on His Mother and foster father. So great an air of majesty appeared on His countenance that, had it not been tempered by incomparable mildness, no one would have dared to address Him, so profound was the respectful awe which He inspired.

Chapter 17

THE RETURN FROM EGYPT
TO NAZARETH.

After six years of exile in Egypt, the Eternal Father expressly ordered the Incarnate Word to return to Nazareth. His Mother, who was praying at His side, saw in His heart that He was conforming Himself to the Divine Will; the Angel, at the same time, made known to St. Joseph that they were to depart, as is recorded by the Evangelist.

After having regulated everything, they distributed their few utensils among the poor, by the hands of the Child Jesus, who had been accustomed to distribute their little alms.

They left Heliopolis accompanied by the holy Angels, and recrossed the deserts they had traversed seven years before. The Blessed Virgin, carrying the Child, rode on the ass they had brought with them in their flight, and St. Joseph led the way. Sometimes he prayed, at others, conversed with his spouse, contemplated the Divine Child, or sang sacred canticles. They soon exhausted their supply of provisions, but the Child Jesus supplied their wants, either by miraculously multiplying the bread, or by the ministry of Angels.

At length, after a tedious and painful journe they arrived at the confines of Palestine, where the holy spouse learned that the cruel Herod was dead, but that Archelaüs, his son, reigned in Judea. Therefore, he thought it best to cross the country of the tribes of Dan and Issachar, in the lower part of Galilee.

They followed the coast of the Mediterranean, leaving Jerusalem to the right, and finally arrived at Nazareth. They returned thanks to God, and St. Joseph went to seek that pious woman, their former neighbor, to whom they had confided the care of their house. Entering this abode, the Blessed Virgin prostrated herself on the earth, and again returned thanks to the Most High for having delivered them out of the hands of Herod. She placed everything in order and resumed her wonted occupations, according to her rule of life.

As Our Lord wished that His holy Mother should be a perfect model of all virtues, He applied Himself with special care to her perfection during the twenty-three years He spent with her in this holy house. To try her in the greatness of her holy love, as well as to exercise her in the most heroic virtues, He deprived her of the gift of reading His interior, which had hitherto been to her a source of inexpressible consolation. He began to treat her with a serious and reserved air, seldom spoke to her, and frequently remained alone.

The tender Virgin Mother, not knowing what had caused so great a change, had recourse to her profound humility. She esteemed herself unworthy of those favors, and was less afflicted for having lost the sight of her Lord than from the fear that she had disgusted Him by her ingratitude. Jesus felt sensibly the affliction of His holy Mother, but did not wish to give any exterior sign of His compassion. Sometimes when His Mother called Him to take the nourishment necessary to sustain life, He did not attend immediately, as He had been accustomed to do; at other times He obeyed, but would not look at her, or speak even one word. Although His exterior manner of acting was so severe, He felt inexpressible interior joy and complacency at seeing such wonderful virtue in a mere creature.

He assumed a still graver air when, at taking Him to rest, she would prostrate herself before Him all bathed in tears and implore His pardon for her want of care during the day. Although He beheld her in such deep affliction, yet He answered her humble petition only by commanding her to depart. This bitter and cruel trial, which was to Mary a martyrdom of excessive grief, was to Jesus a subject of complacency, in proving how great and pure was His Mother's love. After this terrible agony had lasted for thirty days, she prostrated herself at His feet and, bathed in tears, implored Him to tell her if in aught she had been remiss in serving Him, begging Him at the same time not to deprive her any longer of a return of love. Our Lord answered: "Arise, My Mother." At these affectionate words the heart of that tender Mother, so oppressed with grief, was immediately transformed, as it were, and raised to sublime ecstasy, in which her grief was changed into sweet interior consolation of the soul.

But this first affliction was quickly followed by another.

By the law of Moses it was ordained that the Israelites should go to the Temple to adore God three times each year. This law, it is true, was not binding upon women; nevertheless it was resolved that St. Joseph should go thither twice alone, but that the third time the Blessed Virgin and her Son should accompany him. Although Jerusalem was many miles distant, nevertheless Jesus wished to perform the journey on foot, although at so tender an age it would naturally cause Him much pain and suffering. On His first pilgrimage only did He permit Himself to be carried, sometimes by His Mother, at others by St. Joseph. When they rested for the night at some hostelry, He never left His Mother's side, in order that she might be able always to consider and imitate Him in all His actions.

When Jesus had attained the age of twelve years the Holy Family performed one of these pilgrimages, in order to be present at the feast of the Azymes, which lasted seven days. On the last day of the feast they set out to return to Nazareth. Our Lord profited by this occasion to separate from His parents. In order to do this, He availed Himself of the custom of the Jews, for the immense concourse of people divided themselves into groups, the women walking by themselves, and the men doing the same. Children were allowed to remain either with their father or mother, therefore St. Joseph thought that Jesus had remained with His Mother.

At this time Mary's thoughts were diverted from the person of her Son and absorbed in a state of high contemplation; returning to herself and perceiving Jesus to be absent, she thought He was with St. Joseph.

The Divine Child had separated from them at the gate of the city, where the crowd was the greatest. In the evening when the people met together and families were reunited at the appointed place, the Holy Virgin and St. Joseph perceived the absence of the Child and were rendered speechless by surprise and grief. Coming a little to themselves, they resolved to return and seek Him by the road they had just traveled over; meanwhile they accused themselves of great negligence.

The Holy Virgin inquired of the Angels of her guard as to what had befallen her Son, but they gave her no reply. The afflicted parents feared that Archelaüs had heard of the Child and had caused His arrest; or that, by some fault, they themselves had been the cause of His loss. Oppressed with these sorrowful fears, they continued to seek Him without taking either rest or nourishment. Having vainly sought among their friends and relations in Jerusalem, they were about to go into the desert, in the hope of finding him with St. John the Baptist, but this the Angels prevented.

On the third day they wished to go to Bethlehem, thinking that Jesus might have gone thither, but they were again dissuaded by the Angels; therefore they traversed the streets of Jerusalem, inquiring for Him and giving descriptions of His countenance, hair, height and clothing. A woman replied that such a child had come to her door to ask alms, and that whilst giving it to him she had felt tender compassion at seeing a child so gracious and amiable without anyone to take care of him. Hearing this, the afflicted Mother and St. Joseph directed their steps to the hospital for the poor, where they again heard that a child like that described had been there consoling the poor, but he had gone, no one knew whither.

Then the afflicted spouses thought that they might find Him in the Temple, and having asked the Guardian Angels, they encouraged them to seek Him there.

They directed their steps to the Temple, where they arrived just as the dispute going on between the scribes and doctors, in which Jesus had taken part, was about to be terminated; they only heard the last reasons given by the holy Child to prove the coming of the Messias, which was the subject of the discussion.

Ravished with joy at having found her treasure, the Holy Virgin approached her Divine Son and, in the presence of all, addressed Him in the words written by St. Luke: *Fili, quid fecisti nobis sic? Ecce pater tuus et ego dolentes, quaerebamus te*—"Son, why hast Thou done so to us? Behold, Thy father and I have sought Thee sorrowing."

Jesus answered in the words quoted by the Evangelist. Leaving the Temple, they took the direction of Nazareth. As soon as they reached a solitary place, the Holy Virgin satisfied the desire of her heart by prostrating herself at the feet of her Divine Son and asking His blessing. He consoled her by kind and gracious words and by giving her a clearer knowledge than she had had heretofore of the mysteries of His heart, and the reasons which had prompted Him to act towards her as He had done.

The Evangelist has written nothing of the eighteen years which Jesus spent in Nazareth, except that He was submissive to His parents—*et erat subditus illis*—and this because the things that transpired within that holy abode are too sublime for human description. Here it was that our great Queen received the knowledge of all the mysteries, rites and ceremonies of the Church, the falsity of heresies, the errors of the Gentiles, and all the arrangement of the Evangelical Law. She had a foreknowledge of the four Gospels and of all the mysteries which they contain, and this knowledge was so clear and well-defined that no other creature could ever attain it. In a vision of the Divinity, she learned that God wished her to be the Mistress of the New Law of grace, and she received the lights and graces necessary to so exalted an office.

Three years were devoted by Jesus to the instruction of His holy Mother, during which time He gave her three instructions each day. He also continually operated wonders in her soul by the force of holy love; at each instant He added graces to graces already received, gifts to those with which He heretofore had enriched her, and an increase of sanctity to the sublime perfection which she had attained. She learned that not only would the Holy

Sacrament of the Altar be instituted, but that this would occur before her death, and that she would have the happiness of receiving It many times. In view of this wonderful mystery she annihilated herself in the depths of her nothingness, and offered most fervent thanksgiving to God; as a preparation to receive in future time the adorable Body of her Son, she began to offer up every action for this great end, and this ineffable mystery remained from that moment ever present to her mind.

These wonders were usually operated in the humble oratory of Mary, in the house at Nazareth. There did Jesus converse with her on sublime mysteries, there did they pray together, sometimes kneeling, sometimes prostrate in the form of a cross, and again raised from the ground, in the same holy position. Sometimes Jesus spoke to her as a Master, at other times as her Son; sometimes He would be transfigured in His body as He was afterwards on Mount Thabor; and again would be bathed in a sweat of blood, as in His Passion.

Whilst Mary was receiving these divine lessons she attained to her thirty-third year, the age at which the human body has received all its perfections and begins to decline; yet in Mary, age operated no change; at seventy, her complexion and form were as beautiful as at the age of maturity, and this privilege was granted to her sinless body that it might always resemble the Sacred Humanity of her Divine Son as it seemed when He attained His full perfection. This same favor was not granted to St. Joseph; and the Blessed Mother, perceiving the great change in him, begged him to cease from work, saying that she herself would labor for the support of the family. Although the holy patriarch at first opposed this proposition, yet he finally acquiesced, and in order that they might possess nothing superfluous, they distributed his tools among poor carpenters.

From this time St. Joseph gave himself up entirely to the contemplation of the mysteries of which he was the depositary, and to the heroic practice of virtues. The Blessed Mother was enabled to support the family without being compelled to leave her retreat, for a devout woman, who loved her for her virtue, always provided her with work. In this she did not seek for gain, for a little sufficed for all their wants. Mary and her Son never tasted meat; their food consisted of fish, fruits and herbs, and of these they partook with great moderation. She took but very little rest, and devoted several hours of the night to labor, for God allowed her to do so now, more than when she dwelt in Egypt. Sometimes, when her means did not suffice to provide for St. Joseph all those little delicacies which she wished, God would supply the want, sometimes by multiplying what they had, at others, by sending through the Guardian Angels of Mary all that was required.

Chapter 18

THE SICKNESS AND PRECIOUS
DEATH OF ST. JOSEPH.

The suffering and pain consequent to the indisposition of the holy patriarch continued to increase with his years, and his holy spouse was obliged to redouble her labors, not for their support alone, but also that she might be able to procure many comforts for him. She frequently exercised her power over creatures by commanding the viands she prepared to have a more agreeable flavor. His meals she presented on her knees, and also performed the humble office of taking off his shoes when he was unable to do it himself.

During the last three years of his life, in which his sufferings increased, she assisted him day and night, except when she was occupied in serving Jesus or giving Him His meals. Not content with these assiduous attentions, she begged the Lord to diminish the sufferings of her spouse, and inflict them upon herself. She commanded his pains to abate and bade her Angels to console him, which they did, sometimes by conversing with him in visible forms, and again by chanting celestial melodies.

During the space of eight years God had tried

ᴛʜᴇ virtue of the holy patriarch by continual sickness, in order thereby to add to his eternal reward.

The Holy Virgin saw that the hour of his death was drawing nigh, and supplicated her Divine Son to aid him in that last and dangerous hour. The merciful Jesus promised that He would not only assist him, but would raise him to a rank so exalted that he would be the admiration of all the heavenly hierarchies. In reality, during the last five days of his life, Jesus never quitted his side, except when the Holy Virgin took His place. During the nine days which preceded his decease, the Angels, by the order of his blessed spouse, chanted three times a day their heavenly canticles, and the celestial perfume of Paradise, filling the room of the dying Saint, fortified and strengthened him. On the eve of his death he was ravished in an ecstasy which continued for twenty-four hours, for Our Lord strengthened him and enabled him to bear it. In this state he clearly beheld the Divine Essence, as also all that regarded the mysteries of the Incarnation and Redemption, which he had heretofore known only by the light of faith.

He was commissioned by the Most Holy Trinity to announce to the holy patriarchs in Limbo that the time of their deliverance was approaching. Returning to himself out of this ecstatic state, St. Joseph appeared glorious and resplendent. Turning to the Holy Virgin he besought her to bless him, but she humbly asked her Divine Son to give this consolation to St. Joseph, and Jesus blessed him. Then kneeling before the dying patriarch, she asked and received his parting benediction, and respectfully kissed his hand. With great humility St. Joseph begged pardon of his holy spouse for the faults he might have committed against the reverence due to her dignity and merit, and prayed her to assist him in his last moments. After this he addressed himself to his Son, and returned most humble thanks for the favors He had conferred on him, particularly during his illness. He made every effort to throw himself on his knees, but Jesus, who was at his side, taking him in His arms, pressed him to His bosom; in that moment of supreme happiness his pure soul exhaled its last breath. As soon as he was dead, the Angels chanted their celestial harmonies in the holy house, and the Blessed Virgin commanded them to conduct his great soul to Limbo, to remain with the holy patriarchs.

With her own hands she prepared the body for burial, and the Lord vested it with ravishing splendor. It is necessary to remark that the death of St. Joseph was not caused by his great and particular infirmities alone, but was also caused by the fire of his ardent charity. His heart was consumed by flames so ardent that his life had been many times preserved by a miracle; God at length suspended His succor, nature could no longer resist the force of his love, and the link which bound his holy soul to the body was broken.

This kind of death was then more the triumph of divine love than the punishment of Original Sin. St. Joseph died at the age of sixty years. He had lived twenty-seven years with the Blessed Virgin, who, at the time of his decease, was forty-one years and six months old.

The Holy Virgin felt a great natural sorrow for the death of her spouse, because she loved him with tender affection, and this love was increased by her knowledge of the sublime sanctity to which he had attained. She knew that he had been sanctified when seven months in the womb of his mother, and that the fire of concupiscence had seemed to be extinguished in him through his entire life. Never had he experienced the lightest sentiment of an impure or ill-regulated affection. At the age of three years he had received the use of reason, as also infused science and an augmentation of grace in the highest degree. The gift of contemplation had been given him, and at the age of seven years, he had possessed consummate sanctity. He was equal to the Seraphim in purity, and had never had a thought or image contrary to this divine virtue. In fine, by his heroic virtue, he had merited to be chosen as the foster father and adopted parent of the Son of God.

Knowing of all these gifts, and even of many others, the Holy Virgin could not but be sensibly grieved at such a loss.

God has granted some extraordinary privileges to St. Joseph. First, those who invoke him shall obtain from God, by his intercession, the gift of chastity, and shall not be conquered by the temptation of the senses; secondly, they shall receive particular graces to deliver them from sin; thirdly, they shall obtain a true devotion to the Blessed Virgin;

fourthly, they shall have a good and happy death, and in that all-decisive moment be defended against the assaults of Satan; fifthly, they shall be delivered, when expedient for them, from bodily sufferings, and shall find help in their afflictions; sixthly, if married, they shall be blessed with offspring; seventhly, the demons shall have extreme dread of the invocation of the glorious name of St. Joseph.

After the death of the holy patriarch, the Blessed Virgin learned that it was the will of God that she should no longer devote so much time to manual labor, but apply herself more particularly to interior exercises. A few hours' work was sufficient to procure all that was necessary for her wants, for now she restricted herself to one frugal meal in the day. Heretofore she had taken two, but this only that she might be able to keep company with her spouse. She now punctually executed what she knew to be the will of Our Lord with regard to her food, frequently tasting nothing but a morsel of dry bread, and even this only at night.

Although the respect and veneration entertained by Mary for her Divine Son had always been very great, yet these sentiments increased in her after the death of St. Joseph, more particularly in the outward manifestation of them. Having then no witnesses but the Angels, she would prostrate herself before Jesus and remain in this humble position until He would bid her arise. Frequently she kissed His sacred feet, and always presented His food on her knees. Many were the humble contests which arose between her and the Angels with regard to such lowly offices as cleaning the house, etc., which she wished to perform herself, but in which they frequently anticipated her, serving her as subjects do their queen; yet, if she asked them not to perform these actions, they immediately obeyed. Mary most attentively observed all the actions of Jesus; and as He, considering that notwithstanding His sufferings and death, so many souls would be lost through their own fault, was often so extremely afflicted as to be bathed in a sweat of blood, so she, from the same motive, shed tears of blood. Then Our Lord, being moved with compassion, would command the Angels to console her with celestial melodies, or sometimes He Himself would console her by His embrace. She had a foreknowledge of many of the predestined, principally the Apostles, the disciples and the faithful of the primitive Church; therefore, when she afterwards beheld the followers of her Divine Son, she knew them before she spoke to them, and had already prayed for them.

Many other mysteries were operated in this time between Jesus and His Mother, more particularly during the last four years they spent together, which are reserved to be revealed in Heaven for the particular happiness of the elect.

Chapter 19

PREPARATION FOR
THE PUBLIC LIFE OF CHRIST.

Jesus, having attained His twenty-seventh year, began to prepare for His public life. He retired more frequently from the house, and sometimes remained absent from His Mother for three days. She suffered much in those separations, and would often send her Angels to inform Him of the details of her occupations. When He returned to the house she prostrated herself, in order to thank Him for the graces He had granted to sinners. She served Him as a tender and affectionate Mother, and prepared delicate food to support His sacred Humanity. Of this He was often in great need, as He sometimes passed three entire days without either food or rest. She desired to accompany Him on His journeys in order to assist those who would hearken to the divine word, and this desire Our Lord granted by permitting her to follow Him; therefore, from that moment, whenever Jesus went forth from Nazareth, His blessed Mother accompanied Him.

Our Lord began to make journeys in the neighborhood of Nazareth, announcing everywhere the coming of the Messias and accompanying His words by the interior inspirations of His grace, to prepare them to receive Him. He suited His instructions to the quality of the persons who heard Him; to the learned He spoke of the testimonies given in the prophecies; to the ignorant, He alluded to the coming of the Magi and the massacre of the Innocents, thus bringing forward what was most suited to the capacities and dispositions of each. The fruit produced by these divine teachings was great and abundant, although it was done in private and not in public, as afterwards in His three years preaching.

He visited the sick and consoled many in their agony; some He cured without their knowing who had relieved them. The Virgin Mother was generally present on these occasions, and cooperated with Him; she instructed more women than men, for at that time the followers of Jesus were but few in number, as the time destined in the divine decrees for calling them had not yet arrived. The usual companions of Jesus were His Mother and the Angels; these blessed spirits frequently sheltered them from the inclemency of the seasons when they were returning to their home.

To everyone they spoke of the coming of the Messias, the Saviour of the world, but in this regard the poor were more privileged, as being the better disposed, their sins being less heinous, their attachment to worldly goods but slight and their humility greater.

At that time the voice of the Lord came to John the son of Zachary in the desert, as is related in the holy Gospel. He heard this divine Voice whilst absorbed in an ecstasy, in which he was given to understand that he should leave the desert to prepare the way for the preaching of the Word. The holy precursor came forth from his desert clothed in camel-skin, barefoot, pale and emaciated. His appearance breathed an air of gravity, tempered by incomparable modesty and profound humility; his soul was strong, generous and inflamed with love for God and his neighbor; in a word, he was admirably fitted to be the precursor of the Incarnate Word and the teacher of the Jews, a stiff-necked, ungrateful and obstinate people, governed by idolatrous magistrates and directed by proud and avaricious priests.

The Angels had given to John the Baptist, while in the desert, a beautiful cross, before which he performed many exercises of mortification and prayed, extending his arms in the form of a cross. He did not wish to leave this treasure behind him in the desert, therefore he sent it as a present to the Blessed Virgin by the hands of the Angels. She received it with great veneration and bitter grief, because of the mysteries which it presented to her mind. She placed it in her oratory until the dispersion of the Apostles throughout the world, when she gave it to them, with many other precious relics, as we shall see hereafter.

Jesus had now attained His thirtieth year. The Virgin Mother, who had reached the height of her love for Him, was one day raised to a state of sublime contemplation, when she heard a voice from the throne of God, which said: "Mary, My daugh-

ter and My spouse, offer Me thy Son in sacrifice."
The obedient Mary immediately did so with such
great and inexpressible intensity of love that this
sacrifice was incomparably more agreeable to God
than that of Abraham, or all others that had been
offered to Him. In recompense the Holy Virgin was
raised to the clear vision of the Divinity, in which
she was given to see all the mysteries of the
Redemption of men, by the preaching, the Passion
and the death of her Son, to which she was to cooperate by giving her consent. When she returned to
herself out of this ecstasy, Jesus presented Himself
to beg her permission to accomplish in favor of men
all that she knew God had imposed on Him, promising to return again and take her with Him to be
the companion of His labors.

The Holy Virgin cast herself at His feet; Jesus
embraced His Mother, and both, shedding many
tears, made an offering of themselves for the salvation of the world.

The Redeemer directed His steps to the Jordan,
where John the Baptist was preaching and baptizing sinners. Mingling with the crowd, He asked to
be baptized by John, who, enlightened by an interior light, humbled himself before Jesus, begged to
be baptized by Him, and rendered testimony of Him.
But in obedience to the Saviour, he baptized Him,
as is related in the Gospel. At that moment was
heard a voice saying: *Hic est Filius meus dilectus*—
"This is My beloved Son"—and the Holy Ghost
descended on Him in the form of a dove. Thus the
divinity of Jesus Christ was confirmed by the most

glorious testimonies.

Jesus then granted the prayer of St. John by baptizing him with His divine hands and conferring on him the character of a Christian.

Thus He instituted the Sacrament of Baptism, although its promulgation was deferred until after the Resurrection. From the Jordan Jesus retired into the desert, accompanied by the Angels, to the spot appointed by the Divine Will for His retreat.

This was a desert place, overgrown with thorns and briars, in which there was a grotto entirely concealed. He prostrated Himself upon the earth with profound humility and thanked the Eternal Father for having given Him this place, so suitable for a retreat, and He continued His prayer in the form of a cross, interceding for the salvation of men. This was His ordinary prayer whilst in the desert; He generally prayed in the form of a cross, and frequently had sweats of blood.

Many wild beasts came to render homage to their Creator; the birds, in particular, by their joyous songs testified delight at the presence of their God made man.

As soon as Mary knew that her Divine Son had gone into the desert, she retired into her oratory to imitate His actions, as was her custom. There she prayed, and often shed tears of blood for the sins of men. At every moment the Angels revealed to her the actions of Jesus, His manner of prayer and all His divine occupations. She sent many embassies of Angels to visit Him in her name, and she gave them linen which she herself had woven, to be used in wiping away His bloody sweats. So perfect was her retirement during these forty days that the neighbors thought she had departed from Nazareth, as they knew Jesus had done. Having closed her door, she occupied herself day and night in imitating the Redeemer in the desert.

During the forty days she tasted nothing; she made three hundred prostrations each day, as Jesus did in the desert; she united herself with Him in all His adorations, oblations and prayers, when He was tempted. She saw His terrible contest with Lucifer, and imitated Him in the acts by which He confounded His adversary, and thus she participated in His glorious triumph and congratulated Him by the ministry of His Angels. On their return, they, by the orders of Jesus, gave her some of the food they had brought from Heaven, and thus she was strengthened after her long fast.

When the forty days were ended, the Son of God returned thanks to His Eternal Father and prayed for those who, in after times, would, in imitation of Him, retire from the world, either for life or for a time, in order to apply themselves to contemplation, or to the holy exercises of retreat. The Most High promised to show them favor, to cause them to hear in their hearts the words of eternal life and to bestow upon them particular graces. Then Jesus went to find John the Baptist, who gave testimony of Him before all those present. Going into Judea, Jesus remained there ten months, preaching and enlightening the humble and simple with regard to the coming of the Messias. Our blessed Lady also came forth from her retreat and instructed many persons of the neighborhood, announcing to them the advent of the Redeemer of the world, without, however, discovering to them who He was.

Chapter 20

THE PREACHING OF OUR SAVIOUR,
AND THE COOPERATION OF
THE BLESSED MOTHER.

Our Saviour at length began to announce publicly that He was the expected Messias. He first
called two of the disciples of St. John the Baptist
to follow Him; one was St. Andrew, the other, St.
John the Evangelist. After this He called St. Peter,
then St. Philip, who told Nathaniel of the coming
of the Messias, and conducted Him to Jesus: this
latter became the fifth disciple of our Saviour. With
these five He came into Galilee to preach and baptize publicly. The Most High made known to the
Holy Virgin His Will that she should accompany
her Son, and cooperate in the accomplishment of
the work of the Redemption. She testified her
entire submission to the Divine Will, and most
earnestly begged the favor of being allowed to suffer and die in the place of her Son, or at least to
expire with Him.

The disciples, having been instructed in the mysteries of the Incarnation, were filled with an earnest
desire to see, know and venerate the Mother of the
Saviour. They incessantly begged this favor from

the Lord, and when He had graciously granted their
desire, they, in His holy company, turned their steps
in the direction of Nazareth. The Blessed Virgin,
knowing the visit she was about to receive, was very
diligent in preparing the house and providing meals
for her expected guests.

She came to the door to receive her Son and
Saviour; prostrating herself at His feet, she kissed
them humbly and begged His divine benediction.
This she did in the presence of His disciples, that
by her example they might learn how they should
respect and venerate their Master. She received
them into her house and served them at table, not,
however, on her knees, as was her custom with her
Divine Son. As soon as the disciples had retired to
rest, Our Lord entered into His Mother's oratory.
There she prostrated herself to ask pardon for any
want of care she had shown whilst serving Him,
and the Lord consoled her by words of eternal life.
He graciously bade her arise, but at the same time
showed an air of great majesty and serenity and
treated her with more reserve; this He did for her
greater merit. The most pure Mary prayed her
Divine Son to administer to her the Sacrament of
Baptism, which He had instituted. To this He consented, so that she might be united to the number
of His followers.

In order to confer the Sacrament with greater
solemnity He ordered thousands of Angels to assist
at it in visible forms. As Jesus was baptizing His
holy Mother in their presence, the voice of the Eternal Father was heard, saying: "This is My daughter,

in whom I am well pleased," and the Incarnate Word also spoke, saying: "This is My beloved Mother, whom I have chosen; she shall assist Me in all My labors." The Holy Ghost added: "This is My spouse, chosen from among thousands." After her Baptism the great Queen was invited to a marriage to be celebrated in Cana between persons related to her in the fourth degree, on the side of St. Ann.

The Holy Virgin apprised the spouses of the arrival of her Son with His disciples, and as they wished to invite them, the divine Mother persuaded them to do so. As Our Lord entered into their house, He saluted the guests in the following words: "May the peace of the Lord be with you." Afterwards He gave an exhortation to the bridegroom, teaching him what regarded his state, and by what means he might attain to the sanctity and perfection of it. The Holy Virgin performed the same good office for the bride; both these spouses remained ever faithful to their duties. St. John and the other disciples were present at these instructions. It is false to assert, as some writers have done, that St. John was the bridegroom.

Our divine Saviour and the holy Mother sat at the table with the company and partook of every dish presented to them, but always in great moderation. This they did, although they had not such dishes served at their own table, in order not to condemn the common life of men by abstaining and showing singularity in what is not reprehensible, and can be done even with perfection.

It was on this occasion that the changing of the

water into wine was operated, to the great astonishment of the steward of the feast, who was a priest
of the law. He was surprised, because as he held the
first place, and Our Lord and His blessed Mother
occupied the last, he knew nothing whatever of the
miracle. The answer of Jesus to His Mother: *Quid
mihi et tibi, mulier*—"Woman, what is that to Me
and to thee?"—was not addressed to her as a
reproach, but with great mildness. He called her
not "Mother," but "woman," because, for some time
past, He had not used towards her the same tender words as before. St. John calls this the first miracle of Jesus, because it was the first of which He
publicly acknowledged Himself to be the author,
but He had already wrought great numbers of them
in secret.

From Cana Jesus proceeded to Capharnaum,
accompanied by His Mother and disciples. They
remained there for some days, and He immediately
began to preach in divers places. Many pious women
joined the Blessed Virgin, it being more becoming
that she should not be alone. She instructed these
women, repeating to them what she had learned
from the teachings of Jesus.

She also operated many miracles and prodigies,
cured the sick, the lame and the blind, expelled
demons and even raised the dead to life, by virtue
of the power communicated to her by her Divine
Son. The sufferings which she endured in all those
journeys were so great that we can never make an
adequate acknowledgment of them. Many times her
sufferings were so excessive that it was necessary

for God to succor her miraculously; at other times He rendered her body so light that she felt not its weight, and moved as if with wings. When the Lord preached, she listened attentively as an humble disciple, although the finger of God had engraven the Evangelical Law on her heart. She heard the divine word on her knees, to testify her respect for the law and her veneration for the person of Him who delivered it. Knowing that whilst He preached, Jesus prayed His Eternal Father that the divine seed might bear fruit in the hearts of the people, she united with Him in this supplication. She knew the interior state of His hearers, whether they were in grace or in sin, and according to these different states, she experienced different emotions. Seeing that some received not the word of God, she was deeply afflicted and wept tears of blood for their unhappy blindness; on the other hand, when she saw that others corresponded with this grace, she blessed the Lord thousands of times.

Innumerable were the conversions wrought by her prayers, conversations and instructions. She spoke to both men and women, but never in public or in those places destined for the ministers of God. She ate and conversed together with the disciples and the holy women, but her words were always seasoned with prudence and wisdom. Our Lord acted in the same manner, so that no one might doubt that He was really man, and the natural Son of the most pure Virgin.

Mary, on many occasions, gave proofs of her wonderful and admirable humility. It was generally by her means and through her intercession that Jesus operated His miracles, and she was known and recognized as the Mother of that Master so famous throughout Palestine for the wonders He had wrought. This was a great glory for Mary, yet under it, she humbled herself more profoundly than all the Saints have ever done, and she endeavored to prevent the honors which were sometimes rendered to her when she was present at the miracles of Our Lord. The Evangelists have written of two occasions. The first was when Our Lord delivered the man possessed by a dumb [mute] devil. At that time a woman cried out in honor of the Blessed Virgin: *Beatus venter qui te portavit!*—"Blessed is the womb that bore Thee!" Hearing these words, Mary interiorly prayed her Divine Son to turn this praise from her, which He did by the words: "Blessed are they who hear the word of God, and keep it." The other occasion was that recorded in the eighth chapter of St. Luke. Seeing the glory that would be rendered to her by the great concourse of people who had crowded to hear her Divine Son, she again prayed interiorly that He would save her from it.

The Lord heard her prayer, and when a voice cried out, "Behold Thy Mother and Thy brethren," He answered, "My Mother and My brethren are they who hear My word and keep it."

The devil, astonished at the numerous conversions operated by Our Lord, strongly suspected Him to be the Messias, but as John the Baptist also converted many, he was in doubt between the two. He employed every means to learn the truth, and he it was who persuaded the Pharisees to send the embassy recorded by the Evangelist. But the answer given by the Precursor, that he was the *voice*, threw him into great perplexity and uncertainty, for he feared that the words, "I am the *voice*," concealed some mystery and might perhaps signify that he was the voice of the Father, that is to say, the Eternal Word. Therefore he tried to compass his death, and for this end employed Herod and Herodias.

The most Holy Virgin knew all these things and, learning that John was in prison, she sent her Angels to fortify and console him, and sometimes to convey to him necessary food. Knowing afterwards that he was to be beheaded, she prayed Jesus to assist him in person, in order that his death might be more precious in His sight. Our Lord granted her request and asked her to follow Him; immediately, by virtue of the divine power, they found themselves in the prison of the Saint, who was loaded with chains and covered with wounds, for the adulteress Herodias had ordered six of her servants to scourge him unmercifully, one after another, in the hope of thus causing his death, even before the ball and banquet should take place.

At the entrance of Our Lord and His blessed Mother, the prison was filled with light, the chains of St. John fell upon the ground, and his wounds were instantly healed. The Saint prostrated himself on the ground and asked their blessing. After a short time spent in holy conversation, an executioner sent by Herod entered the dungeon, and in the presence of Jesus and Mary, cut off the head of the Saint.

Then a dispute arose between the executioners as to who should convey the head to Herod, during which Mary, taking the precious relic in her hands, offered it to the Eternal Father. Our Lord sent his soul to Limbo, accompanied by legions of Angels; there his arrival caused an increase of joy to the Saints, for they hoped that the time of their deliverance was nigh. All these favors bestowed upon the Baptist had been obtained by the intercession of the most Holy Virgin. Nor was he the only one thus indebted to her; all the Apostles received great graces through her mediation. To her St. John owed his sublime knowledge, and also his beautiful title of "the Beloved Disciple of the Lord"; St. Peter, his conversion after having denied his Master three times; and St. James, his glorious martyrdom. The same is true of the other Apostles. She it was who instructed Mary Magdalen in the mysteries of redemption, and gave her rules to regulate her life in Marseilles. She frequently consoled her during her abode in the desert, sometimes by her own presence, and sometimes by the ministry of the Angels. Judas alone did not profit by the great affection of our holy Queen. Having been affected exteriorly by the doctrine of Jesus, and interiorly by a divine impulse, he had asked to be received among the followers of Jesus.

Our Lord, who rejects no one, received him and granted him many favors, even choosing him to be one of the Twelve. The Blessed Virgin loved him, although she knew, by the gift of infused science, that he would betray her Son. She knew that the disposition of Judas would not be improved by severity, but would rather become more hardened, therefore she treated him with great benevolence and kindness. The goodness shown to him by the Blessed Mother was so remarkable that in their disputes the Apostles spoke of him as being the most favored by the Holy Virgin; even Judas himself never suspected that he could be excluded from this privilege.

Judas was not of very good temper, and the Apostles, who were not yet confirmed in grace, had their faults. Judas often allowed himself to censure these in his brethren, judging them to be greater than they really were, and paid no attention to his own. This habit grew at last into that of detraction; he most frequently criticized St. John because he was the beloved disciple of Jesus and Mary. By these faults he opened the door to others still greater. His charity for God and his neighbor grew cold; he began to regard the Apostles with envy, and to find fault with even their holiest actions. The Virgin Mother saw the perversity of the unhappy disciple, and endeavored to remedy it by frequently admonishing him with the greatest mildness and most powerful reasons; but instead of profiting by her maternal kindness, he became irritated against her, and strove to conceal his faults by the basest hypocrisy. From this aversion to the Holy Mother he passed to contempt for his Divine Master, whose doctrine he condemned, and whose manner of life, prescribed for the Apostles, he found too hard and laborious.

Notwithstanding this unworthy conduct of Judas, Jesus and Mary always treated him in the same manner as at the beginning of his vocation.

This is the reason why the Apostles knew not the evil state of Judas, although they had some suspicion of it, seeing his exterior bad conduct. For this reason, when Jesus said at the Last Supper, "One of you will betray Me," they were all uncertain on whom that sentence would fall; they did not suspect Judas, who had always been treated with extreme kindness by the Redeemer.

Another occasion led him on to his act of treason. As the number of the disciples continued to increase, the Lord wished to give one of them charge to keep the alms, in order to distribute them again, or to pay the tribute to princes. Our Lord spoke of His intention to all the Apostles, without naming anyone in particular. Judas immediately desired to receive this office and begged St. John to obtain it for him by means of the Holy Virgin. But she, knowing that he was actuated by ambition, would not make the request of her Divine Son.

Failing in this, Judas went to St. Peter and the other Apostles and begged them to obtain for him this employment, but he was again unsuccessful. Growing more eager in his desire, he went himself to the Holy Virgin and offered to serve her and her Divine Son in this office, which, he said, he would exercise with more care than the others.

She told him to consider well what it was that he asked, and that it would be better to confide all to the will of God. At these words he became interiorly angry; the Blessed Virgin knew it, but prudently concealed her knowledge.

At first he was ashamed to present his request to Jesus, but finally ambition won the victory, and under the specious pretext of wishing to serve his Master and provide for His little flock, he begged to be entrusted with the care of the alms. Our Lord replied, "Knowest thou not, O Judas, what thou dost ask? Be not so cruel to thyself as to seek thy own destruction, and procure arms to cause thy death." Judas answered, "I desire to serve Thee, and to employ all my strength for the good of Thy society, and I will serve Thee better in this office than in any other." The Lord, by this obstinacy of Judas, justified His conduct in permitting him to enter on this dangerous charge, in which he lost his soul. But having obtained that which he so much desired, his joy was of short duration, because, contrary to his expectations, founded on Our Lord's miracles, the alms were not very abundant.

He was displeased when he saw our great Queen so liberal to the poor, and was also angry with Our Lord because He would not accept the large alms sometimes offered to Him; so far did he carry these feelings that, many months before the death of the Lord, he would frequently withdraw from the Apostles, and even from his Divine Master, whose company he could no longer support.

Two and a half years of Our Lord's public life had thus passed away, and the time for His return to His Eternal Father was drawing near. To guard His disciples against the scandal they would receive from His death, He wished to be transfigured before them.

For this purpose He chose Thabor, a mountain in Galilee, a few miles east of Nazareth, and taking with Him Peter, James and John, He was transfigured before them with all the circumstances related by the Evangelist. While Angels went for the souls of Moses and Elias, the Blessed Mother was transported to the mountain by the ministry of other blessed spirits. There she not only beheld the glorified humanity of her Son more clearly and for a longer time than the Apostles, but she had also an intuitive vision of the Divinity. So great was the impression made upon her by this vision of the glorious life that it was never afterwards effaced from her mind.

On this occasion Jesus prayed His Eternal Father to grant that all those who during their lives would mortify their bodies or suffer for His love should also share in the glory of His Body, and that their souls should participate in the joy of that glory on the day of the General Judgment.

After the Transfiguration, Our Lord went to Nazareth, whither the Blessed Mother had retired, in order that He might bid a last adieu to His country before going to Jerusalem to undergo His sorrowful Passion. He went to Nazareth with His disciples and, after remaining there some days, set out for Jerusalem, accompanied by His beloved Mother, His Apostles and disciples, and by some devout women. He traversed Galilee to reach Jerusalem, and it was at this time that, passing through Bethania, He raised Lazarus from the dead.

This miracle, operated so near Jerusalem, provoked against Him the priests and Pharisees, who, full of jealousy, assembled the council, in which it was resolved to put the innocent Jesus to death, and they ordered that if anyone knew of His whereabouts they should reveal it to them.

After six days the Lord returned to Bethania with His Mother and His disciples, where He was received by the two sisters of Lazarus. Then it was that Magdalen twice poured precious ointment on the head and feet of the Saviour, in her own house and in that of the Pharisee. Judas murmured at it, and from that moment resolved to procure the death of the Saviour; he denounced Him afterwards to the priests and Pharisees. For this end he went to them secretly and said that his Master taught doctrines contrary to the Law of Moses, to the government and the Roman emperor; that He was a lover of good cheer who associated with persons of depraved morals and kept with Him both men and women. All these base acts of the treacherous and wicked Apostle were known to Jesus, who, as God, saw all, and also to the most Holy Virgin, but they, the Models of most perfect goodness, gave him not the least sign of aversion.

The great Queen endeavored by kind and loving words to save the perfidious disciple even from the brink of the precipice on which he stood. To satisfy his avarice, she sometimes presented him gifts which had been bestowed on her by Magdalen and others, and which she had accepted only on his account. But all was ineffectual to touch the heart of him, who only became the more enraged at each act of kindness; nevertheless, he eagerly accepted all that she offered. After Magdalen had poured the precious ointment upon our Saviour, He retired into the oratory of the two sisters. Then, the Blessed Mother, abandoning Judas in his obstinacy, followed Him thither, and, according to her custom, united with Him in His holy exercises and prayers.

There He again offered Himself to the Eternal Father, and Mary imitated Him. The heroic sacrifice of the Mother and the Son was so agreeable to the Eternal Father that He, together with the Holy Ghost, descended visibly to accept it. The Holy Virgin beheld the Sacred Humanity of her Son exalted to the right hand of His Father and heard that verse of the one hundred and ninth Psalm: *Dixit Dominus Domino meo; sede a dextris meis*—"The Lord said to my Lord, sit thou at my right hand." She was surrounded with admirable splendor and inflamed with an ardent charity for the human race. Jesus and Mary spent the night in prayer and holy conversation.

Chapter 21

THE TRIUMPHANT ENTRY OF JESUS INTO JERUSALEM.

The day which corresponds to our "Palm Sunday" being arrived, the Lord went to Jerusalem accompanied by a multitude of Angels, who by their holy canticles praised His ardent charity for men. When He drew nigh the holy city, He sent two of His disciples to the house of a rich man, who dwelt in Bethphage, and with his consent they brought to Jesus an ass and her colt, on which the disciples spread their garments for the Redeemer to mount thereon. Besides that which the Evangelists have recorded of this great event, there happened many other things. The Archangel St. Michael was sent to Limbo to make known to the holy patriarchs this glorious triumph. All those who, in Judea and Egypt, had known Jesus, felt great joy of spirit and interiorly adored the Lord.

God ordained that on this day, so glorious, no one should die throughout the universe. All the demons were compelled to remain in the depths of the abyss.

Having arrived at Jerusalem, the Lord alighted from the ass and went on foot to the Temple, where

He overthrew the tables of those who bought and sold, and expelled them from that holy place. Then He began to teach and to preach, without having taken any nourishment; for among all the people, and even persons of consideration, who had cried out, *Hosanna in excelsis,* not one had invited Him to eat in his house. This was the reason why He returned to Bethania in the evening. The Virgin Mother had remained there all day, retired in her apartment, where she beheld in spirit all that happened to her Divine Son in the city and in the Temple; she heard the acclamations of the Angels in Heaven and on earth, and saw all that befell the demons.

This triumph again caused Lucifer to suspect that Jesus was the true Messias; therefore, he resolved by every possible means to prevent His death, which he feared would be the destruction of his empire. He tried to dissuade Judas from his design of betraying his Master to the Pharisees; he even appeared to him in human form and offered to give him as much money as he desired, if he would but relinquish his design. But the ungrateful man was not worthy to receive the grace to change his desires. Lucifer, having failed in this attempt, tried to persuade the Council not to put Jesus to death on the day of the feast, lest they might raise a tumult amongst the people. Being again unsuccessful, he endeavored by means of Pilate's wife to prevent His condemnation, and he also made many artful suggestions to Pilate himself.

Jesus remained in Bethania until Thursday, to

instruct His disciples and converse with His holy Mother; however, on Monday and Tuesday He paid a visit to the Temple. In His entertainments with His holy Mother, He prescribed all that she should do during the course of His Passion and death. In those discourses and entertainments He did not speak to her with the tenderness of a son, but with the gravity and majesty of a king. On Thursday, at the dawn of day, He called His Mother, who, prostrating herself at His feet, said, "Speak, Lord, Thy servant is at Thy feet." The Lord raised her and announced that the hour of His cruel Passion had arrived. He not only asked her permission to die for the Redemption of man, but also exhorted her to cooperate with Him in the great work. Who can describe the ineffable sorrow which penetrated the most pure heart of the Virgin Mother when she was about to separate from her tender and well-beloved Son? But she resigned herself with the most perfect submission to His Will and begged Him to allow her to accompany Him and generously participate in the cruel and terrible sufferings of His Cross. She prayed Him to give her before His death His divine Body in the Holy Sacrament, which He was about to institute, as He had revealed to her. The Lord lovingly consented; He ordered the Angels to assist her in that moment in visible forms, and recommended her to follow Him constantly in company of the three holy women. Finally, He bestowed on her the divine benediction, both being a prey to ineffable and profound sorrow.

Having taken leave of His tender Mother, He

left Bethania a little before mid-day, accompanied by His Angels. The divine Mother followed Him soon after, in company with the holy women. On the way, Jesus instructed His disciples, and Mary did the same with regard to the holy women. Judas was not present when Our Lord said the words: *Scitis quia post biduum Pascha fiet, et Filius hominis tradetur ut crucifigatur*—"You know that after two days shall be the pasch, and the Son of man shall be delivered up to be crucified"—and he sometimes inquired of the Apostles, sometimes of Mary, and again, even of Our Lord Himself, in what place He would eat the Pasch. Although Jesus knew well the perversity and depravity of His disciple, He answered him only in these words: "O Judas, who can fathom the secrets of the Most High?" The Apostles proposed some doubts to their Divine Master, and He answered them with ineffable prudence and wisdom.

Afterwards He sent St. Peter and St. John to prepare the place for the Last Supper. Near to Jerusalem there stood the house of a rich man who was much devoted to Our Lord, and who believed in His doctrines and miracles; he had received a particular grace which caused him to make a voluntary offering of his dwelling and all that was necessary for the paschal feast. He had caused a large hall to be fitted up for the solemnization of the great mysteries about to be operated.

Chapter 22

THE LAST SUPPER.

Our Lord and His disciples entered into the Supper-room, as did also the Blessed Virgin and the pious women. Then Our Lord requested her to retire into another part of the house and instruct the women who accompanied her in all that was necessary, whilst He would celebrate the Last Supper, from which Judas was not excluded. The Holy Virgin withdrew into another room with the holy women and, prostrate on the earth, became absorbed in a state of high contemplation in which she saw all that her Divine Son did and said, and she gave the necessary instructions and advice to the holy women. After the legal supper, Jesus, with profound humility and a serene countenance, washed the feet of His Apostles.

Having laid aside His mantle and girded Himself with a towel, leaving one end free, He washed the feet of the Apostles, even those of Judas, which He not only washed with great joy and goodness, but also kissed and pressed them to His breast, sending, at the same time, into his heart His interior inspirations. But all was unavailing, for, besides that, the demon tried to prevent every emotion of grat-

itude in his heart. He was also ashamed to break
his word, given in his infamous compact with the
Pharisees; at this moment he would not even cast
a look on the divine countenance of Jesus.

Unable to endure the sight of such profound
humility, Lucifer tried to fly from the heart of Judas
and from the Supper-room, but the Divine Master
would not permit it.

It was at this time that St. John, at the suggestion of St. Peter, begged to know who was the traitor; Our Lord pointed him out by the sign of a
piece of bread dipped in the dish. Many secret things
were communicated by Our Lord to St. John whilst
he leaned on His sacred breast; among others, He
recommended His holy Mother to his care. For this
reason, when He was dying on the Cross, He did
not say, "She shall be thy mother," but only, "*Behold
thy mother*," thus revealing publicly what He had
communicated before in private.

After He had washed His disciples' feet, Jesus
ordered a table to be prepared so as to resemble an
altar, and to be covered with a very rich and beautiful cloth. On this table they laid a plate, and also
a high cup like to a chalice and capable of containing the wine necessary for the designs of the
Lord, who had prepared and foreseen everything by
His infinite wisdom. The master of the house, by
an interior motion of grace, had prepared those vessels so rich and precious.

Our Lord, being seated at the table and surrounded by His disciples, asked first for unleavened
bread, which He laid upon a plate, then for pure

wine, which He poured into the chalice with a small quantity of water. The Blessed Virgin, in her retirement, considered all these things.

The Angels, by the order of the Lord, conducted into this place Elias and Enoch, to the end that the patriarchs of both the natural and the written law might be present at the institution of the Evangelical Law. The Eternal Father with the Holy Spirit appeared in the Supper-room as at the Jordan and Mt. Thabor, but the Apostles did not see them; the vision was given only to the Blessed Virgin and St. John.

After praying for a long time, Our Lord took the bread into His hands and interiorly offered a prayer to the Eternal Father, begging that, in virtue of the words He was about to pronounce, the Sacrament He was going to institute might be perpetuated in His Church throughout all ages. With great majesty He raised His eyes towards Heaven, that is, towards the two Divine Persons; He pronounced over the bread and wine the sacred words of Consecration, by which they were changed into the Body and Blood, Soul and Divinity of our Divine Redeemer. The Holy Virgin in her retreat adored her Divine Son, really present under the Sacred Species; the Angels in Heaven, as well as those present, also adored Him.

Our Lord elevated His sacred Body and Blood so that those present at His first mysterious sacrifice might adore Him. As sovereign High Priest, He communicated Himself [received Communion], and this with such profound awe and veneration that

He experienced fear, as it were, in the sensitive part of His soul. The admirable effects produced on Our Lord's body by His reception of the Holy Eucharist were such as to cause the glory of His soul to be reflected on His exterior, as at His Transfiguration on Mt. Thabor; this wonder was, however, seen clearly only by the Blessed Mother, and in part by Enoch, Elias and St. John.

After this great favor conferred on His body, the holy Humanity renounced all consolation in the inferior part of the soul from that moment until His death.

After Jesus had communicated Himself, He gave the Archangel St. Gabriel a small Particle of the Consecrated Bread, that he might carry It to the Blessed Mother and communicate her; thus, after her Divine Son, she was the first to have the happiness of receiving Holy Communion. She communicated with sentiments of lively faith, ineffable love and respect, profound humility and deepest veneration, such as she had contemplated in the God made man, now present under the holy species. Our great Queen received the miraculous grace of preserving the holy species in her heart from this night until after the Resurrection, when the Apostle St. Peter consecrated, as we shall relate hereafter.

The divine Mother received in this Holy Communion a perfect knowledge of the manner in which Jesus is present in the Blessed Sacrament, as also of all the mysteries which He operated in its institution. She foresaw the ingratitude which men would return for this great and incomparable benefit and, by her prayers, praises, homages, adorations and prostrations, endeavored to make reparation for the outrages which our Divine Saviour would have to undergo from His ungrateful creatures in the Sacrament of the Eucharist.

After Mary had communicated, Our Lord gave the Consecrated Bread to His disciples, bidding them divide It among themselves and partake of It. By these words He conferred on them the sacerdotal dignity, which they began to exercise at this moment by communicating each other. He afterwards ordered St. Peter to communicate Enoch and Elias, in order to fortify them anew.

Another hidden prodigy occurred. Judas, the traitor, when communicating, resolved to preserve the Particle of consecrated Bread and carry It to the priests and Pharisees in order to accuse his Master. The Holy Virgin knew the intention of the perfidious traitor, and commanded the holy Angels to remove the consecrated species from the mouth of the unworthy Apostle. The Angels executed this command and, having carefully purified Them, replaced the Particles on the holy table in an invisible manner, which could be easily done, as Judas was neither the first nor the last to receive Holy Communion.

He was the first heretic in the Church who denied the Holy Sacrament of the Eucharist.

Chapter 23

FROM THE BEGINNING OF OUR LORD'S PASSION UNTIL HIS APPEARANCE AT THE TRIBUNAL OF CAIPHAS.

In the first part of the night which followed the institution of the Blessed Sacrament, our sweet Lord resolved to enter upon His dolorous Passion. Leaving the hall in which He had celebrated the Sacred Mysteries, He gave a long instruction to the disciples. Then also He met His holy Mother, who had come forth from her retreat. Looking at her with a joyful countenance, He said: "My Mother, I will be with thee in thy affliction. Let us accomplish the will of the Eternal Father and the salvation of the world." Then He gave her His benediction and parted with her. She retired to the apartment she had just quitted, because the master of it, having been present at her painful separation from her Son, had offered her, by divine inspiration, the house and all that it contained, to be her abode during her stay in Jerusalem. Here she remained, overwhelmed with sorrow, such as every Christian can imagine, but she did not cease to be present in spirit at all that occurred during that night of agony.

She saw that when Judas was going to the priests and Pharisees, the demon, in visible form, tried to prevent him from selling his Divine Master. She beheld Jesus retiring to the Garden of Gethsemane and falling into profound sadness. She knew that the agony He endured was such as to cause a bloody sweat, produced by the knowledge that His sufferings would, for the wicked, be not only useless, but because of their malice, be also the cause of a still greater chastisement. For this reason He prayed His Father to remove this sorrow, under the name of His *chalice.*

She knew also that after the prayer of Jesus Christ, the Eternal Father sent the Archangel St. Michael to console Him in His pains, by saying that among those whom He would save by His Precious Blood would be Mary, His Mother, worthy fruit of His redemption. She saw that when He found His disciples sleeping, before He awoke them He waited a little, to gaze on them with compassion and weep over their neglect and coldness. Not only was she witness to these and all other things which happened in the garden, but she also imitated, as far as possible, each action of her Divine Son during His Passion.

When Jesus retired with His disciples, she retired with the holy women and prayed to the Eternal Father as Jesus did, that He would take away or suspend every consolation which might prevent her from suffering with her Divine Son, and grant that her body might partake in all the sufferings which He had to endure. Feeling the same profound sadness, she offered up the prayer which Jesus made for sinners and fell into an agony like His, wherein she sweat blood. As the Archangel Michael had been sent to strengthen Jesus, so the Archangel Gabriel was commissioned to do the same for Mary.

When Our Lord returned to visit His disciples, His Mother visited the holy women and exhorted them to be vigilant against the snares of Satan. When Jesus said to the Apostles, "My soul is sorrowful even unto death," she said to the three Marys, "My soul is sorrowful, because my beloved Son and Lord must suffer and die, and I may not die with Him. Pray, my friends, that you may not enter into temptation." In the midst of all these sufferings Mary's heart was not only magnanimous, but also anxious to find means to aid Jesus, her Divine Son. She sent one of her Angels to wipe away, with linen which she gave him, the drops of Blood from the face of her agonizing God.

When the soldiers, accompanied by Judas, set out to arrest Jesus, the most wise Queen, foreseeing the outrages, injuries and ill-treatment which those wicked men would inflict upon Him, invited her Angels to join with her in endeavoring, by their praises and adorations, to offer Him some reparation. Thus while Jesus suffered the ignominious treatment of those wicked men and the treacherous kiss of the betrayer, she offered up contrary acts of love and reverence, by which she stayed the anger of God.

She prayed in particular for Judas, and in consideration of her intercession, God sent into his heart many and pressing inspirations, and other graces, in order to make him enter into himself.

When she saw that by the marvelous power of the words, *Ego sum*, which Our Lord addressed to this wicked band, they and their horses were cast upon the ground, and that the demons also were thrown down and compelled to remain in that position for half a quarter of an hour, she rejoiced and sang canticles of praise in honor of the Most High. Nevertheless, out of compassion for the miserable soldiers, she interceded with Our Lord to permit them to live and give them the power to arise. This He did, and allowed them to exercise all their rage against Him. Again He asked, "Whom seek ye?" and they answered, "Jesus of Nazareth." He answered, "I am He." Upon which they threw themselves upon Him like wild and ferocious animals. When her Son was bound, Mary felt the pain of those bonds and cords as truly as if she herself had borne them; the same is true of all the ill-treatment and blows inflicted upon Him at the time of His arrest, when they tore His garments and pulled out His hair.

She felt no indignation at the flight of the Apostles, but immediately recommended them to Our Lord, and although she was afflicted at the sight of their weak faith, she prayed for them and offered to the Lord all the honor and veneration due to Him from the whole Church. While Jesus was being overwhelmed with blows and entirely given over to the power of His enemies, the Holy Virgin remained in the Supper-room.

Judas, believing from the suggestions of Lucifer that his pardon was impossible, and tormented with the dread of the dishonor which would be heaped upon him by the world for having betrayed his Master, became so excited that he fell into excessive fury against himself. He tried to throw himself from the highest window of the pontiff's palace, but was prevented. He rushed into the streets, uttering cries like a wild beast, biting his flesh, tearing his hair and loading himself with a thousand maledictions.

Seeing him in this state, Lucifer persuaded him to return the money to the priests, hoping thus to prevent the death of Jesus, whom, from the great and admirable patience with which He suffered such unheard-of outrages, he still more strongly suspected of being the Messias. But failing to accomplish this, the tempter increased the despair of Judas and persuaded him to take his life, in the desire thus to rid himself in an instant of much pain and ignominy. To this the unhappy apostate consented, and leaving the city, hanged himself upon a tree.

This horrible death happened on Friday, a few hours previous to the death of our Saviour. His wretched body remained suspended from the tree, with the entrails hanging out, and when the Jews tried to remove and bury it, because such a death gave great glory to the cause of Jesus, they were unable to do so.

In fine, after three days, the demons, by the permission of God, carried the miserable carcass into Hell, whither they had borne his unhappy soul.

The soldiers who had come to seize Jesus, think-

ing on account of His miracles that He was a magician, feared He would escape from them; therefore,
they bound Him very strongly on His sides, arms
and neck, with two long ropes and a heavy chain
which had been used to open and close the prison
gate. At the end of this chain were heavy mana-
cles, with which they fastened His hands behind
His back.

Having thus cruelly bound Him, they set out from
Mt. Olivet with great noise and tumult, some pulling
Him forward, others in the contrary direction, by
which movements they threw Him violently on the
ground. They vented their rage by inflicting blows
on His face, head and body. They tore His garments,
plucked His beard, dragged Him by the hair and
forced the points of their sticks into His sides, struck
Him on the shoulders and dragged Him from one
side of the street to the other. The Lord fell many
times, striking His face against the ground with great
pain, for, having His hands chained behind His
back, His divine face became covered with wounds.
The blows and bad treatment of every kind which
He received are indescribable, yet the meek Lamb
of God bore those frightful cruelties with admirable
patience. Lucifer was in a fury at the sight of such
resignation, and in order to overcome Him, wished
to take hold of the cords, in order to drag Him
more violently. But the Blessed Virgin, who saw all
this in spirit, prevented the execution of this exe-
crable design by depriving him of strength.

They arrived in the city uttering cries and exe-
crations as if they had arrested the chief of male-

factors. The inhabitants rushed to the windows and doors with lights; they loaded our blessed Lord with insults, injuries and opprobrium, calling Him a false prophet, a deceiver, a wicked man, a robber and a perverter of the people: *et cum iniquis reputatus est*— "and with the wicked He was reputed." They conducted Him to the tribunal of Annas, who received Him seated on his chair. Lucifer and an innumerable crowd of demons ranged themselves beside the judge and ceased not to irritate him against Christ, in order to try His divine patience.

Then it was that Jesus received that cruel blow from the mailed hand of the servant whose ear He had miraculously restored in the Garden of Gethsemane. To this outrage Our Lord replied in the well-known words: *Si male locutus sum, testimonium perhibe de malo*—"If I have spoken ill, give testimony of the evil"—which covered the wicked servant with confusion, but wrought no change in his heart. This blow was so cruel that it broke all the teeth of our Divine Redeemer and caused the blood to flow profusely from His eyes, nose and mouth. The Virgin Mother experienced the violence of that terrific blow in such a degree that she shed tears of blood.

Meanwhile John and Peter arrived at Annas' house; and when Peter drew near the fire in the vestibule, the servant asked him in a tone of mockery and derision if he also were not a disciple of the Nazarean. Overcome by shame and filled with fear and cowardice, he denied that he was. After this he left the house of Annas and proceeded to that of Caiphas, whither Our Lord was dragged with still greater derision and there received with laughter, insult and bitter mockery. Nevertheless, He only prayed for His persecutors, and in His supplications His blessed Mother united with Him. Caiphas was seated on a magnificent tribunal, surrounded by the Scribes and Pharisees, as also by Lucifer and his legions, for he was still anxious to know if Our Lord were the Messias. He therefore inspired Caiphas to say: "I adjure Thee in the name of the living God to tell us if Thou be the Christ, the Son of God." At His sweet reply, Lucifer was so enraged that, unable to endure it any longer, he precipitated himself into the bottom of the abyss. By the permission of God, he came out again, being uncertain if Christ had thus spoken in order to deliver Himself from the hands of His enemies. Returning to the court-room, he incited the officers to load Him with blows, to tear His hair, strike Him on the face and trample Him under foot.

The Angels present at this scene were ravished in admiration of the incomprehensible judgments of God, seeing that His Divine Majesty was willing to appear as a culprit, and that the iniquitous judge seemed full of zeal for the honor of God, in whose Name he sacrilegiously pretended to take away the life of Jesus, who remained silent before Him. Here it was that they blindfolded Our Lord, because on His face there shone a splendor which caused great pain and confusion to His enemies. This they attributed to magic arts, and covering His divine countenance with filthy rags, they loaded

Him with outrages and unheard-of insults. All these sufferings were renewed in the person of the Virgin Mother.

Peter found it easy to enter into the house of Caiphas, being aided to do so by the dense crowd and the obscurity of the night. Nevertheless, as he stood in the court, he was perceived by a maid-servant, who, turning to those who stood by, said: "This man also was with Jesus of Nazareth," and one of those present added, "Thou art truly a Galilean, and a follower of Jesus." Then Peter denied the fact and swore he was no disciple of Jesus. He went out from the court, but, his heart being still drawn to his Master by compassion for His sufferings, he could not bear to lose sight of Him, and still remained near for about an hour. Again he was seen and recognized by a relation of Malchus, who said: "Thou art a Galilean, and a disciple of Jesus, for I saw thee with Him in the garden," and again Peter swore that he knew not the man. Then the cock crew for the second time, and the prophecy of Jesus was accomplished—"Before the cock crow twice, thou wilt deny Me thrice." Peter remembered the words of Jesus, who, at that same moment, cast on him a look of mercy. Bursting into a flood of tears, he immediately retired from the house and secluded himself in a grotto called, ever since, "The crowing of the cock." There he wept bitterly for three hours, during which time he returned to grace, and was received into favor by the intercession of the Blessed Mother, who had seen his fall and repentance and, prostrate on the ground, had interceded for him. She even sent one of her Angels to console him—not in a visible manner, because his fall was as yet too recent, but by interior inspirations.

Chapter 24

CONTINUATION OF THE PASSION
UNTIL THE SENTENCE OF DEATH.

Sometime after midnight it was decided by the council that while they would retire to rest, Jesus should be thrown, bound as He was, into a dungeon used for great robbers and murderers. This prison was so obscure that scarcely a ray of light could penetrate into it; it was so loathsome as to be insupportable to everyone. Thither they dragged the Son of God by the cords and chains with which they had bound Him in the garden.

In this dungeon there was a stone or piece of rock to which they chained Our Lord in such a manner that He could neither lie nor sit; then, going out of that loathsome place, they fastened Jesus in and left one of their number on guard. The Angels rendered homage to their God; they wished to unbind Him, but to this He would not consent, wishing to suffer still more; but He bade them console His afflicted Mother.

After the infuriated and intoxicated rabble had taken some refreshment, being excited by the devil, they hastened to the prison, where they unbound Jesus from the rock and placed Him in the middle

of the apartment. They tried to force Him to speak
and to work some miracles, but the Incarnate Wisdom answered them not. They renewed their insults
and outrages, and again blindfolded Him with filthy
and disgusting rags. Striking Him violently on the
neck and face they cried, "Prophesy who it is that
struck Thee."

Lucifer, enraged at His patience, suggested to those
drunken wretches to strip our Blessed Lord quite
naked, in order to load Him with still greater insult
and outrage. But the most pure Virgin, who in spirit
contemplated the dreadful scene, prayed Our Lord
not to permit such an ignominy, and her prayer was
granted. They again bound Him to the rock and
retired from the prison; the Angels compassionated
His sufferings and adored Him. During this time Jesus
interceded with His Eternal Father for those who
tormented Him.

At dawn of day the priests and Scribes assembled together, and the Divine Lamb was again conducted before them. It was a sight most worthy of
compassion to behold that innocent Victim with
His face all bruised, disfigured and covered with spittle, which He could not remove because His hands
were bound. Seeing Him in such a deplorable condition, even His enemies themselves were startled.
They again designedly asked Him if He was the Son
of God, and hearing Him answer that He was, they
cried out that He was worthy of death and sent
Him to Pilate, the Roman proconsul, to whom all
capital cases were reserved.

The sun had already risen when the Blessed

Mother resolved to leave her retreat to follow the steps of her Son. As she was about to leave the house, accompanied by the three Marys and by Magdalen, St. John arrived with the intention of informing her of all that had passed, for he did not know that she had, in spirit, contemplated everything. Having first humbly begged her to pardon the cowardice he had shown in deserting her Divine Son, he related all that had befallen Our Lord during the past night. To this account, the humble Mary listened with feelings of the deepest agony, and her companions shed many tears.

They quitted the house, and as they passed through streets, Mary heard the conversations going on among the people about her Divine Son; yet, far from being indignant at those who spoke ill of Him, she prayed for them.

From her garments, many persons recognized her to be the Mother of Jesus. Some were moved with feelings of natural compassion for her, others insulted her, saying that she had given her Son a bad education. Hearing a great noise and tumult, Mary looked and beheld her innocent Son in the hands of the rabble; prostrating herself upon the ground, she adored Him; at the same moment there passed between them looks which penetrated their hearts with inexpressible grief, and they spoke with each other from the interior of their souls. Then, as they dragged Jesus to Pilate, the afflicted Mother, bathed in tears, followed with the pious women, exclaiming, "My Son, my beloved Son!"

When the Jews arrived at the house of Pilate,

he, although a pagan, had regard for the ceremonial law, which forbade them to enter the praetorium; therefore he came out to interrogate the pretended criminal. The agonizing Mother, with St. John and the holy women, was present at this interrogatory, for the Angels conveyed them to a place where they could see and hear all that was transpiring. Here again the violence of her grief drew from her tears of blood, for she shared intimately in each suffering inflicted on her Son. She earnestly prayed the Eternal Father that Pilate might see clearly the innocence of Jesus. This grace he received in answer to her prayer, but he did not correspond to it fully, although he tried not to condemn Him whom he saw to be innocent. Finding that Jesus had been born in the jurisdiction of Herod, grandson of him who had caused the massacre of the innocents, he sent Him to him.[1] By reason of this deference, these two men who had been enemies now became friends. It is impossible to relate all that Jesus had to undergo from His enemies in this journey from Pilate to Herod, for they were continually excited by Lucifer to further

---

1. We know of nothing more admirable than these details, so precise, so sublime and so capable of inspiring devotion, which we find in all that concerns the Passion of our Divine Saviour. The Queen of Heaven participates in a mysterious manner in the great work of the Redemption of our souls. We ought to read and re-read these pages, which reveal to us such hidden mysteries, which cause us to understand in what sense and under what titles the Blessed Virgin is truly our Mother, the Mediatrix for our salvation and co-redemptrix of mankind.

outrages, in the hope that he might be able to learn if He were truly the Messias.

His afflicted Mother continued to follow the crowd and kept her eyes constantly fixed upon her Divine Son. Although she entered not the house of Herod, she beheld in spirit all that passed there and heard the questions propounded to Our Lord. When He was clothed in the robe of mockery, she fully comprehended the depth of the ignominy thus inflicted. She followed Him with the same constancy when He was conducted back to Pilate. In this painful journey it happened many times that by the pressure of the crowd and the violence of those who dragged Him, Jesus was thrown upon the ground. His veins were opened by the fall and by the blows He received, for He could not rise because His hands were chained and fastened behind His back. Then the prudent and tender Mother commanded the Angels to gather up and preserve the drops of precious Blood, that they might not be profaned and trampled underfoot; she also commanded them to support their Creator, when He would be in danger of falling. But she did not give this order until she had obtained the permission of the Lord, whom she prayed to condescend to the humble petition of His afflicted Mother.

Jesus was conducted back to Pilate, who, seeing the innocence of Jesus and the envy and hatred of the Jews, tried to deliver Him. He spoke with Jesus in private; he also spoke secretly to the chiefs of the synagogue, representing that as there was in the prison an infamous robber, condemned by the people, they should demand the delivery of the Nazarean, and not of Barabbas, which was the name of the homicide and murderer. This custom of delivering a criminal at the feast of the Pasch had been introduced among the Jews in memory of their deliverance from Egypt.

The afflicted Mother was present in Pilate's house and knew his endeavors to deliver her Son. She heard the words addressed him by Procula, his wife, and knew that her embassy had been suggested by Lucifer, who sought to prevent the Redemption of man. The heart of Mary was most cruelly transpierced, but the sword of sorrow was plunged still deeper when she learned that Barabbas was preferred to Jesus.

Pilate, finding that all his endeavors to save Jesus had failed, thought to have Him scourged, in the hope that the Jews might think He was sufficiently chastised and allow Him to be set free; but in this he acted against all justice, for he had already acknowledged the perfect innocence of Jesus.

To execute this flagellation, they chose six young men most remarkable for their strength and barbarous cruelty. They led Jesus into the court, in which there was a column, and removed the handcuffs, chains and cords. They tore off His garments, leaving His sacred person almost entirely naked. The flagellation commenced under the eyes of the afflicted Mother.

Jesus was bound to the column so tightly with little cords that they entered into the flesh, and His divine hands became much swollen. Afterwards they began to scourge Him in pairs, one after the other, with a cruelty of which human ferocity was not capable, but Lucifer had incorporated himself into the hearts of the pitiless executioners. The first two scourged the innocent Jesus with large twisted cords, exerting their utmost violence and greatest fury upon Him. The first blows which fell upon His divine and delicate body inflicted large livid bruises, which swelled to a frightful extent and seemed as if the blood was about to burst from them.

When these cruel men were exhausted by fatigue, they were succeeded by the second two, who, using heavy leather thongs, broke the flesh of the bruises inflicted by the first, so that the Precious Blood not only covered the body of Jesus, but also saturated the garments of the sacrilegious murderers and fell upon the ground.

When exhausted, they were succeeded by a third party, who used as their instruments of torture the sinews of beasts, which were very hard and dry, resembling dried twigs. Their blows, being repeated over the wounds inflicted by the first and second executioners, caused Jesus the most intense agony. But as His divine body was but one entire wound, they could no longer inflict new wounds; their blows, therefore, falling on His sacred flesh, tore out pieces which fell to the ground, and in many places left the bones exposed to sight. Not content with this, they satiated their cruelty by striking Him on the face, hands and feet, and sparing no part of His body. So bruised, torn and disfigured was the countenance of the Lord as to be no longer recognizable.

During all this agonizing scene, Mary, accompanied by the holy women, the companions of her trials, remained in a corner of the courtyard. The cruel blows which fell upon her Son were felt by her, not in her heart alone, but also in her virginal body, and her countenance could no longer be recognized by St. John or the holy women, so great was the change wrought in it by her intense agony and grief, the effect of her profound faith and her perfect knowledge of the incomprehensible dignity of her suffering Son. Amongst all creatures, she alone could fully understand the innocence of Jesus Christ, the dignity of His divine Person, the enormity of the injuries He received, and the indescribable torments He was compelled to suffer. But anxious to see Him die on the Cross, the Jews unbound Jesus from the pillar, and He sank to the ground bathed in His blood. They ordered Him to put on His garments, but one of the wicked wretches had hidden His seamless robe; therefore, while He remained thus naked, they reviled and mocked Him. Some of them, going to Pilate, said that as Jesus pretended to be the king of the Jews, it would be but just to crown Him with thorns. Having obtained his permission, they took Jesus, threw over His shoulders an old purple cloak, placed in His hand a reed for a sceptre and violently pressed on His divine head the thorny diadem.

This crown was plaited of sea rushes, with very long and sharp thorns, which, being pressed upon His head, many penetrated the bones of the head, others protruded at His ears and eyes. After this ignominious and cruel ceremony, they adored as a mock-king Him who, by nature and by every title, was the King of Kings, the Lord of Lords. The whole body of the soldiers placed Jesus in their midst and, in the presence of the priests and Pharisees, loaded Him with injuries and blasphemies; and many, bending the knee before Him, cried out in mockery, "Hail, King of the Jews!" Others struck Him violently on the face; some, taking the reed, struck Him on the head, others covered His countenance with disgusting spittle, while all conspired to load Him with still greater injuries and blasphemies.

Pilate, thinking that these ungrateful and cruel people would be softened by the sorrowful spectacle of the innocent Victim, led Him to a large window, whence he showed Him to them, saying: *"Behold the Man!* What cause have you to fear that He will make Himself king, since He no longer resembles a man, and nothing can be found in Him deserving of death?" But the infuriated mob cried out, "Crucify Him! Crucify Him!"

At this sorrowful spectacle, the blessed Mary, our agonizing Queen, prostrated herself upon the ground and acknowledged Jesus to be true God and true Man; in this act she was joined by St. John, the holy women and the Angels. She supplicated the Eternal Father to give Pilate a clearer knowledge of her Son's innocence; this was why Pilate took Jesus aside and interrogated Him in the manner recorded by the Evangelist, after which He again showed Him to the people, protesting that He was innocent.

The Jews, seeing that Pilate was anxious to deliver Jesus, raised a great tumult and threatened him, if he would not put Him to death. Pilate, much troubled and overcome by fear, seated himself on his tribunal, towards midday, the eve of the Jewish Pasch.

He first washed his hands, blindly seeking thus to free himself from the guilt of the injustice he was about to commit; then he pronounced sentence of death against the Author of Life. Hearing it, all the cruel bitterness and agony of Mary's heart were renewed, and she felt the sword of sorrow pierce her soul, even to its utmost depths. But as the greatness of Mary's sorrows surpasses the comprehension of human intelligence, we must leave the imagination of it to Christian piety. In like manner it is impossible to relate all the interior acts of love, praise, compassion, veneration, sorrow and conformity to the Divine Will which she formed within her most pure heart.

Chapter 25

JESUS ASCENDS CALVARY—HIS DEATH.

When sentence of death had been pronounced against Jesus of Nazareth, the soldiers drew Him aside, tore off the robe of mockery and vested Him in His own tunic, that He might be the better known, and on His head they again pressed the thorny crown. The city was thronged with strangers who had come to celebrate the Pasch, and the streets which led to Pilate's house were filled, as all desired to know what was transpiring.

When Jesus was dragged into the midst of the crowd, a confused murmur arose amongst them, yet nothing could be plainly heard but the insolent expressions of joy, the blasphemies and outrages of the priests and Pharisees.

Among the people there was a great diversity of opinion; many of them had been healed of diseases by Jesus; others had heard His doctrine and embraced it; everyone was filled with anxiety or trouble, according to his different disposition. On all sides there was nothing but confusion.

Out of eleven Apostles, St. John alone was present. When he beheld his Lord and Master publicly led out to be crucified, he was so overwhelmed with grief that he became unconscious, and seemed as if bereft of life. The three Marys were also affected in the same manner, but the Queen of Virtue remained firm and invincible; her magnanimous heart never quailed amidst all her sufferings. She did not experience the same weakness as her companions, but in her exterior deportment remained strong, resolute and ever admirable. Uttering not a cry or a groan, she encouraged the holy women and St. John; she prayed for them to the Eternal Father, and by virtue of her prayer, they regained their wonted strength.

In the midst of all this confusion and in the agony of her untold grief, she never performed the least action but with her accustomed modesty; calm and serene, although she shed tears continually, she remained with her attention ever fixed upon the Divine Jesus.

She prayed to the Eternal Father, offering to Him the Passion and death of her Son, and she imitated the interior acts of the Saviour. She considered the great malice of sin, penetrated the mysteries of the Redemption and invited the Angels to praise and adore the Most High; she prayed also for her friends and enemies. Her love was raised to a high degree, and she experienced a grief commensurate with her love; for this reason, she, at this time, practiced all the virtues in a manner which excited the admiration of the heavenly spirits and the extreme complacency of the Most Holy Trinity.

In the presence of an immense crowd, the executioners presented the Cross to Jesus and laid it upon His delicate shoulders, all torn and covered with wounds, and that He might be able to carry it, they untied His hands, but did not remove the other bonds. They put a chain around His neck and bound His body with long cords; with one they dragged Him forward, with another, backward. The Cross was of very heavy wood and fifteen feet in length. The herald advanced first with sound of trumpet to publish the sentence; then followed the noisy and clamorous multitude, the executioners and soldiers, uttering railleries, taunts, laughter and cries of opprobrium; thus, in frightful disorder, they traversed the streets of Jerusalem from the palace of Pilate to Mt. Calvary.

Our Lord continued His sorrowful journey in the midst of a thousand injuries. Many times He fell to the earth because they dragged Him backwards and forwards, and also because He was loaded with the heavy weight of the Cross. In these falls, the Redeemer received new and numerous wounds which caused Him great pain, particularly those on His knees, and the load of the Cross made a great wound on the shoulder. By dragging and pulling Him violently, they frequently struck His head against the Cross, and each blow forced the thorns still deeper into His head and caused Him more bitter suffering.

At that moment it seemed that all the intensity of faith, knowledge and love were concentrated, so to say, in the heart of the divine Mother; therefore she alone had a true knowledge and just appreciation of the great sufferings and cruel death of a

God-made-man for our redemption. Without ceasing in the attention necessary for exterior things, she interiorly contemplated and, by the depth of her profound wisdom, penetrated into the mysteries of the sacrifice of our redemption, which was to be accomplished by the ignorance of those who were to be redeemed. She worthily and truly appreciated the majesty of Him who suffered because, as next to her Divine Son, she possessed the gift of knowledge in the highest degree, so she most fully comprehended the dignity of Jesus Christ, in whom were united both the human and divine natures, with the utmost perfection of each; therefore, she alone, among all pure creatures, could fully estimate the value of the holy Passion and ignominious death of a God-made-man.

Not only was she an eye-witness of the sufferings of Jesus, but, in her own virginal body, she became the participator in them. In the sorrowful journey to Calvary, it sometimes happened that the Mother of Sorrow lost sight of her Beloved, yet even then she sensibly experienced all His sufferings and cried out, "Ah, my Son! what a martyrdom art Thou suffering!"

Taking her Divine Son as her model, she never allowed herself to receive the least alleviation of her sufferings during the time of the Passion; to her body she gave neither rest nor sleep, food nor drink; in her mind, she suspended every consideration that could tend to allay her grief, except those divine influences communicated to her by the Most High in order to preserve her life.

By means of the Blessed Mother the Most High operated another secret mystery against Lucifer. The infernal dragon and his ministers considered most attentively all that was passing in the Passion, but could not satisfy their doubts. At the moment that Our Lord was loaded with the Cross, they felt their strength to be greatly diminished and, being ignorant of the cause, were filled with rage and sadness. The prince of darkness judged that the Passion and death of Jesus would be the cause of his irreparable ruin and the destruction of his empire. Resolving not to await this event in the presence of Jesus, he endeavored to fly with his companions into the infernal caverns. But his design was frustrated by the will of our great Queen, who at that moment was enlightened by the Most High and invested with His power.

Turning towards the proud Lucifer and his companions, she, with the authority of a queen, forbade their flight and commanded them to be present at the Passion of her Son and be witnesses of all that should take place on Mt. Calvary. The rebellious spirits could not resist her command, because they recognized in her the virtue of the divine power. Therefore, vanquished and enchained, they were forced to accompany Jesus to Calvary, where the Eternal Wisdom had resolved to triumph over Hell from the height of the Cross.

The executioners dragged Our Lord with inexpressible barbarity; their outrages and violence, added to the weight of the Cross, caused Him to fall many times and thus to receive new wounds.

He received continual injuries and railleries from the executioners, who threw on His divine face their spittle and filth in such a horrible manner that they covered His eyes; a great number of persons, being suddenly seized with confusion, were forced to cover their faces with their hands. The afflicted Mother, beholding all this, continually adored her Son carrying His Cross. With great humility she prayed that as she could not lessen the heavy weight of the Cross, and as He would not allow the Angels to help Him to support it, as in her great compassion she ardently desired, yet He would deign at least to inspire the executioners to seek for someone to carry it with Him. Her Divine Son granted her prayer; the soldiers, seeing Jesus so faint, and fearing He would die on the way to Calvary, forced Simon of Cyrene to come to His aid.

Among the crowds of people who followed Jesus, there were many pious women of Jerusalem who compassionated Him and wept over His sufferings. Our Lord, turning to them, said: "Daughters of Jerusalem, weep not for Me, but weep for yourselves and your children," etc., as recorded by St. Luke.

The Cyrenian, taking up the Cross, followed Jesus, who walked between the two thieves in order that He might seem to the people to be a malefactor like them.

According to her desire, Mary was near her Divine Son. What then must have been the agony of her heart to behold Him so near to her, and so cruelly treated! What the sorrow of that Son, to behold His Mother in an agony like that of death!

This must be left to the imagination of the pious soul.

The new Isaac arrived at the mount of sacrifice spent with fatigue, faint from pain, covered with blood and so disfigured as not to be recognizable. His Mother, too, reached the holy mountain, and seeing the executioners about to tear off His garments, she knelt and offered Him to the Eternal Father for the salvation of the world. Having noticed that, according to custom, they gave to the two thieves a drink of aromatic wine, but to her Divine Son one of vinegar and gall, she interiorly prayed Him not to inflict this additional suffering upon His sacred mouth. The Divine Son heard the loving prayer of His Mother; He tasted the bitter draught, but would not drink. It was now the hour of the feast, that is to say, midday.

All the sorrows of the Redeemer were renewed when they violently tore off His seamless robe, which clung to all His wounds. They dragged it over His head, without removing the crown of thorns, and by this violence pulled it off with His garment, thus renewing all the wounds of His sacred head with frightful cruelty and inexpressible suffering. When they again violently pressed on the crown of thorns, the afflicted Mother saw her Divine Son all one wound, and she would have died of grief and sorrow had she not been supported by a miracle of the omnipotence of God.

When the executioners prepared to crucify the Saviour, He prayed to the Eternal Father for the whole race of men, and for those about to crucify

Him, and His merciful Mother united her prayer to His. When the executioners began to bore the holes in the Cross to receive the nails, the loving Mother drew near to Him. She raised His languishing arm and kissed His divine hand; she adored Him with profound veneration, and the agonizing Jesus was a little consoled and strengthened by the beauty of this great soul. They then threw Him violently down upon the Cross; raising His eyes to Heaven, He extended His arms and placed His right hand upon the hole.

He offered Himself anew to the Eternal Father; then with ferocious cruelty they fastened His all-powerful hand with a large, pointed nail, which burst the veins and tore the sinews. The left hand could not reach the second hole, on account of the contraction of the sinews, and also because they had purposely made the hole at too great a distance. Therefore they took the chain which had been fastened around His neck, and fastening it to the manacle on His wrist, stretched the arm with horrible cruelty and nailed it. The blood burst forth and flowed abundantly, causing incredible suffering to the Son and the Mother.

Attaching the chain to His feet, they bound them together, one upon the other, and dragging them with great violence, nailed them with a third nail, larger and stronger than the other two. The Sacred Body was thus nailed on the holy Cross, but in such a state that all its bones might be counted, for they were entirely dislocated and dragged out of place. Those of the breast, shoulders and limbs were entirely disjointed by the cruel violence of the executioners.

Let us here consider the agony of the heart of the poor Mother, and of her virginal body oppressed with all kinds of pain. Ah! my great Queen, thou art without consolation!

After having thus crucified the Lord, those monsters of cruelty began to fear that the nails would be loosened and the Sacred Body fall to the ground; therefore, they determined to prevent it. Raising the Cross, they turned it over in such a manner that our Saviour lay upon His face on the ground, and whilst He was in this position, they riveted the nails. At the sight of this new excess of barbarity the beholders shuddered, and many of the crowd, being excited to compassion, raised a great tumult. Mary had recourse to the Eternal Father and prayed Him not to allow this inconceivable cruelty to be accomplished, according to the intention of those executioners, and she commanded the Angels to assist their Creator.

After the nails had been riveted, they raised the Cross and let it fall into the hole prepared for that purpose. Then those cruel wretches supported the Sacred Body with their lances, making deep wounds under the arms and thrusting the points into the flesh, whilst the others planted the Cross.

At this fearful sight the cries of the people were redoubled, and a still greater tumult was raised; the heart of the dolorous Mother was entirely overwhelmed with deepest anguish. The Jews blasphemed Him, the devout compassionated Him, and strangers were overwhelmed with astonishment. Many dared not look at Him from the horror that they felt. The Sacred Blood was gushing forth from the new wounds and from those which were reopened.

The two thieves were also crucified, and their crosses planted, one on each side of Jesus, that, being in the center, He might seem to be the greatest malefactor. The priests and Pharisees wagged their heads in mockery, and throwing dirt and stones at Him, cried out, "Thou Who canst destroy the Temple of God and in three days rebuild it, save Thyself!" The thieves also insulted Him, saying, "If Thou art the Son of God, save Thyself and us." During all this the Virgin Mother was on her knees, praying to the Eternal Father that He would make known the innocence of Jesus. Her prayer was answered: the earth shook, the sun was eclipsed, the moon darkened and the elements thrown into disorder. The mountains burst asunder, the veil of the Temple was rent, the graves opened and the executioners departed, groaning and contrite, because Jesus, in His agony, had, with excessive charity, offered the prayer, "Father, forgive them, for they know not what they do."

One of the thieves, called Dismas, hearing these words, was interiorly enlightened and filled with sorrow for his sins, this grace being procured for him by the prayers of the Holy Virgin. Reproving his companion, he defended the honor of Jesus Christ and recommended himself to the Saviour, who promised him Paradise.

After the conversion of the Good Thief, Jesus cast a look of inexpressible love upon His Mother and uttered the third word: "Woman, behold thy son," thus giving her to St. John, to whom He said, "Behold thy Mother." It was nearly three o'clock when He addressed to His Eternal Father the fourth word: "My God, My God, why hast Thou forsaken Me?" This interior agony was caused by the Divinity suspending the influence it had exerted on His holy humanity, and also by the thought that great numbers of those who would become His members, and for whom the Precious Blood was so profusely shed, would separate themselves from His Mystical Body and be damned. Therefore He uttered the fifth word, "I thirst," meaning that He thirsted to see men correspond to the gift of their Redemption by giving Him that faith and love which are His due. Then the executioners presented to Him a sponge dipped in vinegar and gall, but, as we have before mentioned, He refused to drink because of the prayer of His Mother. After this He pronounced the sixth word, "It is consummated," to announce that the world's Redemption was accomplished. Finally He added: "Father, into Thy hands I commend My spirit." These words He pronounced in a loud, clear voice; then raising to Heaven His eyes, filled with blood, He bowed His sacred head and expired.

That the loving Mother did not also expire at that moment was due to a miracle of divine power.

By virtue of these last words Lucifer was vanquished, his power crushed, and he and his legions precipitated into Hell. The Holy Virgin remained at the foot of the Cross until evening, at which time they buried the Body of the Divine Redeemer. In recompense of this last sorrow, all that was purely earthly in her body became spiritualized.

Before death, every father of a family makes his will; therefore, Jesus Christ, before pronouncing the seven words, made His will on the Cross in concert with the Eternal Father. It remained sealed and hidden with regard to men, but was revealed to the divine Mother as the cooperatrix of the Redemption. The Divine Jesus declared her heiress and testamentary executrix to accomplish His divine Will, and all was remitted into her hands, as the Eternal Father had remitted all into those of His Son.

Thus our great Queen was charged with the distribution of the treasures which belonged to her Son by virtue of His Divinity, or had been acquired by His infinite merits. She was declared the depositary of the riches of her Son, our Redeemer, that all graces, favors and helps might be given us by the Holy Virgin, and that she might distribute them by her merciful and liberal hands.

Chapter 26

OUR LORD'S TRIUMPH ON THE CROSS OVER DEATH AND HELL—COUNCIL OF THE DEMONS AGAINST MANKIND.

During the whole course of the divine life of Jesus Christ, our Sovereign Good, Divine Providence never permitted that the demons should recognize Him to be God and the Redeemer of the world, and consequently, they never knew the sublime dignity of the most Holy Virgin. Lucifer remained always in his blindness, for although he sometimes thought that Jesus might be God, from the splendor of His miracles, yet again he could not believe it, seeing Him so poor and humble. He was entirely convinced by the glorious triumph of the divine Cross. At the moment when Our Lord received His beloved Cross, Lucifer and his demons lost all strength; they were vanquished and enchained and the end of their chains placed in the hands of the divine Mother, that by the virtue of her Son she might hold him and his legions in subjection. They tried to precipitate themselves into the abyss, but were constrained by the great Queen, to the extreme shame and confusion of Lucifer, to witness the end of those mysteries and to remain around the Cross.

When Jesus Christ began to speak upon the Cross, He willed that the demons should hear Him and understand the sense of His words and the profound mysteries expressed in them.

Hearing Him pray to His Eternal Father for His executioners, they clearly understood that He was the Messias and were filled with rage at His infinite charity. When He promised Paradise to the Good Thief, they understood the virtue of His Redemption; and Lucifer, being unable to endure that sight, humbled his pride so far as to supplicate our great Queen to allow him and his legions to precipitate themselves into the infernal abyss; but this was refused, in order to add to his greater torment.

When Jesus, in recommending His Mother to St. John, called her "Woman," they clearly understood that she was that great *Woman* who had been shown to them in Heaven after their creation; and again that it was she that was to crush the head of Lucifer, as had been foretold him in the terrestrial Paradise.

At the fourth word, which testified the desolation of Jesus, they learned His incomprehensible charity, which led Him to complain to the Eternal Father, not because He was suffering, but because He wished to undergo even more agony, in order to save mankind. But at the words, "I thirst," they were filled with rage, because they saw that He complained not of bodily thirst, but of that ardent desire which He felt in His soul for man's salvation. At the sixth mysterious word, "All is consummated," they received a clear knowledge of the great mystery of Redemption, which was already accomplished, to their eternal shame and confusion. The reign of Jesus was established, and the empire of Satan entirely overthrown.

When Jesus pronounced the words, "Father, into Thy hands I commend My spirit," and bowing His head, expired, the ground opened, and the demon with all his companions was, in a terrific manner, swallowed into the bottomless pit of Hell more quickly than the thunderbolt falls from the clouds. He fell, disarmed and vanquished, and his head was crushed beneath the feet of Jesus and His holy Mother. This rapid fall of the demons was far more humbling and painful to them than their first fall from heaven; and though Hell had ever been a region of darkness, covered with the shadows of death, it nevertheless became on this occasion still more horrible, for the damned felt a new accession of torments from the violence with which the demons were hurled into the abyss. Judas, in particular, suffered horrible torments, for this unhappy man was thrown into a bottomless cavern, into which the demons had tried to precipitate other souls, but had always failed, without ever understanding the cause. From the beginning, this horrible abyss had been destined for him, and those who imitate him, such as relaxed religious and wicked Christians, who, after having received the grace of Baptism, lead a bad life and are damned because they do not profit by the Sacraments, by the Passion of Christ, or by the intercession of His holy Mother.

Lucifer, having, by the permission of God, recovered from the effects of his terrible fall, called together the chiefs of the infernal legions and spoke thus: "Companions, you see that we have lost the empire which we so long maintained over the world, and have been overthrown by the Man-God, and crushed beneath the feet of His Mother. What shall we now do? How shall we ever re-establish our fallen empire? How shall we be able to draw men to us? Will not everyone follow and imitate the Incarnate God? They will walk in His footsteps, give Him their hearts, practice His law, observe His precepts, and no one will ever again listen to our deceitful promises. They will reject the riches and honors with which we try to allure them. Ah! no doubt, after His example, they will love poverty, obedience, purity and ignominy, and thus attain to that eternal kingdom which we have lost. In order to imitate the Redeemer, they will humble themselves to the dust and suffer all things with patience. Nevertheless, my pride fails not. Courage! Let us confer together on the means by which we may still make war against the world, redeemed by the Man-God and protected by His Mother, our terrible enemy." To this difficult proposition some of the most cunning of the infernal chiefs replied: "It is true that men now possess a very mild law, very powerful sentiments, the new example of a Divine Master and the efficacious intercession of this new *Woman*. But human nature is always the same, and things pleasing to the senses have not changed. It is a condition of human nature that when occupied with one object, it cannot pay attention to that which is opposed to it."

Then they resolved to maintain idolatry in the world so that men might never attain to the knowledge of the true God or the mystery of the Redemption, and that, should idolatry be overthrown, they would introduce into the world new sects and heresies, such as the erroneous and infernal doctrines of Arius, Pelagius, Mahomet and other wicked heretics. All these plans were approved by Lucifer, because they aimed at the destruction of the foundation of the blessed and eternal life.

Other demons pledged themselves to devote all their energies to cause parents and heads of families to be careless and negligent in the education of their children and dependents. Others promised to sow discord between husbands and wives, thus to raise hatred and quarrels between them. Others said: "Our office will be to destroy piety and all that is spiritual and divine, and to prevent men from understanding the virtue of the Sacraments, so that they may receive them in the state of sin, or that even if they do not receive in mortal sin, yet they may do so in a state of tepidity and indevotion, for as the benefits which flow from them are spiritual, those who wish to receive the fruit of them must be fervent in spirit. If they have contempt of the remedy, they will be careless about their salvation, and thus become too feeble to resist our temptations; being blinded, they will not perceive our snares and deceits, they will not appreciate the love of their Redeemer or the intercession of this powerful *Woman*."

They unanimously resolved to devote all their zeal and energy to cause the faithful to forget the dolorous Passion of Jesus, that thus they might be led to forget the pains of Hell and the danger of eternal damnation.

It would be impossible to record all the different suggestions and resolutions of the rebellious spirits, whilst they plotted the destruction of the Church and the perdition of her children. It will suffice to say that this infernal council continued during an entire year. Lucifer, having approved the plans of his legions, afterwards excited them all to work earnestly against the redeemed world, but principally against Christians. Animated by rage and fury, he bade them sow discord in the Church, and excite in the heads of families the passions of ambition, cupidity, sensuality and avarice, so that sins being multiplied among Christians, principally among those entrusted with the guidance of others, God might be justly irritated against them for their ingratitude and either refuse His graces or withdraw them from them, and by these means he hoped the way of salvation would be closed against them, and that Hell would triumph.

Whoever reads this chapter should consider that Lucifer is ever the same, that he is still animated by the same spirit of rage and hatred against us, who are so weak. Let us therefore renew our zeal for our salvation and not allow ourselves to be deceived by the false pleasures of the world, of the senses, and of Hell, but have recourse to the Wounds of our Redeemer and live under the protection of our august Queen.

Chapter 27

PIERCING OF OUR SAVIOUR'S SIDE WITH
A LANCE—HIS BURIAL—RETURN OF THE
BLESSED VIRGIN TO THE SUPPER-ROOM.

The Mother of Sorrows remained standing on Calvary, leaning against the holy Cross and adoring the
sacred body of her Son and His divine Person, to
which this most holy body always remained united.
This great Queen continued ever constant in the
interior practice of the most heroic virtues, ever firm
and immovable amidst the impetuous movements of
her most bitter sorrows. The greatest affliction of this
merciful and divine Mother was the culpable ingratitude which men, to their own great detriment and
loss, would return for this incomprehensible benefit.
She also felt great anxiety about the burial of the
divine body of her Son, and how it was to be taken
down from the Cross. Suddenly she beheld a crowd
of armed men approaching Calvary. Her fears were
redoubled, for she dreaded some new outrage to the
sacred body of the Redeemer.

Addressing herself to St. John and the holy
women, she said: "Alas! my sorrow has reached the
highest degree, and my heart is broken within me.
Alas! the executioners are not satisfied with hav-

ing put my Son to death; they now come to commit new outrages on His sacred Body."

It was already the evening of Friday, and the great
feast of the Sabbath of the Jews had commenced;
therefore, that they might be able to celebrate it
without hindrance, they begged Pilate to allow
them to break the limbs of the three who had been
crucified, in order to hasten their death, that they
might be able to remove them at the close of day.
With this intention the soldiers seen by the Blessed
Mother had come to Calvary. Finding the two
thieves still alive, they broke their limbs, which
caused their immediate death, but as Jesus had
already expired, a soldier named Longinus pierced
His sacred side with a lance, and blood and water
flowed therefrom.

As Our Lord was dead, He could not feel the
pain of this wound, but His more afflicted Mother
endured the same agony as if the lance had really
transpierced her heart, yet her bodily pain was less
than that which she experienced in her soul at the
sight of her Son's body being thus outraged. Touched
with pity and compassion for Longinus, she said:
"May the Almighty cast upon thee a look of His
infinite mercy in return for the immense pain thou
hast caused my soul." Her prayer was granted; a few
drops of the sacred blood and water fell upon the
face of Longinus, and he obtained not only his corporal sight, which he had nearly lost, but also that
of his soul, by which he recognized the majesty of
the Lord who had been crucified, was converted
and, weeping for his sins, confessed the Divinity of

Christ, which he publicly preached to those who were around him.

The Mother of Wisdom clearly understood the great mystery of the piercing of the side of the Divine Lord. She saw that from this wound came forth the new Church, washed, purified and invigorated by the virtue of His Passion and death, and that from the Sacred Heart, as from the tree, proceeded branches laden with the fruit of eternal life, which were to spread over the entire earth. The august Mother prayed that all the mysteries thus accomplished might be productive of good for the happiness of mankind. She beheld a number of persons coming towards her, carrying ladders; they were Joseph of Arimathea, Nicodemus and their servants.

When they arrived at the foot of the Cross and beheld the dolorous Mother, they were so moved at the sight of her grief, and at beholding Jesus nailed to the Cross, that for some time they remained motionless, and could neither salute Mary nor attempt to console her. Being strengthened by the Virgin Mother, they took courage and saluted her with humble compassion, after which they prepared to remove the sacred body. Joseph of Arimathea begged Mary to retire a little apart, in order that her sorrow might not be renewed, but ever constant and courageous, she replied: "As I have had the consolation of being present at my Son's death upon the Cross, permit me to have that of seeing Him removed therefrom, for this act of great piety will give me more relief than pain and suffering."

At these generous words they began to remove the mangled body of Jesus. First, they took off the crown of thorns, and having kissed it with great veneration, presented it to Mary, who received it kneeling. Pressing it to her lips, she bathed it with her tears, and St. John and the pious women also venerated it, as they likewise did the nails. To receive the sacred body the Holy Virgin knelt down and stretched out her arms, holding over them at the same time some white linen. St. John supported the head, and Magdalen the feet, while they assisted Joseph and Nicodemus. In this manner, with the deepest veneration and an abundance of tears, they laid the divine body on the bosom of the dolorous Mother. She adored it profoundly, shedding tears of blood caused by her excessive grief.

All the holy Angels present adored the body of their God, although they were invisible to the assistants. St. John did the same, and after him the rest of the faithful followers. St. John and Joseph asked the weeping Mother to allow them to bury the body of her Divine Son, and having embalmed it, they placed it on a litter to bear it to the sepulchre.

The great Queen, although oppressed with grief, called many of the heavenly choirs to assist, with her own Guardian Angels, at the interment of their Creator. The heavenly spirits obeyed, but they were visible only to the Holy Virgin. Then the devout procession of men and angels set out. St. John, Nicodemus, Joseph and the centurion who had been present at the Redeemer's death and confessed Him to be the Son of God, carried the sacred body.

After them followed the Queen of Martyrs, accompanied by the Marys and the other pious women, and many of the faithful who had been enlightened by divine light. Thus they carried the precious remains into the garden, in which Joseph had a new sepulchre, wherein they laid it with the greatest reverence.

Before the stone was rolled against the sepulchre, the loving Mother prostrated herself to adore the body of her Son; the others did the same, shedding many tears. The sepulchre being closed, Mary ordered the holy Angels to remain there as a guard, while she conducted her pious company to Calvary to venerate the holy Cross; after they had done so, they accompanied her to the hall of the Last Supper, whence they returned to their own homes, filled with heavenly consolation. The Holy Virgin, St. John and the pious women remained in the Supper-room. St. John begged the Blessed Mother to take a little rest. "My rest," answered she, "will be to behold my Son risen."

After these words she retired to her room, accompanied by St. John. There she cast herself at his feet, reminded him of Jesus' words upon the Cross, and entreated that, in his office of priest of the Most High, he would, in the future, command her as if she were his servant with regard to all that she was to do.

The Apostle remonstrated with her and tried to prove that the right to command belonged to her as a mother; but all was in vain, for the humble Queen added, "My son, I must always be subject to someone, and certainly, as thou art my son, thou oughtest to give me this consolation in my solitude." To this the Saint answered, "My Mother, it shall be as thou desirest." After this the Holy Virgin begged his permission to retire into solitude, to meditate on the Passion of her Divine Son. She also begged him to procure food for the pious women and to assist them. The Apostle punctually executed these orders, and they separated, to pass the night in sorrowful meditation on the Redeemer's Passion.

At dawn of day on Saturday, St. John entered into Mary's oratory in order to console her and be the first to receive her blessing. At her request he went to seek St. Peter, whom, by the disposition of Divine Providence, he met before he had proceeded many steps. He was coming from the grotto, in which he had wept over his sin and, overwhelmed with confusion, was proceeding towards the Supper-room. The Blessed Virgin had told St. John to give him every mark of love and tenderness, to console him, and bring him to her.

After he had strengthened St. Peter by his kind words, they went together to seek the other Apostles, and having found several of them, they returned to the Supper-room. St. Peter entered first, and prostrating himself at Mary's feet, he cried out with tears: "I have sinned, I have sinned before my God; I have offended my Divine Master, and thee also, O my Mother!" Then, overcome by his tears and grief, he could say no more.

The merciful Mother, placing herself on her

knees, said, "Let us, O Peter, beg pardon of my Son thy Master for thy fault."

The other Apostles joined in their prayer, and, bathed in tears, they prostrated themselves at her feet, begging pardon for their cowardice in having forsaken her Son, their Divine Master. The Mother of clemency bade them arise, promised them the pardon they desired, and also her mediation to obtain it.

After having passed the Sabbath in holy conversation and pious meditation, she retired in the evening to contemplate the divine actions of the most holy soul of Jesus in Limbo, for she clearly beheld everything in spirit. She saw that at the entrance of Jesus into Limbo, that obscure prison was illuminated and filled with heavenly consolation; then the Angels were ordered to conduct the souls detained in Limbo and in Purgatory; being united together, they gave a thousand benedictions and praises to their Liberator. At this sight, the Holy Virgin felt great joy in her soul, yet not in the sensitive part, for she had prayed the Eternal Father to suspend in her every means of consolation during the time that Our Lord would remain in the sepulchre.

This day was terrible to those in Hell, for, by the permission of God, they felt sensibly the triumphant descent of Our Lord into Limbo. The demons were still feeble and crushed by their fall from Calvary, but hearing the voices of the angelic heralds who preceded the Lord, they were troubled and seized with fear, and like serpents when pursued, hid themselves within the infernal caverns.

The confusion of the damned was great and inde-scribable, particularly that of Judas, because on him the demons vented their rage with greater fury and indignation.

Chapter 28

RESURRECTION OF OUR LORD—GREAT JOY OF THE DIVINE MOTHER—OTHER MARVELS.

The Divine Saviour remained in Limbo with the holy fathers from Friday night until Sunday morning, before dawn, when He came forth from the sepulchre, accompanied by the holy Angels and the souls of the just whom He had redeemed.

A great number of the holy Angels had kept guard over the holy sepulchre. By order of the great Queen, some of them had gathered the drops of divine blood and the pieces of sacred flesh, torn by the blows, as also everything which related to the glory of the sacred body or appertained to the integrity of the most holy Humanity.

The souls of the holy fathers, on arriving, beheld at first this divine body covered with wounds and disfigured by the outrages and cruelty of the Jews; then the Angels replaced, with great reverence, the holy relics which they had gathered, and at the same instant the most holy soul of the Redeemer reunited itself to the divine body and communicated to it life, immortal and glorious. Jesus came forth from the sepulchre, shining with heavenly beauty; in the

presence of the holy fathers, He promised to all
mankind the resurrection of the body as an effect
of His, and as a pledge of this promise He commanded the souls of many of those present to reassume their bodies; therefore the Evangelist says,
"and the bodies of many arose."

The Queen of Martyrs beheld all this, and the
sight reflected on her a celestial splendor, so that
she became radiant with beauty and light. St. John
had come, as on the previous morning, to console
her in her desolation; suddenly he beheld her surrounded with rays of glory, so that as before she
was hardly recognizable from the excess of grief, so
now she was so brilliant and transformed, as it were,
that she seemed to have received new life; hence
he concluded that Jesus must be risen.

The great Queen, entirely absorbed in the
thought of her Son's Resurrection, performed heroic
acts of virtue, and her heart became inflamed with
the fire of charity. Suddenly she experienced within
herself a new emotion of joy and heavenly consolation, corresponding to the inexplicable grief she
had suffered during the Passion, and this emotion
was communicated to her body by the soul. To these
admirable effects was added a third benefit of a different nature, which was a new light like that of
Heaven.

After she had been thus prepared, her beloved
Son entered into her room, risen and glorious, and
accompanied by all the holy patriarchs. The humble Queen prostrated herself upon the ground to
adore her Son and Lord, who, raising her, drew her

to His side. In this divine contact, she received an incomprehensible favor of the most exalted kind, a favor which she alone could merit, because she alone was exempt from the sin of Adam; yet even she could not have received it had she not been fortified by her Divine Son. This favor was that the glorious Body of the Son environed the soul of His Mother in the same manner as if a globe of crystal were to surround the sun, and the most pure body of the Virgin Mother became like to one of the blessed. She heard a voice which said, "My beloved, ascend higher." By virtue of this divine voice she was entirely transformed, and clearly beheld the Divine Essence, in which, even in a moment, she found at once her repose and the reward for all the sorrows she had undergone. In this state of ineffable happiness she remained for many hours, and she received as many gifts and graces as was possible for a creature to receive. She afterwards spoke to and recognized each of the holy patriarchs in turn, and they did homage to her as to the Mother of the Redeemer. She spoke in particular with St. Ann, St. Joachim, St. Joseph and St. John the Baptist.

After this visit to His holy Mother, Our Lord willed to visit those who had suffered most during His Passion, as is related by the Evangelist, and except when Jesus was thus occupied in consoling others by His visits, He always remained to converse with His Mother in the Supper-room, where she remained during the forty days which preceded His Ascension.

After His blessed Mother, the Lord was pleased to pay His first visit to the holy women, because they had remained firm in the faith and hope of the Resurrection. The holy Gospel relates that the Marys went to the sepulchre, one Evangelist says, "by night"; another, "when the sun had risen." This apparent contradiction may be thus explained. The holy women left the house before daylight, but when they reached the sepulchre the sun had arisen, because on that day he anticipated the time by three hours, in order to compensate for the three hours eclipse at our Saviour's death. Therefore it is true that by the hour it was still night, yet it was day, by reason of the sun's being risen.

During the forty days after the Resurrection which Jesus spent with His holy Mother, His divine presence produced in her most wonderful effects. She also conversed many times with the holy fathers, and being the Mother of Wisdom, knew the graces and favors they had received from the Most High and the prophecies they had made regarding the divine actions of the life and death of Jesus Christ. At her invitation they often joined with her in praising the Lord; ranged in order, they formed a magnificent choir in which each sang a verse, to which the divine Mother answered, and in these canticles she alone gave more glory to the Most High than all the Saints together.

In this happy time another wonder was operated; this was that all the souls of the faithful who passed to eternity during those forty days were conducted to the Supper-room, and those who were pure were immediately beatified; those who were condemned to Purgatory had not this happiness, and were deprived of the sight of Jesus risen, some for three days, others for four or five. Then the great Mother of piety and mercy satisfied for them by adorations, prostrations, genuflections and many other acts of religion, after which satisfaction they were admitted to the sight of the Lord and the enjoyment of His presence; then prostrating themselves before the Virgin Mother, they expressed their thanks.

The Evangelists record many apparitions of Jesus after His Resurrection; although they make no mention of that to St. Peter, it is, nevertheless, certain that the Lord of Goodness appeared to him after the holy women. Regarding St. Thomas, it is well to know that he was drawn from his incredulity by the prayers of the Holy Virgin, to whom the Apostles complained of his obstinacy in his own opinion and his refusing to believe their words. The merciful Mother replied to them with kindness and mildness, telling them that the judgments of God are profound and that He would draw great good from the incredulity they so much condemned. Then she offered a fervent prayer to obtain from the Lord the remedy, which was afterwards given to St. Thomas.

Some days before the Ascension, as the Holy Virgin was in the Supper-room, the Eternal Father and the Holy Spirit appeared to her upon a throne of ineffable beauty, on which the Incarnate Word also ascended. At this sight, the humble Mary withdrew into a corner of the room, where, prostrate on the ground, she annihilated herself and adored the Most High Trinity with profound veneration.

The Eternal Father ordered the Angels to conduct her before His divine throne. When they had done so, she heard a voice saying, "My beloved, ascend higher," and she was raised to the august throne of the Divinity. The Eternal Father recommended the Church to her, saying: "My daughter, I confide to thee the care of the Church founded by My Son, and also the new law of grace which He has published to the world."

The Holy Ghost communicated to her the sovereign wisdom and grace, and the Son established her in His place to govern the faithful.

Then the three Divine Persons, addressing the choir of Angels, proclaimed her the Sovereign and Queen of all created things, Protectress of the new Church, Mother of fair love, Advocate of sinners, with many other beautiful titles.

On the day of His glorious Ascension, Jesus made the same discourse to the one hundred and twenty persons assembled in the Supper-room. "My dear children," said He, "I return to the Father, from whose bosom I have descended for the salvation of the world, but in My place I leave My Mother to be your Consoler, Advocate and Mediatrix, that you may hear and obey her. And as I have already told you, he who will see Me, will also see My Father, and he who will know Me, will also know My Father, so I say to you, he who will know My Mother will know Me, and he who will hear her, will also hear Me. Whoever will offend Me, will offend her, and he that will honor Me will also honor her. You shall consider her as your Mother, your Mistress, your Superior and your Advocate. She shall decide all your doubts and difficulties, because I will be with her unto the end of the world, even as I now am, although it is in a manner which you do not as yet understand." The Lord spoke thus because He was really in her under the sacramental species, which she had received at the Last Supper and still preserved in her heart.

"You shall also," continued Our Divine Lord, "acknowledge Peter as head of the Church, over which I have constituted him My vicar. You shall regard John as the son of My Mother, for such I named him when on the Cross."

After these words, Jesus made known to the Blessed Mother that He was about to command the assembly of the faithful to begin to pay her that homage due to her as the Mother of God, and that He would leave it as a precept to His Church that she should receive such veneration. But our humble Queen earnestly begged Him not to give her at that time any honor but that necessary for the accomplishment of the office He had imposed on her, and not to allow the faithful to pay to her any deeper veneration than that which they had given her up to that time, so that all worship might be addressed to Him and in His name. The Lord granted her humble request, but reserved to Himself the right to make her known to the world at a time more suitable and opportune.

Chapter 29

ASCENSION OF JESUS INTO HEAVEN—
SINGULAR FAVORS GRANTED TO
HIS BLESSED MOTHER.

Whilst Our Lord was in the Supper-room with His blessed Mother, it happened, by a particular disposition of Divine Providence, that many of the faithful and pious women besides the three Marys and Magdalen congregated there to the number of one hundred and twenty. The Divine Master filled their hearts with holy fervor. He instructed His disciples and enriched the Church with the sacred mysteries and Sacraments. At length arrived the happy hour in which, as the true heir of eternal felicity, He was to ascend to His Eternal Father. Begotten from all eternity and consubstantial with His Heavenly Father, He was to assume into Heaven His Sacred Humanity in order that all the prophecies concerning His coming, life, death and redemption might be accomplished. He thus wished to seal all the mysteries by that of the Ascension, at which He promised to send the Holy Ghost, for the Comforter would not come until Christ had ascended into Heaven, because He and the Father were to send Him to His well-beloved Church. In order then to worthily celebrate this joyous and auspicious day, He chose the one hundred and twenty as witnesses, viz., the most holy Virgin, the twelve Apostles, the seventy-two disciples, Magdalen and Martha, Lazarus their brother, the three Marys and many others of the faithful, both men and women. At the head of this little flock which represented the entire Church, Jesus, the Divine Shepherd, left the Supper-room and walked through the streets of Jerusalem with His most pure and tender Mother by His side. Thus they advanced in the direction of Bethania, about two miles from Jerusalem, towards Mt. Olivet. The company of the Angels, and also of the Saints who had been taken out of Limbo and Purgatory, followed the Lord all radiant and glorious, singing canticles of praise, but they were visible only to Mary.

The Resurrection of the Lord was already known throughout all Jerusalem and Palestine, although the priests and Pharisees had, out of envy and hatred, tried to prevent the news being spread abroad. Divine Providence so willed that this holy procession passed on unnoticed, and that no one but these one hundred and twenty beheld the Lord.

When they reached the summit of Mt. Olivet they ranged themselves in three choirs; the first, the Angels; the second, the Saints; and the third, the body of the faithful and the Apostles. The latter separated into two parties, and Jesus placed Himself in their midst. Prostrating herself at the feet of her Divine Son, the august Mother adored Him as true God and Redeemer of the world, then she begged Him to bestow on her His last benediction, and all present followed her example.

The Divine Lord blessed them with a joyous countenance, full of majesty. Joining His hands, He began to ascend slowly out of their sight, leaving upon the mountain the imprint of His sacred feet. With a scarcely perceptible motion, He arose in the air, drawing after Him the loving eyes and ravished hearts of His first-born children. And as the attraction of the sun causes the motion of the inferior planets, thus Jesus triumphant drew after Him the Angels and the glorified Saints, who accompanied Him.

But the new and hidden mystery operated on this occasion by the power of the Most High was that of taking with Him into Heaven His most holy Mother, there to give her that place due to her as His Mother and acquired by her merits, to be possessed by her in due time, for all eternity. The Almighty willed that while the Blessed Mother was in Heaven, she should still remain in the company of the faithful on Mt. Olivet.

The blessed Queen was then exalted with her Divine Son and placed at His right hand, as had been foretold by David (*Ps.* 44), and there she remained during three days. It was becoming that, at that time, this mystery should be concealed from both the Apostles and the faithful, for had they seen Mary ascend with Jesus into Heaven, their affliction would have been too great. As they beheld their divine and beloved Master receding gradually from their sight, they gave vent to their grief in sighs and tears, and when a luminous cloud hid Him from their eyes, their sorrow became still deeper.

The Eternal Father and the Holy Ghost, attended by all the blessed spirits, descended on a cloud to meet the only begotten and Incarnate Son and His Virgin Mother. Then both those Divine Persons, according to our manner of understanding, embraced them with a kiss of ineffable purity, which caused a new joy to all the choirs of Heaven, who sang: "Open, O Princes, your eternal gates, and let the great King of Glory and the Queen of Virtues enter. Already has His liberal and infinite mercy given to men the power of acquiring with justice the rights they had lost by sin, and of meriting, by the observance of His law, eternal beatitude as His brethren and co-heirs. In order to increase our joy, He brings with Him the Mother of piety, who gave Him the body in which He has vanquished Satan. Our Queen is replenished with such grace and beauty that she fills with joy all those that behold her."

This procession, so admirably arranged, arrived in Paradise with incomprehensible joy. The Angels ranged themselves on one side, the Saints on the other, and Jesus Christ and His august Mother passed through their midst. All rendered to Christ supreme adoration, and to Mary, the co-redemptrix, the veneration due to her, singing canticles of praise in honor of the Author of grace and life. The Eternal Father placed the Incarnate Word at His right hand on the throne of the Divinity. The great Queen remained humbled in the depth of her nothingness, because of her extraordinary humility and wisdom. She abased herself in the knowledge that she was a mere creature, and this admirable humility of their Queen was to Angels and men a new motive for joy. The voice of the Eternal Father was heard, saying, "Ascend higher, My daughter"; and her Divine Son also called her, saying, "Arise, My Mother, and come to the place which I will give thee." The Holy Ghost added, "Come, My spouse, My beloved, receive My eternal embrace."

Then to the whole celestial court was made known the decree of the Most Holy Trinity, which gave to the august Mother the seat at the right hand of her Son, on the throne of the Blessed Trinity, and she was offered the choice of returning to the world or of remaining in Heaven. Arising from the throne, she prostrated herself before the Blessed Trinity and, in imitation of her Son, showed herself ready to labor for the good of the Church and to relinquish the ineffable joys of Heaven. This heroic act of charity was so agreeable to God that, having purified and enlightened her, He raised her to the intuitive vision of the Divinity and surrounded her with glory. Thus, like the industrious bee, she descended from the Church Triumphant to the Church Militant laden with the flowers of the most pure charity, to make the sweet honeycomb of the love of God and her neighbor for the young children of the primitive Church, whom she raised to be strong and robust men, who afterwards became the foundation of the great edifice of the Church.

But let us return to Mt. Olivet. There the faithful remained with eyes upturned towards Heaven, weeping and lamenting because they could no longer behold their Divine Redeemer. The merciful Mother cast on them a look of tenderness and, filled with compassion for their sorrows, prayed her Divine Son to console them; therefore, He sent to them two Angels clothed in white and resplendent with glory. After they had been thus comforted they departed from Mt. Olivet and returned to the Supper-room, in company with the Blessed Virgin, where they persevered in prayer, expecting with earnest desire the coming of the Holy Spirit promised to them by the Redeemer.

After the Blessed Mother had enjoyed in her soul during three days the glory of Heaven, the Divine Majesty ordered an innumerable company of angels from every choir to accompany her to the earth, and she was carried on a bright cloud to the Supper-room. The human mind cannot conceive the beauty and exterior brightness with which the august Queen came from Paradise. It was necessary that the Most High should conceal them from those who beheld her. St. John alone had the privilege of seeing her in this splendor. Descending from this cloud of light, she prostrated herself upon the ground and in her heart humbled herself beneath the dust; she abased herself before God in a manner not to be expressed by human tongue. She was entirely absorbed in her Beloved and so disengaged from all created things as to be a subject of admiration to the Angels, who wondered at seeing a pure creature so exalted and so full of gifts and with such a great fund of the beautiful virtue of humility.

The evangelist St. John was rendered worthy to see her descend from Paradise; he was ravished with astonishment and seized with such humility that he remained a whole day without daring to present himself before the Queen of Angels. But at length, being impelled by love and devotion, he came to the august Mother, and seeing her incomparably more brilliant than was Moses when he descended from Mt. Sinai, he prostrated himself upon the ground, overpowered by emotion. The merciful Mother hastened to him and, kneeling, said, "My son and my master, thou knowest that the obedience that I owe thee directs all my actions; as thou art to take the place of my Son in commanding all my actions, be kind enough to exercise this power over me, to give me the consolation of obeying." Hearing these words, the holy Apostle was filled with astonishment and confusion, knowing the greatness of the divine Mother; nevertheless he promised to do as she desired, in order to leave to the Church a singular example of humility.

If, then, we wish to be the children and true servants of this divine Mother, let us endeavor principally to imitate her holy humility.

Chapter 30

HOLY EXERCISES IN THE SUPPER-ROOM BEFORE PENTECOST.

The divine Mother had been left on earth to direct the Church and be the Mistress of the Apostles, and as such she was regarded by the faithful assembled in the Supper-room; nevertheless, the great Queen never spoke in their midst, unless when commanded by St. Peter or St. John, for she had begged her Divine Son to inspire them with His orders, that she might obey them as Himself. Therefore she executed all that they desired, as if she were their humble servant and the least among them, and as such did she ever act and speak among the primitive faithful. After she descended from Heaven, she consoled them all with kindness, exhorted them to banish sadness and filled them with consolation.

She assembled them together twice a day in the Supper-room, and being commanded by St. John or St. Peter to speak, explained to them for one hour the mysteries of faith, as if she were conversing with them, rather than teaching them as their Mistress and Queen. She explained the mysteries of the Hypostatic Union and all those contained in the

ineffable and divine Incarnation. After this she bade
them entertain themselves for one hour longer on
the counsels, promises and doctrines they had
learned from their Divine Master; to consecrate
another part of the day to the recital of the *Pater
Noster*, with some psalms; and to employ the rest
of the time in mental prayer. In the evening they
took some slight nourishment of bread, fruits and
fish; thus by prayer and fasting they prepared for
the coming of the Holy Spirit. She incited them
to mental prayer, teaching them its excellence and
necessity, because the noblest occupation of the reasonable creature is to raise his mind above created
things to meditate on the divine, and that nothing
should be preferred to this holy exercise.

By these holy lessons, the Mother of Wisdom and
the Mistress of Charity enlightened the minds and
inflamed the hearts of the Apostles and disciples,
filling them with fervor and disposing them to
receive the precious gifts of the Paraclete, which
she told them they would receive in an abundance
corresponding to their dispositions. She caused them
to practice perseveringly and courageously both
interior and exterior acts of virtue, also genuflections, prostrations, acts of religion and veneration
and other acts of adoration in honor of the infinite greatness of the Most High. Every morning and
evening she went with great humility to receive the
blessing of the Apostles, first that of St. Peter or
St. John, and then of the others, according to
seniority.

At first they were amazed at beholding their

Mother and Queen prostrate at their feet and refused to bless her. But as the Mother of Wisdom, possessing the plenitude of all science, she made them understand that by the greatness of their priestly office and the sublimity of their sacerdotal dignity, it was their right to bless her, and hers to receive that benediction. Then they complied with her request, to the great edification of the faithful. The words of the Holy Virgin were mild, fervent and efficacious in touching the hearts of the primitive faithful and in leading them to the practice of what was most fervent and heroic in virtue.

Surprised themselves at their feelings, they said: "We truly find in this pure creature that doctrine and consolation of which we have been deprived by the departure and absence of our Divine Master, for by her works, words, counsels and conversation, so full of grace, humility and sweetness, she teaches and persuades us as did our amiable Redeemer when He conversed with us. Let us dry our tears, because, although deprived of the presence of our Divine Master, He has left to us this Mother and Mistress."

When they had recourse to her for advice, it is impossible to say with what humility, modesty and clearness she satisfied them, and she explained mysterious and hidden things with great light and clearness, because as the Mother of Wisdom, she knew how to accommodate herself to everyone and adapted herself to the capacity of each. Ah! if the Apostles had but left in writing all that they knew and learned of the august Mother, all that they saw and heard during her lifetime, particularly during those days which preceded the Descent of the Holy Ghost, we would certainly have a greater knowledge of the sublime doctrine of Christ and the incomparable sanctity of our great Queen. From her explanations and the effects they produced, it was clearly shown that her most holy Son had communicated to her a kind of divine virtue like to His, except that in Him it was as a fountain and source, and in her as the channel by which it was to be conveyed to the souls of men.

The apostleship of the unhappy Judas was, as David says in *Psalm* 108, left vacant by his treason and despairing death; therefore, it was necessary to elect another worthy of the apostolate, for it was the will of the Lord that at the Descent of the Holy Ghost, the number twelve should be complete as when first chosen by their Divine Master. In a conference held with the eleven Apostles, the Blessed Virgin made known to them this order of the Most High; they unanimously approved what she proposed and begged her as their Mother and Mistress to choose him whom she knew to be most worthy of the office of an Apostle.

Although the great Queen knew well who would be chosen, because the names of the Twelve were written in her pure and burning heart, nevertheless she knew by her profound wisdom that it would be most suitable to leave this care to St. Peter, that he might begin to exercise his office as sovereign Pontiff and head of the Church. Therefore she humbly charged him to make this election in the presence of the disciples and others there assembled, that thus they might see him discharge his office as chief of the Church. St. Peter faithfully performed all that she desired. In the Acts of the Apostles, St. Luke records the manner of this election.

During the days that intervened between the Ascension and Pentecost, St. Peter, having convoked the one hundred and twenty who had assisted at the Ascension of Our Lord, spoke to them and announced that now was about to be accomplished the prophecy uttered by David regarding Judas, who, having been chosen from among the disciples to be an Apostle, had unhappily prevaricated and had hung himself with a halter; therefore, it was necessary that one should be elected to fill his place among the Apostles and be a witness of the Resurrection of the Saviour, adding that he must be of the number of those who had followed Jesus from the beginning of His preaching.

Having heard these words, the faithful agreed to obey St. Peter as to the manner in which the choice should be made, and he determined that they should choose two from among the seventy-two disciples. They chose Joseph, commonly called "The Just," and Matthias, and decided that he on whom the lot would fall should be numbered among the Apostles. Their names were written on separate tickets and thrown into a vase; all united in fervent prayer that the Lord would reveal His Will in the choice they were about to make. Then St. Peter arose and drew the ticket of St. Matthias, who was joyfully recognized and accepted as the legitimate Apostle of Jesus.

The divine Mother knelt to receive his blessing, as did also the rest of the faithful. From that time they persevered in fasting and prayer until the Descent of the Holy Spirit.

Chapter 31

THE DESCENT OF THE HOLY GHOST—
WHAT HAPPENED TO THE HOLY VIRGIN.

It is impossible to imagine the loving solicitude of the Blessed Virgin or her ardent charity in strengthening the weakness of that pious yet still imperfect assembly. The Apostles themselves doubted the coming of the Holy Spirit; as the Mother of Piety, she came to their aid and dissipated their doubts when, feeble and vacillating, they said that the Holy Ghost would not come as had been promised. With great charity she reassured them, saying: "All that my Divine Son said has been entirely accomplished; He said in particular that He would suffer and rise again, and all has been verified. If, then, He has promised to send the consoling Spirit, without doubt He will come to console and sanctify us." At these words they became so united that from that time there was not the slightest discord in this devoted assembly; they were all of one heart and one soul, and had but one sentiment and one will. Although in the election of St. Matthias there had been no disputes nor contention, yet this was the effect of the earnest exhortations of the divine Mother. This great union of charity among the disciples was an additional cause of torment to the demons.

The Queen of the Angels and Mother of Grace already knew the time and the hour in which the Holy Spirit was to come. The days of Pentecost, which were fifty after the Resurrection of the Redeemer, being accomplished, the great Queen saw the holy Humanity of the Person of the Word reminding the Eternal Father of His promise to send into the world, by particular communication, the Holy Spirit, the Comforter. As Advocate and Mediator, He presented His wounds and merits; He offered also the ardent desires of His holy Mother, who still remained in the world. The august Virgin united herself to the prayer of her Son, sometimes by extending her arms in the form of a cross, and again by prostrating herself upon the ground. She saw that the Most Holy Trinity willed to console the infant Church, and this knowledge she communicated to the Apostles and other disciples, exhorting them to pray with fervor and to beg the Holy Spirit to descend, because He would speedily come.

While they prayed, uniting themselves to their Queen with great fervor, at the hour of tierce, they heard frightful thunder and impetuous wind, accompanied with a great splendor like lightning, and a fire which seemed to invest the Supper-room and fill it with light; this divine fire spread itself over this holy assembly and rested on the head of each one in the form of a tongue of this same fire, in which the Holy Spirit came. They were all filled with divine influences and sublime gifts; at the same time it produced in the Supper-room and in Jerusalem diverse effects.

Those effects in the Holy Virgin were many and admirable; she was elevated and transformed into God, the Consoler, and during the same time enjoyed the beatific vision of the Divinity, in which she alone received more gifts and ineffable communications than all the rest of the Church, and her glory in this moment surpassed that of all the Angels and Saints. She alone rendered greater thanks, praises, honor and glory to the Most High for having sent the Divine Spirit, than the whole Church united. Thus the Lord, being pleased with the lively and fervent thanksgivings of the pure dove, the divine Virgin, resolved to appoint her again to the government of His Church. At the same time, all the gifts, favors and graces of the Holy Spirit were renewed in His blessed Spouse with new effects and divine operations.

The Apostles were also filled with the Holy Spirit and an admirable increase of justifying grace, and they alone were confirmed in grace, never more to lose it. They received infused habits of the seven gifts, *viz.*: wisdom, understanding, knowledge, piety, counsel, fortitude and the fear of the Lord. They were renewed and fortified to be worthy ministers of the New Law and founders of the Church, for this new grace and multiplicity of gifts communicated to them a divine virtue which urged them sweetly and efficaciously to all that is most heroic in virtue and most sublime in sanctity. It operated also in the other disciples and the faithful, according to the disposition of each.

St. Peter and St. John were particularly enriched with sublime gifts, the one as chief of the Church, the other as the son of the great Sovereign of the universe. The divine and beautiful light which filled the Supper-room spread itself abroad, and all those who had been well-disposed towards the Redeemer, at least by acts of compassion, were interiorly enlightened by a new light, which disposed them to receive the doctrine of the Apostles.

The contrary effects of the Holy Spirit upon the inhabitants of Jerusalem were no less marvelous, although more hidden. In punishment of their incredulity the enemies of the Lord were terrified by fearful thunder and lightning. Moreover, all those who, with remarkable rage and cruelty, had participated in the sufferings and death of Jesus, were prostrated to the earth and remained for three hours, as if deprived of life. The men who had scourged Him were suddenly struck dead, being suffocated in their own blood, which burst from them as they fell. The barbarous and ungrateful Malchus, who had given the cruel blow, was not only struck dead suddenly, but was carried off by the demons, both body and soul. The rest of the Jews were chastised by severe pains and horrible maladies; the chastisement was extended even to Hell, for the demons and the damned felt a greater oppression of pain and particular torments, which lasted for three entire days; Lucifer and his demons yelled and roared with terror and fury.

O Holy Spirit, adorable and all-powerful, the holy Church calls Thee the *Finger of God*, because Thou proceedest from the Father and the Son, as the finger from the body and the arm. Thou art God, like the Father and the Son, infinite, eternal and immense. Ah! triumph over the wickedness of men and, by the merits of Jesus Christ and His divine Mother, communicate to us Thy gifts. Amen.

Chapter 32

THE APOSTLES LEAVE THE SUPPER-ROOM
TO PREACH—MIRACLES OPERATED
BY THE DIVINE MOTHER.

On the Sunday on which the Holy Ghost descended, the Jews were celebrating in Jerusalem a solemn feast; therefore, among the crowd there were many strangers, who, together with the inhabitants, were much surprised at the new marvels which they had seen in the Supper-room, and they hastened thither to learn their cause. The holy Apostles, hearing the noise made by so great a concourse of persons, begged their divine Mistress to allow them to go forth and instruct the people by their preaching, and they began to instruct the people. After having lived retired during fifty days, they resolutely appeared abroad, and the words which fell from their lips were like rays of light profoundly penetrating the hearts of their hearers, who, looking on each other with astonishment, said: "What is this that we see in our days? Are not these men who speak to us Galileans? How then do we all understand them in our own language? Jews and proselytes, Romans and Latins, Greeks, Cretans, Arabs, Parthians and Medes, we all understand them in the language of our own country."

This miracle wrought many different effects in the minds of the hearers, who were divided by contrary opinions, according to their different dispositions. Those who listened with devotion received great knowledge of the Divinity, and the redemption of man, which were the subjects on which the Apostles preached; by the power of their fervent words they were excited to learn the truth and, illuminated by divine light, they conceived a lively horror for their sins and deplored them. All bathed in tears, they hastened to throw themselves at the feet of the Apostles to learn what they should do to gain life everlasting. Others, on the contrary, being hardened, were indignant at what they heard and, instead of profiting by the divine word, called the Apostles the inventors of novelties, while many of the Jews, still more wicked, regarded them as drunkards. St. Peter, as head of the Church, rose to deny the blasphemy and, speaking very forcibly, convinced them by the texts of the prophets, as related by St. Luke in the *Acts of the Apostles*. Then they cried out: "What shall we do to obtain salvation?" St. Peter answered in a loud voice: "Do true penance, receive Baptism, and your sins shall be pardoned, you shall also receive the Holy Spirit." Three thousand persons were converted, instructed and baptized; and the incredulous departed, covered with confusion.

God wished that the three thousand converts should be of different nations in order that, on their return to their own countries, they might spread

the evangelical doctrine and the grace of the Holy
Spirit, and that the faithful thus dispersed might
form but one Church.

The Apostles returned to the Supper-room to
relate to the divine Mother all that had occurred;
they took the new converts with them, that they
might see and venerate her. From her retreat she
had observed all that passed, for when the Apostles went forth from the Supper-room she had prostrated herself to pray for the conversion of those
who had come to hear St. Peter; she implored God
to give the Apostles the light and inspiration necessary to persuade and move their auditors, and sent
many of the Angels of her guard to their assistance.

When the Apostles led into her presence the
reward of their labors, the first fruits of the Passion
of her Son and the Descent of the Holy Ghost, she
received them as the Mother of piety, with the greatest charity, love and sweetness. St. Peter said to
them, "Beloved brethren, this is the Mother of our
Divine Master and common Redeemer, Jesus, in
whom you have received the Faith; this Queen is
His true Mother, who conceived Him by the operation of the Holy Ghost in her chaste womb and
gave Him to the world by a miracle, remaining
always a most pure Virgin, a Virgin before childbirth, in childbirth and after childbirth. Receive her
then as your mother, your protectress, your mediatrix with the Divine Majesty, and through her you
will receive light, consolation, the remedy of sin
and of all the miseries of this frail life."

By this exhortation and by the interior lights

obtained for them by the divine Mother, they were filled with celestial consolations, and prostrating themselves on the earth, they begged her benediction. The Mother of humility refused to give it in the presence of the priests, but St. Peter begged her to afford this consolation to the pious faithful. She immediately obeyed the head of the Church and, with the humble serenity of a queen, gave her blessing to the new converts, who at that moment were replenished with heavenly consolations. Seeing that the divine Mother obeyed St. Peter, they begged him not to allow them to depart from her presence without hearing some words which might encourage them still more. St. Peter, believing it would be well to afford them this consolation, turned to the divine Queen and said, "Hear the prayers of these faithful, thy children." The great Queen obeyed, and, as the Mother of wisdom, spoke to them with zeal and humility; they were animated with fervor, edified and filled with light and admiration, and, after receiving her benediction again, returned to their homes.

From this time the Apostles and disciples continued, without interruption, to preach and work miracles. During the octave they catechized the three thousand converts, with many others who received the Faith, and afterwards baptized them. The women, after having heard the Apostles and received the divine light, went to Magdalen and the Marys to be catechized, for all the holy women who had received the Holy Ghost had also received the gift of tongues and of working miracles.

The news of this wonder spread quickly through the city of Jerusalem and the neighborhood, and they brought all the sick, the infirm and the possessed to be healed, who received the health of both body and soul with the light of faith. Thus were spread abroad the holy faith, doctrine and counsels of Jesus Christ. The faithful loved poverty, purity, peace and humility; they sold all they possessed, and brought the price to the feet of the Apostles in order to free themselves from the danger of sin. They regarded all as their brethren and were content with what was given them by the Apostles. This was the Golden Age of the Church of Jesus Christ, when faith was lively, hope firm, charity ardent, humility true and sanctity admirable.

It would be impossible to record in this abridged life all the miracles and admirable works operated by the Queen of Angels in the primitive Church. She never lost a moment or an occasion of doing some signal favor for the Church in general, or any of the faithful in particular; she incessantly prayed to her Divine Son for the spiritual and temporal necessities of all, because she knew He would refuse her nothing. She exhorted, taught, gave counsel, light and graces to everyone, for she was the treasurer and dispensatrix of the gifts of God. For this reason, during the years that she lived in the Church, the number of those who were damned (as compared with other times) was very small, and on the contrary, there were more saved during those few years than in many centuries after—that is, among the faithful.

The happiness of this Golden Age of the Church may well excite our envy, but we should consider that we were all present to the mind and heart of this merciful and divine Mother while she lived, for she saw and knew us all in the order of time and in the succession of the children of the Church in which we would be born, and she prayed for us as earnestly as for them. In Heaven she is still the same; her charity is not less ardent; her intercession and protection not less efficacious. All the fault lies with us, who do not live with the same fidelity as did the faithful in those days.

The care which she took of the Apostles, as Mother of Mercy, cannot be described. She never ceased to animate them and all the ministers of the divine word; she exhorted them to great works and reminded them of the purity of intention they should have in the miraculous works they performed and by which her Divine Son had begun to establish and propagate the faith in His Church. She recalled to their minds the great virtues which the Holy Ghost had communicated to them to make them worthy ministers, the assistance of the omnipotent arm of the Most High, of which they should acknowledge their continual need, and the unceasing thanksgiving they should render for the marvels which they operated. She taught the same doctrine to the apostolic college and was herself the first to practice it by the genuflections, prostrations and praises which she rendered to the Lord with continual thanksgiving.

Many converts begged to confer with her in secret

regarding their interior, and as a true mother, full
of tenderness, she always consoled them, because
she knew the hearts of all, with their affections and
inclinations, and applied to them the proper and
salutary remedies. The women, in particular, after
having spoken and conferred even once with the
great Queen, were inflamed with charity and
brought her precious stones and objects of great
value; others despoiled themselves of their rich ornaments and laid them at the feet of their divine Mistress, but she generally refused to accept anything.
If, however, it appeared well to do so, she encouraged them to carry their gifts to the Apostles, that
they might distribute them with justice and charity among the necessitous faithful; and the humble
Queen showed as much gratitude as if she herself
had received their gifts. She received the poor and
sick with ineffable goodness and love, and healed
a great number of inveterate diseases; she relieved
many of their secret wants by means of St. John,
for she watched over all, without ever omitting anything which regarded the virtues.

The Apostles and disciples occupied themselves
in preaching and catechizing, and the holy women
also instructed the faithful; as for the Blessed Virgin, looking upon herself as the servant of all, she
saw that the necessary nourishment was provided,
and even waited on them herself. She served the
priests upon her knees and, with incredible humility, begged to be allowed to kiss their hands; towards
the Apostles she showed still greater veneration,
because in them she recognized the sublimity of

grace and saw that they were environed with splendor and filled with the Holy Ghost.

Chapter 33

THE APOSTLES AND DISCIPLES ASSEMBLE TO RESOLVE SOME DOUBTS—ST. PETER CELEBRATES THE FIRST MASS—ACTIONS OF THE BLESSED VIRGIN.

The Apostles continued to preach assiduously, and confirmed their words by miracles and prodigies. The number of believers continued to increase, and seven days after the Descent of the Holy Ghost they were already five thousand. This abundant fruit was due to the fervent prayers of the great Mistress of the Church.

St. Peter, St. John and the rest of the Apostles appeared in the presence of the divine Mother, who received them with great veneration, and placing herself on her knees, she humbly begged the benediction of the head of the Church. After he had given it, St. Peter spoke in the name of all the others and said to the divine Mistress that the new converts had been instructed in the necessary articles of the Faith and ought to be baptized, but that they asked her advice, in order to learn the will of God. The prudent Mother replied: "My Lord, thou art the chief of the Church and the vicar of my most holy Son; therefore, all that thou wilt do in His name shall be approved by His Divine Will, and my will is with thine and that of my Son."

Then St. Peter ordered that on the following day, which corresponds to Trinity Sunday, holy Baptism should be given to the catechumens who had been converted that week. Some of the assembly thought it would be best to give the Baptism of St. John the Baptist, which was that of penance, but St. Peter and St. John, with the Blessed Mother, decided that the Baptism of Jesus Christ should be administered; that the matter should be water, and the form, "I baptize thee in the name of the Father, and of the Son, and of the Holy Ghost," because our Saviour had designated this matter and this form and had baptized many in this manner with His own divine hands. Although we read in the *Acts of the Apostles* that they baptized in the name of Jesus Christ, we must understand this of the author of the Sacrament, and not of the form, in order to distinguish this Baptism from that of penance, which had been established by St. John, for to baptize in the name of Jesus signifies the same thing as to give the Baptism instituted by Jesus Christ, because the form is the same as that taught by the Divine Master.

On the following day the catechumens reassembled in the Supper-room, and St. Peter begged the divine Mother to instruct the new converts more perfectly by her fervent words. The Mother of humility said to them with great modesty: "My children, the Redeemer of the world, my Son, and true God, because of the love He has for men, has offered to the Eternal Father the sacrifice of His divine

Body and Blood, in consecrating and concealing Himself under the species of bread, under which He has willed to remain present in the holy Church, in order that His children might have a sacrifice to offer to the Eternal Father, and might also possess the food of eternal life and a most assured pledge of that which they hope for in Heaven.

"Thus, by means of this Sacrifice, which contains all the mysteries of the life and death of the Son, we can appease the Eternal Father, and in Him and by Him the Church will render the actions of thanksgiving and praise which are due to Him as God and sovereign Benefactor. To you, O priests, to you alone belongs the right to offer it. It is my desire, if it be agreeable to you, that you commence to offer this unbloody Sacrifice, in order to testify our gratitude for the ineffable benefit of Redemption which Jesus Christ has operated for us, and for the descent of the Holy Spirit upon His Church. The faithful in receiving it will begin to relish this Bread of Eternal Life and its divine effects. Among those who have been baptized, they who are capable of it and well-disposed may be admitted to receive it, but Baptism is the first and necessary condition."

All the Apostles and disciples agreed to the desires of the Mother of wisdom, and returned her thanks; they determined that after the Baptism of the catechumens, St. Peter as head of the Church should celebrate the first Mass. St. Peter consented and, before leaving the assembly, proposed to settle another difficulty, regarding the manner of distributing the alms and the goods offered by the converts.

The fatal example of Judas prevented many from wishing to undertake this office, and different suggestions were offered. The great Mistress of virtues listened to all in silence, for, although mistress, she, by her incomparable humility, esteemed herself the disciple and servant of all.

St. Peter and St. John, seeing the diversity of opinions, begged the divine Mother to settle the difficulty. Then with great humility she exhorted all to practice voluntary poverty in imitation of the Divine Master, and proposed to them to choose six or seven persons of solid virtue to receive the alms and offerings by which the faithful were to be supported, so that the Apostles might be free to preach the Gospel; thus no one in the Church could regard anything as belonging to himself any more than to his brethren. If the alms were not sufficient for all, the seven persons should ask for aid in the name of Jesus Christ. All approved this advice of the Queen of Angels, so full of wisdom, and they chose seven men of solid virtue to receive alms and provide for the faithful.

The great Queen begged the blessing of the Apostles, who immediately went forth to preach, and the disciples began to instruct the catechumens and prepare them for Baptism. The divine Mother, accompanied by the holy Angels and the Marys, went to prepare and adorn the hall in which her Divine Son had celebrated the Last Supper; she swept it herself and arranged it for the celebration of the Holy Mass. She begged the good master of the house to give her the same ornaments that had been used on the Thursday of the Last Supper, which he did immediately, because of the veneration he entertained for the Holy Virgin. She also prepared the unleavened bread and wine needed for the Consecration, with the little plate and chalice used by the Redeemer.

She took care to have vessels filled with pure water, that holy Baptism might be conferred with more facility and propriety.

After these preparations, the merciful Mother retired to pass the night in acts of love, genuflections and thanksgivings; she offered fervent prayers to the Eternal Father that the new converts who were to receive Holy Communion on the next day might do it in a manner pleasing to the Divine Majesty, and the same prayer she offered for those who were to be baptized.

On the morning of the following day, the octave of the Descent of the Holy Ghost, all the faithful and catechumens, with the Apostles and disciples, assembled together in the hall. St. Peter made a discourse to show the excellence of Baptism and its divine effects; he told them they would be marked with an interior character as members of the mystical body of the Church, and regenerated as children of God and heirs of glory by means of justifying grace and the remission of sins. He exhorted them to observe the law of God, and announced the truth of the holy Sacrament of the Altar; they were filled with fervor, and the Apos-

tles gave Baptism with their own hands with great
order and devotion; the catechumens entered by
one door, and after having been baptized went out
by another, being conducted by the disciples.

The divine Mother was present at all, and retiring to the corner of the room, blessed and praised
the Lord. She saw that the faithful were renewed
by the divine Blood of the Lamb, and knew the
graces they received; and even in the sight of those
present a most beautiful and sensible light descended
on the newly baptized.

After the Baptism of more than five thousand
persons, while they rendered thanks to God, the
Apostles placed themselves in prayer and prepared
with the rest of the faithful to receive Holy Communion. They prostrated themselves upon the earth,
adoring the infinite goodness of God and confessing their unworthiness to receive so great a gift.
Then they recited the canticles and psalms which
the Lord had said. St. Peter took in his hands the
bread already prepared, and, raising his eyes to
Heaven with great devotion and profound recollection, pronounced over the bread the divine words
of the Consecration of the Sacred Body of Jesus
Christ.

The Supper-room was at that moment filled with
ravishing splendor and an infinite multitude of
Angels, and in the sight of all the assistants, this
divine light was especially directed towards the great
Queen. St. Peter immediately consecrated the wine
in the chalice, and with the Sacred Body and Precious Blood he performed the same ceremonies as

the Saviour; that is to say, he elevated them, that they might be adored by all. After this, he communicated himself, then the other Apostles, as had been regulated by the Holy Virgin. The divine Mother communicated from the hands of St. Peter, the heavenly spirits being there present with ineffable respect. Before reaching the altar, the great Queen performed three acts of humility; she prostrated herself upon the earth, to the great astonishment of her Guardian Angels, and the edification of the assistants, who were moved to tears. Then, being entirely recollected and ravished in the Lord, she returned to the place where she had been kneeling.

It is impossible to explain in words the divine effects operated in this great creature by the Holy Communion, for she was entirely transformed, elevated and absorbed in the embraces of the divine love of her most holy Son, whom she had received in her pure heart. While the divine Queen was thus elevated, the holy Angels, by her own desire, surrounded her, that the assistants might not know the divine effects, which it was not suitable that they should discover.

After the Communion of the Queen of Angels, the other faithful communicated, but of the five thousand who had been baptized, only one thousand received Holy Communion, because they were not sufficiently disposed and prepared. The manner in which the Holy Sacrament was on that day administered was as follows: St. Peter communicated the Apostles, the Holy Virgin and all those who had received the Holy Spirit, under the two species of bread and wine. The faithful who had been baptized, afterwards received only under the species of bread. This difference was not made because the converts were less worthy of receiving one species than another, but because the Apostles knew that by receiving only under one species they received Jesus wholly and entirely in the Holy Sacrament, and again because there was no precept to communicate under both.

After the Communion, St. Peter finished the holy mysteries by prayers and acts of thanksgiving, after which they spent some time in meditation. The great Queen returned thanks to the Most High in the name of all, in which the Divine Majesty took His complacency; He heard and accepted the prayers of His Beloved for all the children of the Church, both present and future.

Chapter 34

A NEW MIRACLE OPERATED BY JESUS IN FAVOR OF HIS HOLY MOTHER.

It is incontestable that the favors which the divine Mother received from her Son after she descended from Heaven to direct the Church were ineffable. If, in effect, they had previously been very great, they were from this moment augmented in an incredible manner, in order to show that He who communicated them was infinite and that the capacity of this wonderful creature, chosen and elected from among all others to receive them, was immense. The great and incomparable miracle was that the sacramental species of the divine Body of Jesus remained in the ardent heart of the Virgin Mother until the next Communion, which she received the succeeding day. It is unnecessary for us to seek other reasons than those which caused the favors with which the all-powerful God singularly endowed this great Queen, namely, His holy Will and infinite power, by which He operates all that He wishes with weight and measure. It suffices for Christian piety to know that this pure creature was the natural Mother of God, and that she alone among all creatures was worthy to be such.

Again, as this marvel was unique and without example, it would be great blindness to seek precedents by which to persuade ourselves of what God has operated for His Mother, because He has done for her that which He never did and never will do for other creatures, for Mary is established and raised above the order of all [other] created beings.

This principle being admitted, it is the will of the Most High that, by faith and the divine lights, we may discover the propriety and justice by which His almighty arm wrought those marvels in favor of His most holy Mother, that we may thus come to know and praise Him in her and by her, and may understand how our hopes and destinies are certain and assured when in the hands of this powerful Queen, whom God has made the depositary of the whole strength of His love.

We must consider that the Holy Virgin lived thirty-three years with her Divine Son, and that she never left Him from the instant the Divine Majesty became incarnate, even to His death on the Cross; that she nourished Him, served, accompanied, followed and imitated Him, performing all her holy actions as mother, daughter, spouse, beloved and servant. She enjoyed His presence, His conversation, His doctrine and the favors which, in consideration of her merits and homages, she received during her mortal life. Jesus then ascended into Heaven, and the greatness of His love and every reason obliged Him to take with Him His beloved Mother, that He might not be deprived of her and that she might not remain in the world without Him.

But the ardent charity which both the Son and the Mother entertained for men interrupted in some manner, as much as was possible, this bond of love, by obliging the merciful Mother to return to the world to confirm the infant Church, and the Divine Son to send her and permit her to remain separated from Him during the necessary time. But as the Son of God is all-powerful and could reward this privation of happiness in a possible manner, owing to the immense love He bore His Mother, He willed to remain with her in this manner, otherwise she would have suffered inexpressible pain in being deprived of His presence during such a great number of years.

The Divine Son supplied for all in remaining always under the sacred species in the divine heart of His Mother; thus He abundantly rewarded her for all the happiness she had caused Him during His life on earth. Then He had frequently left her to apply Himself to the work of our Redemption; on such occasions she had been much afflicted, because she feared that on account of His great fatigues He would not return. Again, when He was with her, she had ever beheld in spirit the Passion and the death of the Cross which awaited Him, and this sorrow diminished the happiness she felt in His society. But when the Passion was accomplished and He was seated at the right hand of His Father, yet, at the same time, was present in her heart under the sacramental species, the august Mother fully enjoyed His sight and presence without fear or apprehension, for, with her Son, she possessed the Most Holy Trinity.

By this favor conferred on His blessed Mother, Our Lord fulfilled the promise He had made to remain with His Church until the consummation of ages, for in these first years the Apostles had neither temples, tabernacles nor other places in which to preserve the Blessed Eucharist; therefore, all the Particles were consumed on the same day.

The Holy Virgin was the temple and the tabernacle in which, during some years, the Lord was preserved under the consecrated species, and thus the Incarnate Word was ever present in His Church. Although He was not preserved in this holy tabernacle for the use of the faithful, He was there, without doubt, for their advantage and for other sublime ends; for the Mother of piety prayed, asked and supplicated for all the faithful in the temple of her heart and adored Jesus in the sacramental species in the name of the whole Church. By means of this merciful Mother, Jesus rendered Himself in her, present in the Church, and was united in a certain manner to the mystical body of the faithful. This great Queen rendered that age the most happy, in preserving in her heart, her Son under the holy species, as if in a tabernacle, for in her He was always adored, venerated, loved, praised and honored in a perfect manner and was never outraged, offended or profaned, as He frequently is in our churches. In Mary, Jesus found in abundance the delights which, from all eternity, He had wished to take among the children of men.

The perpetual presence of Jesus in the Church had been resolved on that He might rejoice with us; His Divine Majesty obtained this end, and He could not have done it so completely in any other manner than by remaining under the sacramental species in the heart of His beloved Mother, burning with love. She was the proper sphere and true center in which He found His repose, for all creatures except her were to Him only a strange place, as in none else did He find the fuel for the fire of His Divinity which burns always, because it is infinite charity.

The manner in which the Most High operated this new miracle was as follows: When the Holy Virgin received the sacramental species, they did not enter the stomach, in which food is digested and the natural aliments transformed, in order that the consecrated species might not be mingled with the little nourishment taken by the great Queen to preserve her life and might not be consumed. Therefore, Jesus, in the sacramental species, did not enter the stomach, but, by a miracle, placed Himself in the very heart of Mary, as the reward for the precious blood it had furnished for the Incarnation of the Word at the formation of the most holy Humanity, to which He united Himself hypostatically. If sacramental Communion is, with reason, called a continuation of the Incarnation, it was just and becoming that the divine Mother should participate in this continuation in a singular and particular manner, because she had also concurred in a miraculous and singular manner to the Incarnation of the Eternal Word.

It is true that the heat of the heart in healthy

persons is very great, and that nature, ever provident, sends air which gives ventilation to temper this natural heat which is the principle of life; but in the noble and perfect organization of the Sovereign of the universe, the heat of the body was very great and was still further augmented by the ineffable affections of her ardent heart; nevertheless, the sacramental species were not consumed, and this was another miracle. Yet we cannot wonder at this in a creature so pre-eminent, who was herself the miracle of miracles and contained them all within her.

This favor commenced at the first Communion which she received from the Lord at the Last Supper: the Holy Species were preserved until the second Communion, which she received from the hands of St. Peter, when, as she swallowed the second, the first was consumed. Thus, in this miraculous manner, from that day until the last hour of her life, Jesus, under the sacramental species, remained in her sacred heart. By this privilege, and that of the continual abstractive vision of the Divinity, the Holy Virgin was so divinized, and her faculties elevated so much above all that the human mind can conceive, that it is impossible to explain it. Who among mortals, and even among the Seraphim, could ever know the ardor of the divine love which burned in her most pure heart?

Who could comprehend the impetuosity of the flood of the Divinity which inundated this City of God? Very frequently the Body of Jesus appeared to her all-glorious in her most pure heart, at other

times with the natural beauty of His most holy
Humanity. She knew all the mysteries contained in
the Holy Eucharist, and all other mysteries; but that
which to her was beyond all price was that her most
holy Son, being in the sacramental species in her
most pure heart, found more joy in being with her
than with all the Saints and Angels together. Let
us then reanimate our faith in her, raise our hope
and be inflamed with love for God, and for so holy
a Mother; let us implore her aid in our necessities,
for she is all-powerful, most merciful and full of
charity.

Chapter 35

THE MOST HOLY VIRGIN KNOWS THAT LUCIFER IS PREPARING TO PERSECUTE THE CHURCH—WHAT SHE DOES TO DEFEND THE FAITHFUL.

The great Queen, being raised to a higher degree of grace and sanctity, considered with profound wisdom the little flock which increased each day and, as a watchful mother, from the summit of the mountain on which she had been placed by the omnipotent arm of her Son, carefully observed the infernal snares. Being in prayer, she saw Lucifer with an innumerable crowd of demons coming forth from the caverns of Hell, into which they had been precipitated at the death of the Redeemer; full of rage and hatred, they came to wage war against the Church with implacable fury. She saw Lucifer come on earth and search through it carefully; then he turned towards Jerusalem, there to vent his hatred against the sheep of Jesus Christ.

When the insidious dragon recognized the fruit of the Saviour's Blood, the sanctity of the converts, the facility of returning to grace, his hatred and fury were redoubled. He made violent efforts to introduce himself into the room in which the faithful were assembled, but he could not do so, being repulsed by their ardent charity and perfect union. He surrounded the place with his demons and prowled on every side in the hope of devouring some of the sheep, but his infernal malice was frustrated. Then the powerful and merciful Mother turned with majesty to the infernal dragon and said to him: "Who is like to God who dwelleth in high places? From the height of His Cross, the Almighty has vanquished and overthrown thee. He commands thee to cast thyself with thy companions into the abyss, and in His name, I give thee the same command, in order that thou mayest oppose no obstacle to the glory of God."

She prostrated herself upon the ground and humbly begged the Lord to come to the aid of the Church. Lucifer and his legions fell immediately into the depths of Hell, and the Lord spoke thus to His Mother: "My dear Mother, be not afflicted at the snares which Satan sets for My Church, for, from the evil which he will do, I will draw good for My greater glory and his eternal confusion." Then the Lord permitted Lucifer and his demons to return to the earth; but finding they could not approach the new Christians, they went to the Scribes and Pharisees and suggested to them to prevent the preaching of the Apostles. They filled them with envy and hatred, and therefore they assembled the council that had witnessed the miracle wrought by St. Peter and St. John when they cured the lame man at the gate of the Temple.

The members of the council called the Apostles

and forbade them to teach in Jerusalem, but St. Peter replied with intrepid courage that they could not obey, because God had commanded them to do the contrary. The Scribes, covered with confusion, set the two Apostles at liberty, who went to inform the Holy Virgin of all that had occurred, but she already knew it, having seen all in a vision. The faithful began to pray, and a short time afterwards received the Holy Spirit, who descended visibly upon every one of them.

Some days after occurred the unhappy fall of Ananias and Sapphira, who, after being baptized, sold all their possessions, but did not bring the whole price to the feet of the Apostles. When St. Peter asked them if they had brought the whole price they lied to him, and immediately fell dead at his feet. The faithful were seized with great fear at this occurrence, and when the Apostles preached publicly in the city upon this chastisement, a great number of persons were converted. But the magistrates and Sadducees, filled with envy and hatred, threw St. Peter and St. John into prison.

The Queen of the Angels saw all this in prayer and interceded fervently with the Lord for them; she sent one of her Guardian Angels to break their chains, set them at liberty and lead them out of prison. Then she sent other Angels to fight against Lucifer and his companions, that they might not interfere with the preaching of the Gospel. St. Peter and St. John, after their deliverance, went to visit the Holy Virgin; she received them on her knees and said: "Now, my children, I recognize you to be true disciples and imitators of your Master, because you suffer injuries for His name, and with joy and contentment aid Him in carrying His Cross. May His omnipotent arm bless you and communicate to you His divine virtue." She kissed their hands and, kneeling, served them at table. The great Queen loved all the faithful with wonderful tenderness, but the Apostles in a more particular manner, for she regarded them as priests and founders of the Church.

In order to increase the number of the faithful, it was necessary that the Apostles should leave Jerusalem in order to preach and baptize in the neighboring places. Seeing that they were about to separate from the Queen of Angels, Lucifer took courage, for in his pride, he did not fear the Apostles. But the more he laid plans for their destruction, the more did the merciful Mother pray for them with ardent charity and profound wisdom; and in her meditations she discovered all the snares and ambushes of Hell and all that befell the preachers of the Gospel. In their necessities, she sent her Guardian Angels to assist them, animate and console them, and above all to expel the demons from the countries in which the Gospel was being preached by the Apostles. In every pain or disquiet, they received the aid of their merciful Mother.

She exercised the same charitable solicitude in behalf of the faithful, and although they were very numerous in Jerusalem and Palestine, she knew them all and aided them on every occasion, not only in the necessities of the soul, but in those of the body also. Some she cured of their maladies, and others, to whom health would not be expedient, she assisted, visited and served with her own hands. Her love for the poor it would be impossible to describe; she frequently gave them food, made their beds and took care of their houses as if she had been their servant. The humility, charity and solicitude of the Queen of the Universe were so great that she filled them with joy and consolation. When they lived at too great a distance to receive her personal care, she sent one of her Guardian Angels to assist and aid them by holy inspirations. Her maternal care was particularly exercised in favor of the dying; she assisted many in the last combat and aided them by efficacious words and holy exhortations, until their eternal salvation was secured.

She felt great compassion for the souls in Purgatory and aided them by her prayers, which she offered with her arms extended in the form of a cross, to which she added prostrations, genuflections and other exercises of mortification, by which she satisfied for them. Then she immediately sent one of her Angels to deliver those souls and present them to her Divine Son in her name, as the property of the Lord and the fruit of His Blood.

A poor woman of low condition who had been baptized in the beginning with the five thousand persons fell dangerously ill, and her sickness being prolonged, she fell from her first fervor and committed a sin by which she lost the grace of Baptism. Lucifer, who ardently desired to win some souls among the first children of the Church, assumed the form of a young woman in order to deceive her, and God permitted this for His greater glory. The demon urged her to separate herself from those persons who believed in the Crucified. The unhappy woman gave her assent to the words of the evil spirit and added: "But how shall I act with regard to the Queen, who is so good and gracious that I cannot help but love her?" "Oh!" replied the demon, "she is more wicked than the others, and you must abhor her in particular. This is most important, otherwise the magistrates and high priests will persecute you, and you will be unhappy. If you will return to your former religion, you shall be cured and be very content." The pretended woman departed, leaving that unhappy soul corrupted by her words.

One of the seventy-two disciples who were accustomed to visit the sick entered the house of this woman and, seeing her possessed by the demon, zealously exhorted her to detest her error, but in vain; she refused to make any reply. Seeing her obstinacy, the disciple informed St. John, who went immediately to visit her and tried with great fervor to draw her out of the snares of the demon, but with the same result. The great Apostle was much afflicted, and acquainted the Holy Virgin with the circumstance, in the hope that she would apply a remedy. The Mother of God cast an interior look on the sick woman and discovered her dangerous condition.

Filled with compassion for that poor, misguided sheep, she prostrated herself upon the earth and prayed and supplicated her Divine Son to apply a remedy to her evil. But the Lord answered not; not because the prayer of the Holy Virgin was disagreeable to Him, but because He desired to listen longer to her charitable pleadings. The Mother of Mercy was not discouraged, but continued to intercede with the Most High; in the meantime she sent one of her Angels to protect her from the snares of the demon and to aid her by holy inspirations. The Angel obeyed, but the woman resisted the grace of God.

Deeply afflicted at her deplorable blindness, the Mother of Mercy continued to pray most fervently, saying: "My Lord, God of mercy, look down upon this worm of the earth; chastise and afflict her, but do not allow this soul, marked with Thy divine character and purchased by Thy Blood, to be deceived by the serpent and become the prey of his malice." The great Queen persevered in prayer, but the Lord delayed to answer, in order that she might give still further proofs of the invincible love of her heart and her ineffable charity for the faithful. She arose from prayer and called St. John to accompany her to the house of the sick woman. She had proceeded from the oratory but a few steps when she was stopped by her Angels, who said: "Great Queen, we cannot allow thee to walk through the city when we can carry thee." Then she was placed on a throne of most brilliant clouds and transported to the chamber of the poor, agonizing woman, who was abandoned by all because she could no longer speak; she was surrounded by a crowd of demons

who awaited the moment in which they might bear
her soul to Hell.

At the sight of the Virgin Mother, they precipitated themselves into the infernal abyss. She
approached the sick woman, called her by her name
and, taking her by the hand, spoke the sweet words
of eternal life, by which she fortified the unhappy
creature. Returning to herself, she said to the Queen
of Angels: "My Queen, a woman who visited me a
few days ago persuaded me that the disciples of Jesus
had deceived me and told me that I should separate myself from them and from thee."

"My daughter," replied the Mother of beautiful
love, "the woman who appeared to thee was the
demon, thy enemy. I have come then, on the part
of the Most High, to give thee eternal life. Return
then—to the true Faith, and acknowledge Jesus to
be the true God and the Redeemer of the world.
Invoke His name, and beg pardon for thy faults."

The poor woman, truly contrite, wept bitterly and
received the Sacraments from the Apostles, who had
been called to her aid by Angels. Filled with joy,
she expired, invoking the names of Jesus and Mary.
She was cleansed from all her sins and the punishment due to them, and was by Mary sent immediately to Heaven, attended by heavenly spirits.
Then the most Holy Virgin was borne back to her
oratory, in which she prostrated herself and thanked
the Most High by new canticles of praise.

The Lord willed all these things in order that
the Angels, the Apostles, the Saints in Paradise and
even the demons might know the incomparable

power of the most Holy Virgin; and that as Queen of all creatures she had power over all, and that nothing that she would ask could be refused to her.

Chapter 36

THE VIRGIN MOTHER'S PRUDENCE IN THE
GOVERNMENT OF THE FAITHFUL—
WHAT SHE DID FOR ST. STEPHEN.

Among the innumerable qualities which the Holy Virgin possessed were that plenitude and abundance of wisdom and divine science, worthy of the Mother of God, established as Mother and Mistress of the Church. She knew all those who had embraced the Faith and discovered their passions, their character, the degree of grace and virtue to which they had attained, the merit of their labors, the end and motive of their actions. She, at the same time, penetrated the secret of divine charity; thus she dispensed the affections of her eternal charity justly and equitably, so that she loved no one either more or less than she should.

Among the holy souls who merited the love of this divine Mother was St. Stephen, one of the seventy-two disciples; for, from the time he began to follow the Saviour, the most Holy Virgin had regarded him with special and singular favor. She knew also that this Saint was chosen by the Master of Life to defend His honor at the price of his blood. The Saint was possessed of great amiability and natural goodness, and grace rendered him still more amiable to all. Because of these rare qualities, to which were united the most heroic virtues, the Divine Mother loved him tenderly, and he was filled with heavenly benedictions. She returned thanks to the Most High for having created this soul, which would receive the crown of the first of the martyrs.

The happy Saint faithfully corresponded to the benefits he received from his Divine Master and His Mother, for he was meek and humble of heart. He had the greatest veneration for the Mother of Mercy and humbly questioned her upon the most profound mysteries, for he was learned and well-instructed, full of faith and replenished with the Holy Spirit.

The Mother of Wisdom answered all his questions; enlightened, strengthened and loved him; and in order to fortify his faith more strongly, revealed to him that he would be the first martyr of Jesus Christ. This news filled St. Stephen with an ardent desire of martyrdom, so that, filled with grace and strength, he performed great prodigies and freely and courageously disputed with and confounded the high priests. He first presented himself to dispute with the Scribes and principal doctors of the Mosaic Law, as if he feared that some other would bear away that first crown, and he sought every occasion to defend the name of Jesus Christ.

The infernal dragon perceived the Saint's desire, and in his hatred tried to prevent him from confessing publicly the faith of Jesus of Nazareth; he wished to persuade the Jews to put him to death secretly, but the great Queen, who knew the design of Lucifer, delivered the Saint out of his snares. On three principal occasions she sent one of her Angels-guardian to deliver the Saint out of a house in which the Jews desired to make away with him privately. The Angel delivered him by rendering him invisible to the enemies of the Church; he presented himself before the great Queen and, full of gratitude for her benefits, thanked her with great humility. At other times, the Holy Virgin, by means of her Angels, prevented him from going into the streets and even from leaving the Supper-room. Burning with an ardent desire of martyrdom, he would lovingly complain to the Queen of Angels, saying: "Ah! my Queen and my refuge, when then shall the happy day arrive on which I shall sacrifice my life for the glory of my Jesus?"

The loving pleadings of the Saint caused an incomparable joy to his divine Mistress, and she replied to him with sweet and maternal affection: "My son, most faithful servant of the Lord, the hour appointed by the Lord will arrive, and thy beautiful desires shall not be frustrated." The purity and sanctity of St. Stephen were so great and of such eminent perfection that the demons looked on him from afar without daring to approach him. They tried to alienate others from him as much as possible, but, on the contrary, he was beloved by Jesus and His holy Mother, and even by the Apostles, who ordained him deacon. He merited to be the first martyr of the Church, as is related by St. Luke in the *Acts of the Apostles*. While the Saint was preaching with his accustomed zeal, he was arrested and dragged before the Jews, who accused him of all kinds of deception. The merciful Mother, having a knowledge of this, sent an Angel to assist and strengthen him. When he was examined, he confounded his judges and accusers by his profound wisdom and strength of mind, so that being overcome and unable to make any reply, they closed their ears and raised a horrible outcry. The Saint was afflicted only because he had not received the blessing of the tender Queen. Seeing his desire, she resolved to console him; she addressed herself to the Lord, who, seconding the charity of His Mother, sent many Angels from Heaven, who, with the Angels of her guard, conducted her on a brilliant cloud into the council hall. There she was visible to the Saint alone, who, environed with light, became wholly resplendent and beautiful as an Angel. The tender Mother gazed on him with merciful eyes, spoke to him words of eternal life, blessed him and prayed the Eternal Father to fill him with the Holy Ghost. Her petition was immediately granted, for the Saint showed publicly his invincible courage and profound wisdom by proving the Divinity and Incarnation of Jesus by the incontestable words of Holy Scripture.

The great Queen was still present, rejoicing at the zeal and courage of the Saint, when the heavens were opened and Jesus appeared at the right hand of the Father.

The Saint rendered testimony to the glory of His Master, and the perfidious Jews accused him of blasphemy; for this reason he was condemned to be stoned as a blasphemer. They threw themselves furiously upon him and dragged him out of the city to be put to death. The Holy Virgin gave him her benediction, encouraged and took leave of him with great kindness; she commanded her Angels to accompany and assist him until death. She returned to the Supper-room, from whence she contemplated his martyrdom and shed tears of compassion and joy.

When before his death the Saint, kneeling, cried out in a loud voice, "Lord, lay not this sin to their charge," she joined in his prayer with incredible joy, seeing him so faithful an imitator of the Redeemer, who had prayed for His enemies. He expired, and his magnanimous soul was conducted to Paradise by troops of Angels and the Guardian Angels of Mary; there it was received with inexpressible joy by Jesus, who gave it a place of eminent glory, to the great joy of the whole celestial court. When the Angels returned to their Queen they rendered her thanks in the name of the Saint for the love and favors she had granted to him. This glorious martyrdom took place nine months after the Redeemer's death, on the 26th of December, the Saint being thirty-four years old. The prayer of St. Stephen, joined to that of the Mother of God, obtained the conversion of St. Paul.

Lucifer was covered with confusion by the constancy of the holy martyr and by the presence of the great Queen, and he resolved to irritate the Jews against the Church, so as to cause its entire destruction. The enemies of the Church, at his instigation, assembled together and resolved either to banish the Christians out of Jerusalem, and even from Judea and the country of Samaria, or to put them to death. Then they raised a great persecution, as is recorded by St. Luke, on account of which the Holy Virgin, with the Apostles and a small number of the faithful, retired into the Supper-room; the other disciples left the city and preached the faith of Jesus Christ with great constancy.

The Lord did not permit that any of those concealed in the Supper-room should be molested, and the disciples dispersed throughout Galilee were the only ones persecuted. Saul was named head of the persecutors. It is impossible to describe the vigilance and solicitude of the Divine Mother during the persecution. She caused the body of St. Stephen to be sought after and buried; she also procured the cross which the holy martyr had carried on his breast, for the Queen of Angels from the time of the Descent of the Holy Ghost had carried one on her breast, and her example had been imitated by all the faithful.

She also ordered that all the little things that had been used by him, and as much of his blood as possible, should be gathered together and preserved with great veneration. In the presence of the Apostles and other disciples, she pronounced a magnificent eulogy on his great merit and commanded Lucifer and his demons, as authors of the persecution, to cast themselves immediately into Hell. She assembled the Apostles, animated, consoled and strengthened them for the persecution;

she sent the disciples into Judea and Samaria to preach the Gospel of Jesus crucified, who always strengthened them.

She sent many of her Angels Guardian to accompany the disciples, and others to assist the faithful in their last agony. She also sent the Apostles from Jerusalem to wherever they were needed, as in the case of St. Peter and St. John, who departed for Samaria. She had a certain knowledge not only of the present, but also of the future. She disposed of her own particular affairs and those of the Church in such a manner that she always had time to retire into her oratory. There she prostrated herself on the earth, abased herself even to the dust, thinking that she was unworthy for the earth to support her; and she prayed and wept for the salvation of men and the conversion of sinners.

The great Mother of Wisdom considered that the disciples who were separated to preach the adorable name of her Son and His holy Faith had not as yet any determined rules by which they might teach the faithful with uniformity, that they might all believe the same truths. She then assembled all the Apostles, and spoke to them by the mouth of St. Peter, with whom she had previously conferred. "My brethren," said he, "as we must now separate, in order to spread the Church founded by the Blood of our Divine Master, and to preach to the entire world, it is fit that we determine the mysteries which it will be necessary to propose explicitly to all believers."

All the Apostles approved the proposition; the

vicar of Jesus Christ celebrated the Holy Mass and communicated the Divine Mother and the Apostles. When Mass was ended they invoked the Holy Spirit and prayed fervently for some time. After this they heard a great noise, as when the Holy Spirit descended the first time; the room was again filled with admirable splendor, and they were enlightened and illumined in a more perfect manner. Then the great Mistress of the Church told them that each one should pronounce the words with which the Holy Ghost would inspire them, and St. Peter began.

St. Peter—I believe in God the Father Almighty, Creator of Heaven and earth.

St. Andrew—And in Jesus Christ, His only Son, Our Lord.

St. James the Greater—Who was conceived by the Holy Ghost, and born of the Virgin Mary.

St. John—Suffered under Pontius Pilate, was crucified, died and was buried.

St. Thomas—Descended into Hell, the third day He arose again from the dead.

St. James the Less—He ascended into Heaven, and sits at the right hand of God the Father Almighty.

St. Philip—From thence He shall come to judge the living and the dead.

St. Bartholomew—I believe in the Holy Ghost.

St. Matthew—The Holy Catholic Church; the Communion of Saints.

St. Simon—The forgiveness of sins.

St. Thaddeus—The resurrection of the body.

St. Matthias—And life everlasting. Amen.

Then a voice was heard, saying, "You have determined well," and our great Queen, with the Apostles, chanted hymns of praise and thanksgiving to the Most High. She thanked them all, then, kneeling at the feet of St. Peter, made her profession of the Catholic Faith by reciting the Creed, which she did in her own name and that of the whole Church, saying to St. Peter, "My master, I acknowledge thee as the Vicar of my most holy Son, and in thy hands, I, a vile worm of the earth, in my own name and that of all the faithful, confess and believe all that you have decided as infallible and divine truths of Catholic faith, and in these truths I praise and bless the Most High, from whom they proceed."

Then she kissed the hand of St. Peter, the vicar of Jesus Christ, and also those of the other Apostles.

Chapter 37

THE HOLY VIRGIN SENDS THE CREED TO THE DISCIPLES—THE APOSTLES SEPARATE FOR DIFFERENT PARTS OF THE WORLD—CONVERSION OF SAUL—OTHER MIRACLES OF THE GREAT QUEEN.

As soon as the Apostles' Creed was composed, the Holy Virgin and her Angels made a great many copies of it and sent them by the ministry of the Angels to the disciples dispersed throughout the country of Samaria and Galilee, and in a short time it was spread everywhere. A year had already elapsed since the Redeemer's death, and the Apostles wished to divide among themselves the provinces of the world, in order to enlighten them by the light of Evangelical doctrine. By the counsel of the divine Queen, they resolved to spend ten days in fasting and prayer; they had adopted this custom since the Descent of the Holy Ghost before deciding on any important affair. After this time, St. Peter celebrated the Holy Mass and communicated the divine Mother and the Apostles, and uniting in fervent prayer they invoked the Holy Spirit. St. Peter renewed their ardor by recalling to their minds that which had been ordained by the Divine Master.

After his discourse they all beheld an extraordinary splendor and heard a voice which said: "Peter, My vicar, assign to each the provinces and let each draw his lot; I will assist him with My spirit and light."

St. Peter said: "My Lord, I offer myself to suffer and die in order to follow my Redeemer and my Master in preaching His holy name, now in Jerusalem, afterwards in Pontus, Galicia, Bithynia, Cappadocia and the provinces of Asia; I will establish my see first at Antioch, afterwards at Rome, where shall be established the chair of Christ, in order that there the chief of the Church may reside.

"The servant of Christ, our dear brother Andrew, shall follow Him by preaching in the provinces of Scythia, of Europe, in Epirus, Thrace and the city of Patrae in Achaia. He shall govern that province and the rest as far as possible.

"The servant of Christ, James the Great, shall follow Him by preaching in Judea, Samaria and Spain, from whence he shall return to Jerusalem.

"Our dear brother John shall obey the will of our Saviour and Master, which was manifested by Him on the Cross; he shall fulfill the duties of a son towards our Mother and Queen; he shall serve her with the respect and fidelity of a child and administer to her the divine Sacrament of the Eucharist. He shall take charge of the faithful in Jerusalem, and when the Blessed Mother shall have been called to Heaven, shall follow his Master by preaching in Asia Minor and by watching over those churches until the time of his persecution, when he will be banished to the isle of Patmos.

"The servant of Christ, our dear brother Thomas, shall follow Him by preaching in India and Persia, among the Parthians, Medes, Hyrcanians and Bactrians; he shall baptize the three Magi and instruct them in all things, for they expect and await him.

"The servant of Christ, our dear brother James the Less, shall follow Him in being pastor and bishop of Jerusalem, where he shall preach to the Jews and unite with St. John in assisting and serving our divine Mother.

"The servant of Christ, our dear brother Philip, shall follow Him in Phrygia, Asiatic Scythia and the city of Hierapolis.

"The servant of Christ, our dear brother Bartholomew, shall follow Him in Lycaonia, part of Cappadocia, and in Asia; then he shall proceed to India, and finally to Asia Minor.

"The servant of Christ, our dear brother Matthew, shall first instruct the Hebrews, then he shall go into Egypt and Ethiopia.

"Our brother Simon shall go into Babylonia, Persia and Egypt; our brother Thaddeus into Mesopotamia; he shall afterwards unite with Simon to preach in Babylonia and Persia.

"Our brother Matthias shall go into Ethiopia and Arabia, and shall finally return into Palestine.

"May the spirit of the Most High direct, govern and assist us."

When St. Peter had finished speaking, they heard a great noise, the Supper-room was filled with splendor and from the midst of this light proceeded a voice, which said: "Let each one receive the lot which has been given him." They prostrated themselves on the earth and said: "Sovereign Lord, with great promptitude and lively joy of heart we will obey Thy words and those of Thy vicar. Our spirits rejoice, being full of Thy sweetness."

The Most High gave them a new gift of strength, and they all became inflamed like the Seraphim.

The Queen of Angels was present at all and knew the divine operations within the Apostles and herself, for she participated in the divine effusions more than all the others together.

She possessed all that knowledge suited to her as Sovereign, Mistress, Mother, Directress and Queen of the Church, with regard to all creatures. At the same time she begged the Most High for the courage and perseverance necessary for the Apostles to preach to the whole world, and received the assurance that they would be particularly assisted, which filled her with joy. Kneeling down, she wished them all great success in the name of her Divine Son. Then she kissed their hands and promised always to pray for and be ready to serve them; finally, she humbly begged the blessing of each.

Before they dispersed, the Apostles made every effort to soften the hearts of the perfidious Jews, whom they wished to call first to the Faith; they visited the holy places in Jerusalem, venerated them with much piety and tenderness and kissed the ground sanctified by the Divine Redeemer.

The maternal solicitude of the great Queen was truly admirable. Assisted by her Angels, she had prepared for each of the Apostles a long woolen tunic, similar in color and form to that of Jesus Christ, in order that they might be dressed alike. She also made with great skill twelve crosses, which she affixed to their pilgrim's staffs, that they might carry with them a sign of that which they preached. She gave to each the tunic and staff, also a small metal reliquary containing three thorns from the crown of her most holy Son, some pieces of the linen worn by the Lord in His infancy, and some also of that which had been stained with His Precious Blood at His circumcision or during His Passion. The Apostles received her gifts with veneration and shed many tears; they thanked their great Queen and, prostrate on the ground, venerated the holy relics; finally they embraced one another, and the first who departed was St. James the Great.

At this time happened the conversion of Saul, to which the Mother of mercy contributed. Saul had a noble, magnanimous and courageous heart. Lucifer, considering his natural disposition, surrounded him with terrible suggestions in order to make him the instrument of his fury. Saul gloried in his knowledge of the Mosaic Law and in his zeal for the traditions of the rabbis; for this reason he believed it was unjust to abolish the law revealed by God for another law of a crucified man. He went to the high priests and obtained ample power to persecute unto death the partisans of the new and odious sect, and

Lucifer suggested that he should not only cause the destruction of the Apostles, but also of the Mother of the Nazarean, the pride of the demon drawing him into this folly.

But Saul was horrified at the suggestions; he thought it would be infamous to treat with cruelty a woman so noble and generous, for he had seen her assist with intrepid love at the Passion of her Son; from that moment he had conceived great esteem and affection for her and had felt compassion for her sorrows. Saul was advancing towards Damascus with a numerous retinue of young men, his companions and other persons, but chiefly accompanied by Lucifer and an infinite number of demons.

The great Queen beheld all in a vision; she saw the snares of Lucifer and knew that Saul would yet become a pillar of the Church. She prostrated herself upon the ground and prayed to the Lord, offering herself to suffer and die for the Church and Saul's conversion. "Thou, O Lord," said the humble Queen, "hast established Thy slave as Mother of the Church and advocate of sinners, without any merit on my part: hear my humble prayers, help Thy children; the torrent of Saul's sins have not extinguished Thy infinite charity." At the same time the great Queen saw that her Divine Son, touched by her prayers, appeared to Saul in immense glory and that Saul, enlightened both interiorly and exteriorly by the celestial light, fell from his horse at the words of Christ: "Saul, Saul, why dost thou persecute Me?" Full of fear he replied: "Who art Thou, Lord?" The

Lord answered: "I am Jesus whom thou persecutest," etc., as is related in the *Acts of the Apostles*.

Thus, from a persecutor, he became a vessel of election and an Apostle of Jesus Christ. The great Queen, having seen all this, returned thanks to the Most High; she was the first to celebrate the feast of this admirable conversion, on which she invited the Angels and Saints to praise God by canticles of thanksgiving.

After Paul had been instructed and baptized by Ananias, he heard the disciples speak of the goodness and excellence of the Mother of God; full of confusion at the remembrance that he had been a persecutor of the Church, he feared he was not agreeable to the great Queen.

At the moment in which he had been divinely enlightened, he had learned that she had been the mediatrix for his conversion: nevertheless, the unworthiness of his past life humbled and deterred him, for he judged himself unworthy of a place in her pure and ardent heart. His fears were known to the divine Mother and, being aware that a long time must elapse before Paul could come to see her, she, moved by maternal affection, did not wish him to suffer such a long delay; therefore, she sent one of her Angels to the new Apostle at Damascus to assure him of her affection and intercession and to bless him in her name. Having received this visit, Paul felt his heart dilated and filled with joy and grace; he humbly begged the messenger to thank in his name the divine Mother, the true mother of piety and his mediatrix. The celestial ambassador related to his Queen all that had occurred, and she experienced great consolation and renewed her thanksgivings to the Most High.

It is impossible to explain or to understand the rage of Lucifer when, by the divine light of Jesus Christ, he and his demons were precipitated into Hell, like serpents entwined within one another and thrown upon the earth; nevertheless, the Most High permitted that, for His glory and the greater merit of His Church, the princes of darkness should arise and assemble in council; they knew not that the great Queen of the Universe discovered all their designs. They resolved to take revenge on God and the Virgin Mother by destroying the Church. O proud demons, full of blindness, Hell is powerless! It cannot even cause the death of a vile insect without the permission of God; how much less, then, destroy a Christian!

The divine Mother begged her Son to oppose the insensate hatred of Lucifer, and, raised into sublime ecstasy, she saw that the amiable Redeemer at the right of His Father prayed Him to grant all that His Mother asked. She saw also that the Eternal Father received her prayers with complacency, and that, regarding her with great goodness, He said, "Mary, My daughter, ascend higher." At the same moment He dispatched from Heaven an innumerable multitude of Angels, who, raising her from the earth on which she lay prostrate and bathed in tears, conducted her both body and soul before the throne of the most Holy Trinity, which was manifested to her by a most sublime vision. Abased in the most profound humility of her heart, she felt and saw herself placed on the throne of the Divinity at the right of her Son, to the great joy of all the Saints and blessed spirits. Being asked what she desired, she replied: "Nothing but the exaltation of the holy Name of God and that the faithful be assisted in the persecutions which Lucifer is preparing." The most Holy Trinity promised to aid the Church, and with regard to Lucifer, to her was confided the charge of combating and overcoming him.

After receiving the divine benediction, she was borne to her oratory by the Angels; there, prostrate on the ground, she, with wonderful humility, abased herself beneath the dust, shed many tears and thanked the Most High for this new favor. She conversed with her Angels on the government of the Church and sent them to the Apostles and disciples, particularly to St. Paul, to warn them against the infernal snares and assure them of the aid of grace and their final victory over Hell. She called together St. Peter, St. John and all the disciples who were in Jerusalem and warned them of what would befall them; she also confirmed the news of Paul's conversion.

St. James the Great was at this time in Spain, and had established in Granada twelve disciples who preached the holy name of Jesus. The Jews who resided there, being excited by Hell, rose in fury and took measures to arrest them all. They loaded them with chains and dragged them out of the city to massacre them. Having bound their feet, they had already raised their swords to kill them. The holy

Apostle ceased not to invoke the all-powerful name of Jesus, his Master, and also of Mary, the divine Mother. He cried in a loud voice: "Most Holy Virgin, succor me in this hour; remember me and my children; most pure Mary, come to my aid! O Mary, O Mary, ever pure!" St. James repeated these last words several times; they penetrated the tender and loving heart of the merciful Mother, who had seen and heard all in a vision. She raised her eyes to Heaven, for she wished to aid her beloved St. James, but, ruled by her heroic prudence, she did not wish to command as Queen. She prostrated herself on the earth and, with many tears, begged her Son to aid him.

Immediately the thousand Angels of her guard appeared in human forms and revealed to her the will of the Most High. Without delay they formed a throne of the most brilliant clouds, on which they transported her to the place where St. James and his disciples awaited the stroke of death. She appeared to the Apostle only and, with a joyful and tender countenance, said: "James, my son, Apostle of Jesus, have good courage, and be delivered from thy chains." At the same instant the Jews fell to the ground, the demons were precipitated into Hell and St. James and his disciples set free.

After receiving the precious benediction of the divine and merciful Mother, they left the city to avoid the fury of the Jews, their persecutors. The great Queen left with St. James one hundred Angels of her guard, to assist and guide him in Spain and to defend and aid him in the propagation of the Gospel.

Chapter 38

NEW PLOTS OF LUCIFER AGAINST THE CHURCH—THE BLESSED VIRGIN LEAVES JERUSALEM AND OPERATES NEW WONDERS.

The most Holy Virgin watched with maternal and inexpressible solicitude over the propagation of the Church, and prayed most fervently to God for it. In her ardent prayer, she was many times ravished in God and heard Him say: "My daughter and beloved spouse, thy faithful love, greater than that of all other creatures, makes Us find in thee the plenitude of Our complacency; ascend to the throne of God, that thou mayest be absorbed in the abyss of Our divinity, as much as is possible to a pure creature. Take new possession of Our glory; we remit all Our treasures into thy hands; Heaven is thine, with the earth and all things; enjoy during thy mortal life the privilege of being blessed above all the Saints. Let all creatures and nations serve thee; enter thou into the participation of all the goods of Our eternal society; understand the great designs of Our Providence, and take part in Our decrees. Let thy will be one with Ours, and one also be the motive by which We shall dispose all things for Our Church."

All these ineffable favors were hidden from Lucifer; filled with pride, he held many councils with his demons, in which he laid dark snares against the Church and planned a new war for its entire destruction. The peace enjoyed by the Church was favorable for the conversion of the faithful, but on the other hand, persecution was necessary to increase their merit and to prove them; therefore God caused them to succeed one another, as in the following centuries; it was for this reason that He allowed Lucifer to come forth from Hell. The fury of the infernal dragon was at its height; he would have wished to destroy the whole world if it were in his power, and he brought with him out of Hell two-thirds of his accursed and cruel companions. They travelled quickly over all the earth, in order to find the Apostles and disciples, while Lucifer remained near Jerusalem.

The evil spirits on their return gave an exact account to their unhappy chief; he bade some of them remain near the Apostles and disciples to persecute them, and others to excite the Jews and Gentile magistrates against the Christians; he assigned a great number of them to Herod, to provoke him to persecute the Christian name. Lucifer tormented the just by secret temptations and suggestions, inspired them with pusillanimity, raised in their mind illusions and a thousand other things, such as he does even at the present day with spiritual persons who wish sincerely to love God.

Nothing was hidden from the Divine Mother, who, adoring the dispensations of Providence, redoubled her prayers, tears and cares for the faithful. She gave advice and counsel to all who dwelt with or near her; she exhorted, urged and animated them to suffer and die for the love of God; yet, in the midst of these solicitudes the Mistress of Virtues always preserved a calm exterior and a countenance full of majesty; never did the sorrows of her heart cause her to appear sad, or her amiability to be disturbed in the slightest degree. She cast herself at the feet of St. John with a joyful and humble countenance, and having begged his blessing and kissed his hand, asked and obtained permission to speak. "My master and my son," she said, "the Most High has revealed to me the terrible persecutions which threaten the Church; the proud dragon has come forth from the infernal caverns with legions of evil spirits inflamed with fury, in order to destroy the mystic body of the Church. This city will be the first to be disturbed; they will take the life of one of the Apostles, and the others will be cruelly ill-treated, by the suggestions of Hell, the Lord thus permitting it. I would wish to assist them as their Mother, but it is the will of God that I leave Jerusalem, if you consent; you, whom I regard as my master and my superior."

It was then resolved that they would depart to Ephesus, a city situated on the confines of Asia Minor.

After having regulated everything necessary at Jerusalem, she recommended to the Lord the Apostles and her servants; she supplicated Him to defend them, to humble the pride of Lucifer and to defeat the machinations of Hell. The Lord replied that He would look on the Church with mercy, would fill with grace and benediction all those who would invoke the all-powerful name of Mary, and would remit all His treasures into her hands. She received an order that before setting out for Ephesus, she should visit St. James in Spain, to console him and bid him return to Jerusalem.

Immediately her Angels-Guardian, with others who had descended from Heaven, formed a glorious chariot of brilliant clouds, in which they placed their great Queen and bore her to Saragossa in the province of Arragon, singing the *Ave Maria*, the *Salve Regina*, and the Psalms, to which the great Queen responded by the words: *Holy, holy, holy is the God of glory; may He take pity on the children of Eve.* The blessed Apostle was near the walls of the city, occupied in prayer; among the disciples some slept and others prayed, when the music of the Angels, sounding from a distance, filled them with celestial joy. The royal throne of the Queen of Angels, surrounded by a globe of light, rested in sight of the Apostle on a pillar of jasper, prepared by the Angels.[1] The Divine Mother appeared visibly to the blessed Apostle, who, prostrate on the earth, venerated her as the Mother of the Creator of all things. With great kindness, she gave him her benediction in the name of her Son, saying at the same time, "James, servant of the Most High, be

---

1. These facts are admitted as true by the traditions of the Church of Spain. To this day we hear of the Virgin *del Pilar*, at Saragossa.

blessed by His all-powerful hand." All the Angels answered, "Amen." "My son James, this place shall be blessed. Here thou shalt raise a temple to the honor of my name; it shall be a house of prayer and a source of graces. Thou shalt afterwards return to Jerusalem, and offer thy life as a sacrifice to the Lord."

The Angels erected a column on which they placed a holy and beautiful image of the great Queen. St. James and the Angels venerated it and celebrated the feast; they sang canticles of praise and thanksgiving to the Blessed Mother, who, after giving them her benediction, returned to Jerusalem. The Apostle, with the help of Heaven, erected a chapel on that holy spot.

The Holy Virgin having been reconducted to her oratory in Jerusalem, returned thanks to the Most High for the favors granted to the Church, and for four days continued her prayers for His assistance, during which time St. John prepared all things necessary for their voyage. On the fourth day, the 5th of January, of the fortieth year of our Redemption, the great Queen took leave of the pious master of the house of the Last Supper and of all those who dwelt there; they were all in great affliction. She begged St. John to permit her to venerate those sacred spots consecrated by the blood of her Divine Son, and she commanded her Angels to watch over and guard them.

At her return she knelt at the feet of St. John to implore his benediction; she thanked the faithful who wished to give her money, objects of value and the means of traveling agreeably on sea, but seated only on a poor ass, the great Mistress of Humility commenced her voyage, accompanied by the disciple St. John. For her consolation in this journey, all her Angels Guardian became visible to her under corporeal forms, and placing her in their midst as their Sovereign, they rejoiced and consoled her by hymns and canticles of praise.

On arriving at the port they found a vessel ready to depart for Ephesus; on this they embarked, and thus did the Star of the Sea first sail upon its waters. She immediately began to consider the sea. She knew its profound depth, its immense extent, its interior arrangement, its sands, its rocks and all its treasures, its tide and ebb and the variety of its fishes; from the grandeur of that element she raised herself to the contemplation of the immensity of God. She recommended to the Lord all those who should afterwards sail on the sea, and the Lord gave her His divine word that He would promptly aid all those who, in tempests, would invoke the Holy Virgin, Star of the Sea. Then considering the different species of fish, she commanded them to render homage to their Creator; and it was most wonderful to see them appear in the sea in sight of their great Queen, to testify by their movements their obedience to their Sovereign and their desire to praise the Most High. After receiving her benediction they dispersed. St. John shed tears of tenderness at this spectacle, and the sailors were filled with wonder and admiration, although they were ignorant of its cause.

They arrived happily at the port of Ephesus, and immediately after landing, the great Queen began to work many marvels and extraordinary miracles. She first returned thanks to God for the benefits she had received, then began to heal the weak and infirm, who were freed from their evils by the mere sight of her. A great number of the faithful who had fled from Palestine and Jerusalem to avoid the persecution came to meet her and offer their houses and themselves for her service, but the Queen of Virtues thanked them all and went to dwell with some pious women who lived in retreat; they gave her two rooms, one for herself, the other for St. John. As soon as she had retired into her apartment, she prostrated herself with her face to the earth, according to her holy custom, to return thanks to the Lord, and she offered herself in sacrifice for the good of the city. She then called her Angels Guardian, some of whom she sent to inform the Apostles that she dwelt in Ephesus and that she would always come to their aid; others she sent to the disciples afflicted by persecution. It was at this time that St. Paul, fleeing from Damascus, because of the persecution of the Jews, was aided and consoled by the Angels of the Mother of Piety; he went to Jerusalem, where, being in prayer in the Temple, the Lord bade him leave the city, to escape the persecution.

St. James left Spain, accompanied by one hundred Angels; he embarked for Italy, and from thence for Asia, preaching everywhere the Gospel of Jesus Christ, until he arrived safely at Ephesus and appeared before the Holy Virgin. He cast himself at her feet, shedding tears of happiness and joy, and humbly thanked her with profound affection for the favors he had received from her. The Divine Mother immediately raised him from the ground, reminding him that he was a priest, but she, only a useless servant; then, casting herself on her knees, she begged his blessing. The Apostle St. James remained some days with the Holy Virgin and his brother St. John, and related to them all that had happened in Spain. At the moment of departure, the great Queen said to him: "James, my son, these are the last days of thy life. I desire to make thee penetrate into the intimate charity of God, by which thou hast been called. Whilst we thus live, I burn with the desire of making thee know this love, and I offer myself to do, with the divine grace, all that which, as thy true Mother, I can do for thee."

"I thank thee, O great Queen and Mother of my Redeemer," answered the Saint, shedding many tears; "I ardently beg thy maternal benediction that I may give my life for Him who has first sacrificed Himself for me. I supplicate thee, O merciful Mother, not to abandon me at the moment of my martyrdom."

The great Queen, attentive to his words, replied: "I will offer to the Most High thy prayers and desires."

By these and other words of eternal life, the Apostle was consoled and fortified. Burning with the desire of martyrdom, he received her blessing, and with many tears bade farewell to his dear brother John and set out for Jerusalem.

Chapter 39

MARTYRDOM OF ST. JAMES—HE IS
ASSISTED BY THE DIVINE MOTHER—
IMPRISONMENT AND DELIVERANCE
OF ST. PETER—MANY MARVELS.

St. James arrived in Jerusalem when the city was
aroused against the disciples of Jesus Christ; their
hate and fury had been incited by Lucifer, who
burned with the desire of destroying the Church.
Entering into the city, the holy Apostle began to
preach the glorious name of the Crucified with a
zeal so ardent that many of those who heard were
unable to resist the divine fire of his words and
were converted. Lucifer, feeling himself enfeebled
by the presence of St. James, became still more furious; he went to the high-priests and principal Jews
to excite them to greater rage and hatred of the
name of Christ. They chose two magicians
instructed in the Mosaic law and the art of magic
to dispute with St. James and confound him. One
was called Hermogenes, the other Philetus, his disciple.

The dispute was begun by Philetus, who publicly
proposed to the Apostle many difficulties, which
gave the Saint an opportunity of clearly demon-

strating, with the aid of divine light, the revealed truths; his adversary was converted, and the Jews covered with confusion. The new convert dreaded the dangerous enchantments of his master, who continued obstinate in error, but the good Saint strengthened him and gave him a holy relic—some of the linen worn by Jesus. St. James, like the good pastor, preached to the sheep confided to his care. After some days, the Jews again engaged Hermogenes to embarrass and confound St. James; the Pharisees, Scribes and doctors of the Mosaic law reassembled, but all the efforts of Hermogenes were vain and he was obliged to confess the Faith of Jesus Christ. Hermogenes and Philetus were both instructed and baptized, to the great confusion of Judaism and the extraordinary fury of Hell, which had thus lost two of its ministers. The Divine Mother by her prayers and tears contributed to these conversions and others effected by St. James; she beheld all from her oratory, whence she exercised a particular care over her beloved Apostle. Hermogenes and Philetus, through fear of the Jews, left Jerusalem and went into Asia, but relaxing from their fervor, afterwards apostatized from the Faith of Jesus Christ.

Lucifer, having become more furious by the conversion of Hermogenes and Philetus, excited the Jews against the holy Apostle and filled them with great hatred. They bribed two centurions of the Roman militia to put him in prison and chose Abiatar, a priest, and Josias, a scribe, to hasten the execution. St. James preached to the people in the public place of Jerusalem and announced the mysteries of religion with great fruit. The unworthy ministers, inflamed with fury, gave the signal to the Roman soldiers; the Saint was arrested and a rope placed about his neck, as a disturber of the government. He was conducted before Herod, the son of Archelaüs, the declared enemy of the name of Jesus, who had raised the first persecution against the disciples; he immediately sentenced the Saint to be beheaded.

It is impossible to describe the joy of the holy Apostle when he beheld approaching the happy moment in which he would give his life for Jesus, who had first died for him. Remembering that the divine Mother had promised to assist him, he invoked her from the depths of his great soul. She was wholly occupied in the care of the Church, and in particular of the Apostles, when she beheld a multitude of Angels descending from Heaven, some of whom went to the Apostles, while others entered into her oratory. They formed a throne of clouds on which they conducted the divine Queen to the place at which the holy Apostle was to suffer martyrdom. He was there healing the sick, delivering the possessed, obtaining graces for all and praying for his enemies. The Saint beheld her clothed with celestial splendor and surrounded by an infinite number of blessed spirits; at this sweet sight he was transported with joy and cried out: "O holy Mother of my Jesus, my protectress, consolation of the afflicted, refuge of those in sorrow! give me thy benediction, which I ardently desire. Let thy most pure hands be the altar of my sacrifice; I commend my soul to thy care." At these words his head was struck off; the great Queen received the soul of her beloved son James, and placed it beside her on the throne. She conducted it to Heaven and presented it to her glorious Son; this caused an increase of joy and glory to all the inhabitants of the heavenly court. The Holy Virgin rendered thanks by a canticle of praise to the Most High, and her soul was filled with new graces and celestial benedictions. Having received additional helps and favors for the Church, she was reconducted to her oratory in Ephesus, where, prostrate on the ground, she humbled herself beneath the dust and rendered thanks to God for all His benefits. Then she sent an Angel to aid the disciples in taking care of the holy body of the martyred Apostle, which was carried first to the port of Joppa and afterwards to Galicia in Spain.

The Jews, excited by Lucifer, became more furious at the death of the holy Apostle; they went to Herod to beg him to order the arrest of St. Peter, who was in Jerusalem. He was immediately cast into prison and the Jews were anxious to put him to death without delay. The disciples, who wished to save the Head of the Church, addressed themselves to the divine Mother by fervent prayer. She was at Ephesus, nevertheless her merciful eyes were on all places, and she principally watched over the vicar of her Divine Son. She prostrated herself and with prayers and tears begged of the Lord the life of St. Peter; her Divine Son appeared to her and said: "My Mother, moderate thy sorrow. That which thou desirest shall be accomplished, for thou art the

Queen; command and govern the faithful; dispose of all things."

"My omnipotent Lord," replied she, "as Thy goodness is infinite, command Lucifer and his demons, who are troubling the peace of the Church, to cast themselves into the infernal abyss."* By the efficacy of these words, they were immediately thrown into Hell, vanquished and deprived of strength. She sent an Angel to deliver St. Peter, who retired to a place of safety. The most prudent Mother of the Lord rendered thanks for all that had been done.

---

*We believe this should read "I command Lucifer . . ." in accord with *The Mystical City of God* (Vol. 4, "The Coronation," p. 366).—*Publisher, 1997.*

Chapter 40

HEROIC VIRTUES EXERCISED BY THE
HOLY VIRGIN AT HEROD'S DEATH—
FRUITS OF ST. JOHN'S ZEAL AT EPHESUS—
MARY'S TRIUMPH OVER LUCIFER.

The divine Mother reflected profoundly within herself upon the state of the Church, with which she was charged then, as she will always be, because she is its protectress and merciful Mother. She felt great consolation at beholding its Chief at liberty, and Lucifer in chains at the bottom of the abyss. There still remained Herod the persecutor of the Church to cause her affliction, for she knew that he had resolved to utterly exterminate the faithful, therefore she ceased not to implore the divine aid with great humility and many tears. Directed by her sovereign prudence, she spoke to one of the highest of her guardian spirits in the following words: "Minister of my Lord and God, I pray thee to go before the throne of the Most High, to expose to Him my affliction, and in my name, beg Him to allow me to suffer for His servants, but not to permit that Herod's orders be executed, for he wishes to destroy the Church." The Angel accomplished his embassy and brought her this reply:

"The Lord of armies says: 'Thou art the Mother, Queen and Mistress of the Church; pronounce then the sentence against Herod.'" The humble Mother of Piety was somewhat troubled; she bade the Angel return to the Lord and say that she offered herself to do penance and suffer the most cruel torments in favor of Herod, that he might be saved.

The Angel returned with the answer: "Herod is obstinate in his perversity; he rejects inspirations and does not follow the lights of Heaven; for this reason, he does not cooperate in the fruit of the Redemption." The heart of the tender Mother was moved, and for the third time she sent the Angel to the Most High to say that as the Mother and advocate of sinners, it was impossible to her love to condemn any creature, the work of His hands. The Angel brought the reply: "Thou art the Mother of sinners, but it is of those who wish to be converted, not of those who remain obstinate and hardened and do not wish to change their lives; still less of those who, like Herod, despise the divine grace"; he added, "thy sentence as Queen of the Universe shall be executed."

Then raising her eyes to Heaven and shedding many tears, she said: "Thou art just, O Lord, and Thy judgments are equitable; I would suffer a thousand deaths to gain this soul, if it had not rendered itself unworthy of the mercy of God, but as it is the obstinate enemy of God, unworthy of His eternal friendship, by a just judgment I condemn it to the death it has merited, that he may no longer persecute the Church and may not merit still greater chastisements in Hell."

She sent an Angel to Caesarea, where Herod was at that time. Being touched by the hand of this spirit, he died a most miserable death, being eaten by worms.

After the death of St. James and the imprisonment of St. Peter, he had gone to Caesarea to reconcile the Syrians and Sidonians. One day, as he spoke before the assembly, clad in his royal robes, the people, in order to flatter him, cried out, "He is a god!" In the height of his foolish pride, Herod believed the impious exclamation, and thus filled up the measure of his iniquity. He had persecuted the Apostles, had mocked the Divine Redeemer, had caused John the Baptist to be beheaded and had committed a public and scandalous adultery with Herodias, his relation, with other innumerable abominations.

The Angel returned to Ephesus, and the merciful Mother, on learning of the death of the unfortunate man, wept over the loss of this damned soul, yet adored the justice of God. After this death the Gospel spread rapidly, not only in Galilee and Judea, but also in Ephesus, by means of St. John's preaching. The divine Mother gave instructions in the neighboring cities also; she wrought great miracles, delivered the possessed, healed the sick, helped the poor and necessitous in their houses, or in places to which she caused them to be conveyed. She kept with her a supply of medicinal plants for those who needed them, as also bread and garments; above all, she took care of the dying;

she healed, consoled and enlightened them.

The fruits of her charity in those souls destined for Heaven were so abundant that whole volumes would not be sufficient to contain them. It would be difficult also to describe the fury of Lucifer; raising his proud head from the bottom of the infernal caverns into which he had been cast by the divine Mother—full of rage and hatred, he called around him his evil companions and told them of his intention of laying before the Most High his just complaints against this great *Woman*, as he had done with regard to Job; otherwise Hell was overcome. He immediately executed this design, God permitting it for the greater glory of His Mother. He alleged to the Most High that he was of an angelic nature, infinitely superior to the condition of her who was formed of dust and ashes; therefore he demanded her destruction.

The great Queen prayed incessantly for the Church, and saw in spirit the battle which Lucifer was preparing against her, and she wept and prayed for her defense and final triumph. Her affliction was very great because she saw Lucifer adored as God by the blind idolaters, and her heart was so filled with grief at the thought that he dwelt in the temple of Diana, that she would have died, had not God preserved her life. The temple was served by idolatrous virgins, who, though pagans, were lovers of purity. "Thy infinite charity," said the Virgin Mother, "has established me as Mother and guide of virgins who are the most precious portion of thy Church. Do not, then, permit them to be consecrated to Lucifer, thy implacable enemy." At this moment St. John entered the oratory. Mary turned to him and exclaimed, "O my son! my heart is filled with bitterness on account of the sins committed against God, but particularly in the temple of Diana."

"My Queen," answered the Saint, "I have beheld abominable scenes enacted in that placc, and I have been moved to tears at beholding Lucifer adored with that worship due to God alone, but it is only thyself who canst apply the remedy to this evil."

Mary entreated St. John to join with her in prayer to obtain a remedy for this evil. St. John obeyed and entered the oratory; the great Queen prostrated herself on the ground and, shedding many tears, persevered a long time in prayer with great fervor, so that she was almost in an agony from the vehemence of her grief. The Divine Son appeared and said: "My Mother and My dove, be not afflicted. All that thou hast asked of Me shall be accomplished without delay. Order and command, as all-powerful Queen, whatever thy heart desires." At these words the heart of the divine Mother was all inflamed with zeal for the honor of God. She arose, and with regal power commanded the demons, who dwelt in the profane temple of Diana, to fall into Hell; they were immediately compelled to cast themselves down. She bade her Angels to destroy that temple, and of its inmates to leave only nine women alive.

By this event St. John took occasion to preach the faith and open the eyes of the Ephesians to the

errors in which the demon had so long kept them.
Many were converted, but others remained incredulous and obstinate, and after the Blessed Mother
had left Ephesus they built a second temple to
Diana, although much less beautiful and magnificent than the first. It is this second temple that is
spoken of in the *Acts of the Apostles.*

Mary unceasingly continued her prayers for the
propagation of the Faith and the exaltation of the
holy Church. Her Angels appeared to her under
visible forms and said: "Great Queen, it is the will
of the Most High that we conduct thee before His
throne." The Holy Virgin answered: "I am but dust,
and the slave of the Lord. May His holy will be
done." Placing her on a throne of light, they presented her to the Most Holy Trinity. The Being of
God was manifested to her in an abstractive vision,
and she adored it most profoundly. The Eternal
Father said: "My daughter and My dove, thy desires
for the exaltation of My name, and thy prayers for
the propagation of the Church, are agreeable to My
divine heart; in recompense thereof, I confide to
thee My power, that thou mayest defend My honor
and glory by the triumph thou shalt obtain over
the ancient pride of My enemies by crushing their
head." "Behold!" answered she, "the last of Thy
creatures, who is ready to obey Thy divine designs."
The Eternal Father added: "Let all the heavenly
court know that I choose and name *Mary* as the
head and Queen of My armies, that she may van-
quish all My enemies and triumph gloriously over
them." This decree was confirmed by the other two

Divine Persons. All the blessed spirits responded: "Let Thy will be done in Heaven and on earth!"

Afterwards, by God's order, the great Queen was adorned by six Seraphim with a sort of light, like an impenetrable buckler, as invincible to the demons as the sanctity of Mary, and resembling even the strength of God Himself. She was illuminated by six other Seraphim with a divine splendor which shone on her beautiful and most pure countenance and inspired terror into the demons. Six others added to her faculties a new and divine virtue, which corresponded to all the gifts with which she had been loaded from the first and glorious instant of her conception, so that she could, at will, hinder or stay the most hidden thoughts or strongest efforts of Lucifer and his companions, and from this moment all Hell was subject to her will and good pleasure. The three Divine Persons then gave her their full benediction. Abasing herself in the depths of her nothingness, she returned thanks to the divine Trinity and was borne back to her oratory; the blessed inhabitants of Heaven chanted, *"Holy, holy, holy is the God of armies!"* She lowered herself to the dust and returned thanks to the Lord for His great mercies, and entered into herself to prepare for combat.

She beheld coming forth from Hell a frightful dragon, with seven heads, from which, with great rage and fury, he vomited forth fire and flames. He was followed by a great number of other dragons, who all proceeded towards Ephesus, where dwelt the courageous and invincible Queen. They excited each other by ferocious cries, saying: "Let us go and annihilate our enemy, since the Most High has permitted us to attack her. She is but an earthly creature."

Having transformed themselves into angels of light, the whole army entered into her oratory. Lucifer was the first to speak and his words were full of his venom, which is pride. "Thou art all-powerful, O Mary! great and courageous among women. The whole world honors and glorifies thee, because of the marvelous virtues it knows thee to possess and the great wonders thou dost operate. Thou art worthy of this glory, since no other person is equal to thee in sanctity."

Whilst he, with his false tongue, uttered these incontestable truths, he endeavored to raise in her imagination thoughts of complacency; but all his arrows fell harmless on her humble heart, for all the torments of the martyrs would have caused her less sensible pain than those evil suggestions. To repulse them she made frequent acts of profound humility. Beholding this heroic annihilation of herself, Lucifer cried out to his companions, "Ah! the pains of Hell are less torment to me than the profound humility of this great woman!" Then crushed and vanquished by her, they threw themselves into the abyss, and the august Mother returned thanks to the Most High for this first victory.

Chapter 41

THE HOLY VIRGIN RETURNS TO JERUSALEM—OTHER VICTORIES OVER LUCIFER.

The persecution of the Church had abated at the death of Herod, and the Apostles were preaching with freedom and reaping admirable fruit. Sts. Paul and Barnabas were in Asia Minor, as also St. Peter, who had gone thither from Jerusalem to avoid the persecution of Herod. Many difficulties were arising among the faithful with regard to circumcision and the Mosaic law, particularly at Jerusalem. They wrote to St. Peter as their chief to settle these controversies, and said that it would be well for him to come to that city; they begged him to write for the Divine Mother to come also. St. Peter wrote, humbly begging her to come to Jerusalem, and making known to her the necessities and desires of the faithful.

The great Queen, receiving this letter some time after and learning it was a message from St. Peter, received it kneeling and kissed it with respect, but would not open it, because St. John, who was preaching, was not present. As soon as he entered, she gave him the letter, saying that it was from the

Vicar of Jesus Christ and the head of all the faithful. The Apostle humbly inquired what it contained, to which the Mother of Humility answered: "Thou wilt know by opening it first and reading it; then thou canst tell me what it contains." The Apostle did so, and they deliberated together whether she had better leave Ephesus to return to Jerusalem. She said: "My son and my lord, command what thou thinkest best, and thy servant will obey." St. John added: "We must obey the Head of the Church." She replied: "Prepare everything for the departure, and we will go, if such be thy desire."

While the Apostle was preparing everything for their journey to Palestine, the Holy Mother assembled the virgins, her disciples, who dwelt in Ephesus, and announced to them her departure. She exhorted them to perseverance in faith, humility, purity and the exercise of holy virtues, and assured them of her love and protection before her Son, their spouse. She established as Superior over the seventy-three virgins the venerable Mary, one of those who had been saved from the ruin of the temple of Diana; she was called "Old Mary" because she was the most aged, and also the first to whom the great Queen had given her name in Baptism. Kneeling at her feet and shedding many tears, they begged her benediction; after having received it they continued in retreat, because they lived together as if in a monastery.

The Holy Virgin bade adieu to her neighbors, and when the time of departure arrived she begged the Apostle's blessing. Then they left Ephesus, having resided there for two years. She was accompanied by her Angels, who appeared to her all armed for combat, by which she understood that a battle with the infernal dragon was imminent. She warned St. John that he might prepare himself by prayer, and might not fear. The vessel on which they embarked had no sooner set sail than there burst upon them a tempest more fearful and terrific than had ever been or ever will be again. The waves rose in their fury even to the clouds, and threatened to engulf the vessel. Sometimes the billows would crash against it, as if they would burst it asunder. Sometimes it was raised high on the crest of a wave, again it sank into the abyss. The rush of the waves, the howling of the winds, the cries of the sailors and the fury of the demons against the vessel caused great alarm to St. John, so that turning to the august Queen, he said: "My Queen, ask thy Divine Son to calm the tempest."

During this time Mary had preserved a great interior peace and showed a perfect serenity, because of her great contempt for Hell and her perfect magnanimity. Considering the peril of the navigators, she was touched with compassion, and as a mother, filled with charity at the sight of their dangers, she prayed to the Lord for them. She answered the Apostle, "Be not troubled; this is the time to wage the battles of the Lord, who will triumph over His enemies by strength and patience. I have asked the Lord not to allow anyone in this vessel to perish. He sleeps not, He is with us." From these words, the Apostle regained his interior peace and tranquillity of soul.

On the fourteenth day of the tempest, Lucifer gathered all his strength for a last effort. The vessel was thrown on the side, the extremities of the antennae touched the foaming billows and the water poured in with great violence. The sailors were discouraged and frightened at so imminent a danger, but suddenly, Jesus, descending from the height of Heaven, appeared and said: My beloved Mother, I am with thee in thy tribulation.

Although under any circumstances this sight and these words would have caused her ineffable joy, nevertheless they were still more precious to the divine Mother in this danger, because of the compassion she felt for the poor afflicted people. "My Mother and My dove, I desire that all creatures be obedient to thy orders; command, and thou shalt be obeyed." Then by the virtue of her most holy Son, she bade Lucifer and his companions quit the Mediterranean Sea; she commanded the winds and the sea to be calm, and they obeyed; the Lord then departed, leaving her replenished with benedictions. On the following day they arrived safely in port and returned thanks to God for their deliverance.

After landing, they took the road towards Jerusalem, she having previously begged the blessing of St. John, and thanked him for having accompanied her in all her dangers. By the permission of God, all the demons met her again on her journey and assailed her by a thousand suggestions against the holy virtues, but the Tower of David turned their darts against themselves. Arrived at

Jerusalem, she wished to visit the holy places, but judged that she should first go to the Supper-room, to visit St. Peter and render obedience to him. When she arrived there she cast herself at his feet, begged his blessing and kissed his hand as the Sovereign Pontiff. St. John related what they had suffered, and all the disciples of Jerusalem came to venerate their Mistress with tears of joy. She visited the holy places, and then prepared herself for her works of virtue. Lucifer and his companions appeared before her in horrible shapes and even wished to threaten her, but were enfeebled by the divine Mother's heroic acts of virtue; thus, a prey to frightful torments, they were obliged to fly, completely vanquished.

One day, when she was visiting the holy places, being arrived at Mt. Olivet, the Divine Son appeared to her with ineffable tenderness; He divinized her, raised her above all terrestrial things and loaded her with divine favors so great that she became entirely transformed into her Divine Son. On her return to the Supper-room Lucifer renewed the assault, but seeing new power and strength in his enemy, he acted like the scorpion, which, when surrounded by fire, stings itself and dies. They all fled, uttering cries of rage and saying, "Ah! if this woman were not in the world, we would destroy it, and, we really could, were it not for this enemy." Lucifer tried to tempt the newly baptized and suggested to them not to abandon the rites of the Mosaic law, principally that of circumcision. The converted Jews were obstinate on this point, while the Gentiles who had embraced the Faith did not wish to be circumcised; but the great Queen destroyed all the demon's snares.

Sts. Paul and Barnabas came from Antioch to Jerusalem; they knelt before the Mother of God and shed tears of joy at finding themselves in her presence; it was also a great consolation for the merciful Queen to behold those two Apostles, so dear to her Son and herself. In this interview with the divine Mother, St. Paul had an ecstatic vision in which he learned and comprehended all the prerogatives of this *Mystical City of God*, so that he beheld her as if vested with the Divinity. Full of admiration, veneration and holy tenderness, he exclaimed: "O Mother of pity and clemency! pardon this man, this miserable sinner, for having persecuted thy Son, my divine Lord, and His Church."

The humble Queen answered: "Paul, servant of the Lord, if He who created and redeemed thee has again called thee to His intimate friendship, how can His servant refuse to pardon thee? He has made thee a vessel of election; my spirit glorifies and exalts Him." The Apostle returned his earnest thanks and begged for her protection and patronage, as did Barnabas also. St. Peter had called together the Apostles and the disciples who dwelt at no great distance from Jerusalem, and in the surrounding country; they assembled in the Supperroom, and he begged the divine Mother not to leave them. He spoke to all and exhorted them to endeavor by prayer to obtain the light of Heaven and the assistance of the Holy Spirit, and during six days they persevered in prayer. The great Queen having prepared the Supper-room with her divine hands, the chief of the Church celebrated the Holy Mass, communicated the Apostles, the divine Mother and then the disciples. A great number of Angels descended, robed with celestial splendor; they filled the place with heavenly light and perfume.

When the sacrifice was ended, St. Peter proposed the difficulties and recommended all to present their supplications to the Lord during ten days. The great Queen retired into her oratory and during the ten days neither ate nor drank, but continually interceded with the Most High in behalf of the Church. When she prostrated herself after receiving the Holy Communion, she was raised to Heaven both in soul and body. Whilst she passed through the region of the air, seated on a chariot of light and attended by a numerous cortège of Angels, God willed that Lucifer and all the demons of Hell should appear in her presence, and to their great pain, should recognize the incomparable elevation, grandeur, majesty and sanctity of that great *Woman* whom they so much hated and so cruelly pursued. They also saw that she preserved in her heart Jesus under the sacramental species and was as if invested with the Divinity, so that, by the participation of the divine attributes, she confounded, humbled and annihilated them. At the same moment they heard a voice proceeding from the throne of the Divinity, saying: "With this invincible buckler, I will ever defend My Church." Enraged at these words, the devils cried out: "Let the Almighty again cast us into the abyss, but let Him not cause us to remain in the presence of this *Woman*, who inflicts on us the torture of a thousand hells. Let the Almighty deliver us from this cruel agony, which renews that which we endured when precipitated from heaven, for now is accomplished the threat of the chastisement which we were sentenced to receive from this great *Woman*, who is the marvel of His omnipotent arm."

All the demons were kept in these sufferings during a long space of time, and when they tried to fly into the abyss they could not do so. They were also tormented by the presence of their all-powerful enemy until she, with regal authority, precipitated them into the deepest pits of Hell, from which fall they suffered new and cruel torments.

Prostrate before the sublime throne of the Divinity, she adored Him profoundly and prayed for the Church, that the Apostles might receive the necessary lights, of which she was fully assured. She saw her Divine Son presenting to the Father His Mother's zeal, and at the same time she beheld, coming forth from the divine essence, a most beautiful temple, all resplendent and magnificently adorned, and the heavenly inhabitants also beheld it. This temple placed itself on the bosom of Jesus Christ, who united it to His holy humanity and immediately placed it in the hands of His holy Mother. Receiving it, she was again filled with splendor, and being absorbed in the Divinity enjoyed the Beatific Vision. At the sight of these favors the Angels said:

"Thou art holy, holy, holy, and all-powerful in the works of thy hands." She was reconducted to her oratory, bearing in her hands the mysterious temple of the holy Church, and she continued her prayer for nine days.

At the end of that time St. Peter again celebrated the Holy Mass and communicated all, after which they invoked the Holy Spirit and St. Peter spoke, as is related in the *Acts of the Apostles*. The difficulties were decided, the answers written and sent to Antioch. When they were read there, as also at Jerusalem, the Holy Spirit descended visibly in the form of tongues of fire. After the council the Holy Virgin, with all those assembled at it, returned thanks to God; St. Paul and St. Barnabas took leave, and she presented to them some holy relics of the Infant Jesus and some sacred thorns; then they departed, fortified by grace and joyful under the protection of the divine Mother. Lucifer roared like a lion at finding himself unable to approach the great Queen; he brought there some magicians of Jerusalem, and engaged them to take the life of the Blessed Mother by their diabolical arts. The unhappy men presented themselves many times in her presence, but her great and infinite piety touched and converted them; nevertheless, only one of them received the light of the Gospel and was baptized, to the great rage of Lucifer.

Chapter 42

FINAL TRIUMPH OF THE HOLY MOTHER— THE STATE TO WHICH THE LORD EXALTED HER.

The reader of this history will be filled with admiration at seeing the great triumphs of this pure creature, a descendant of Adam, over Lucifer, and will ask why we find no mention in the Holy Scriptures of these marvels. St. John, at least, the adopted son of the divine Mother, who lived, spoke, acted and traveled with her—why, when he wrote, did he pass over in silence the great glories of the divine Mother of God?

In the *Apocalypse*, the Saint *has* spoken of the divine Mother, principally in the twelfth and twenty-first chapters, but he has done so in a mysterious manner for two reasons.

First, because the Virgin's triumphs are so sublime that no one could ever comprehend or explain them; he has written mysteriously, that the Lord might make her known in His own time, and again, because the Virgin Mother bade him write in this way.

Secondly, because that, although Lucifer's revolt was prompted by his desire of elevating himself, contrary to the will of the Most High, yet its primary cause had been Jesus Christ and His Virgin Mother, whose excellence the apostate angels, in imitation of their chief, refused to acknowledge. And although the battle with St. Michael was waged on account of this revolt, nevertheless, it was not with the Incarnate Word, nor His Mother in person, but only with that mysterious *Woman* manifested in the heavens, with all the mysteries contained in her, as Mother of the Eternal Word who was to take human form in her womb. It was then necessary that when the time arrived in which those admirable mysteries were to be accomplished, that the battle against Christ and His divine Mother should be renewed in person, that they themselves might triumph over Lucifer and accomplish the threat already uttered against him, first in Heaven, and afterwards in the terrestrial paradise: *Ipsa conteret caput tuum*—"She shall crush thy head." (*Gen.* 3.)

All this was literally verified in Jesus and His Mother, for the Apostle says that He was tempted in all things, but without sin. (*Heb.* 4.) This was equally true of the divine Mother, and as this battle corresponded to the first, and was to be for the demons the execution of the threat announced by means of that *sign*; this is why the Evangelist has written it in the same mysterious words.

The head of the old serpent was crushed in order to finish the combat, and commence the new state which Divine Providence wishes to give to the great Queen in recompense of her virtues.

Then her Divine Son prepared her by favors so

great as to surpass all that intelligence can comprehend or explain. The Almighty raised this pure creature, elected to be the Mother of God, to an ineffable state, for the Holy Virgin received all that it is possible for the Divine Being to communicate exteriorly, and contained within herself a concentration of graces, which may be said to be infinite, so that in herself alone she formed a hierarchy superior to those of all other blessed creatures.[1]

Lucifer, having received permission to make war only during a short time, reassembled all his forces; he convoked the princes of darkness and excited them against their enemy, whom he knew to be the *Woman* who had been shown to him in the beginning of the creation. For this combat, Hell was depopulated, and the demons, in one body, attacked the Holy Virgin in her oratory. The first assault of this terrific combat was directed principally against her exterior senses by a medley of noises, roarings, cries and terrible tumult, as if the great machinery of the world was being completely destroyed. Some of the demons assumed the appearance of angels of light; others, retaining their frightful shapes, acted between them a terrific combat, shrouded in darkness, hoping thus to fill her with terror and alarm, with which in effect they could inspire any crea-

---

1. This is literally the celebrated thesis of the incomparable Doctor Suarez, who teaches that the Holy Virgin alone has more graces and merits than all other creatures together. All the Doctors unite in this opinion, and therefore the Church honors the august Queen of Heaven with a particular worship.

ture, however holy, were she of the common order of grace.

But the Queen of Virtues remained constant and invincible; far from being troubled or disturbed, she did not even change countenance, although the dreadful battle lasted for twelve hours. They presented false revelations and interior lights, made suggestions, promises and menaces and tempted her to all vices and in every way. She conducted herself in so courageous a manner, performed such heroic acts of virtue and combated with such courage and love that Divine Justice loudly demanded in favor of the triumphant Queen that her enemies should be put to flight.

The Incarnate Word descended from Paradise into her oratory, as a judge seated on a throne of majesty, surrounded by an infinite number of the most sublime celestial spirits, by many patriarchs and by St. Joachim and St. Anne, all glorious and resplendent. At this sight, Lucifer and the demons wished to fly, but the divine power retained them against their will and chained them; the ends of those deadly chains were placed in the pure hands of the divine Mother. A voice was heard, saying: "At this moment the wrath of the Omnipotent is about to fall on thee; a woman, the descendant of Adam and Eve, shall crush thy head, and the sentence which was pronounced against thee in the heavens, and afterwards in the terrestrial paradise, is about to be accomplished." (Cf. *Gen.* 3:15).

The great Queen was elevated to the right hand of her Son; there came forth from the Divinity a splendor, which clothed her with brightness like that of the sun; the moon was placed under her feet, to denote that she trampled beneath them all sublunary things; a diadem of twelve stars was placed on her head, to symbolize those divine perfections which had been communicated to her in the highest degree possible to a pure creature. She seemed to be with child, thereby to indicate that she had in her the Being of God, and the immense love corresponding proportionably to that gift. She moaned gently, like her who had given Jesus Christ to the world, in order that all creatures, knowing Him, might enter into participation with Him (but they placed resistance to Him), and she desired and procured Him by her tears and sighs. This great sign is described in the *Apocalypse*, Chapter 12, as it was formed in the divine understanding. She was shown in the heavens to Lucifer, who appeared under the form of a fiery dragon with seven heads, crowned with seven diadems, with ten horns, as author of the seven deadly sins and all heretical sects.

He presented himself to combat in the presence of the most Holy Virgin, who was to give to the world the spiritual fruit of the Church, by which it was to be perpetuated. The dragon waited there until she should bring her Son into the world, in order to devour and destroy the new Church if possible, and his envy increasing, he fell into a fury at seeing this *Woman* so powerful to establish the Church, and enrich it by her merits and protection.

Notwithstanding the hatred and rage of the

dragon, she brought into the world a male Child,
who governs all nations with an iron rod, and this
male Child is the Spirit of justice and strength of
the same Church, the true Fruit of the Holy Virgin; and because she has brought forth Jesus Christ,
and given life to the Church by her merits and care,
she governs it, and will always maintain it in a
purity of doctrine against which error shall never
prevail. St. John adds that this Fruit was brought
before the throne of the Divinity, and that the
Woman retired into solitude, in which she was
nourished during one thousand two hundred and
sixty days; that is to say, that the Fruit of the great
Woman, be it sanctity in the spirit of the Church,
or in particular souls, reaches the divine throne on
which is Jesus Christ, the natural Fruit, in whom
and by whom she has begotten and nourished it.
The divine Mother retired into solitude, the sublime state to which she alone was elevated by grace,
and there the Lord nourished her during those days
which she spent in that state before passing into
another.[2]

Lucifer knew all this before the great *Woman* was
hidden from him, and he then lost the hope with
which his pride had been nourished during four
thousand years, that of conquering this *Woman*, the
Mother of the Incarnate Word. Feeling his head

_____

2. We do not think there can be found a more sublime expo-
sition of the 12th chapter of the *Apocalypse* than this. We
feel that the Spirit of God, which directed the pen of the
Apostle, has also inspired the commentator.

crushed by her great virtue, he became furious, yet, at the same time, so much enfeebled that he could not fly from her presence without her permission. "O insensate children of Adam!" cried he, "why do you follow me, and give up life to meet death? How great is your blindness, when you have with you the Incarnate Word, and so powerful a Woman, both vested with the same nature! Your ingratitude is certainly greater than mine; I am even constrained by this great *Woman* to confess this truth."

St. Michael, who defends the honor of the Incarnate Word and His holy Mother, commanded and imposed silence on the furious Lucifer; and the Lord of armies thus spoke to the great Queen: "My beloved Mother, who hast so perfectly imitated Me, thou art the worthy object of My infinite love! Thou art the stay, the queen, the sovereign and the mistress of My Church! Thou dost possess the power, which I as the God All-mighty, have confided to thy holy will! Command, then, anything that thou pleasest to the infernal dragon!"

She commanded the demon, that whilst she dwelt on earth he should not spread the poison of heresy in the Church, and she also bade his legions cast themselves into Hell. Then through the Supper-room resounded the voice of the Archangel, saying: "Now are established the strength, the salvation and the reign of God, and the power of His Christ, because the accuser of our brethren has been precipitated from Heaven, and vanquished by the blood of the lamb." (*Apoc.* 12.) The Archangel announced by these words, that, by virtue of the triumphs of

Jesus and Mary, the Church which is the kingdom of God was already established and that we should assuredly triumph in all our battles against Hell, if we would but invoke the names of Jesus and Mary.

In the same manner as the mysteries of infinite and eternal wisdom were accomplished in the Virgin Mother, so did she raise herself to degrees of more sublime sanctity. As Mother of Eternal Wisdom she considered the pride of Lucifer, and the destruction of his infernal power, and humbling and abasing herself in the depth of her nothingness, acknowledged all to be the real effect of her Divine Son's Redemption; and as she had been coadjutrix in the Redemption, it is impossible for us to comprehend the admirable effects produced in her most pure heart by this first consideration.

Finally, reflecting within herself on the works of the Lord, the flame of divine love was increased in her and became a true fire, which filled with admiration even the blessed Seraphim, so that she could never have supported the ardor of her impetuous desires to plunge herself entirely into the immense ocean of the Divinity, if her natural life had not been miraculously supported. She was equally drawn by this same charity towards the faithful, her dear children, who depended much more on her than do plants and flowers on the influence of the sun; this was why her inflamed heart was continually drawn by a sweet and powerful attraction towards God and her neighbor. These two loves tended to elevate her to the most sublime heights, as she desired always to separate herself from all creatures, to unite herself more perfectly to the Divinity without any mixture of created things; but she was drawn in a contrary direction by her love for the Church, and the faithful whom she had borne by charity. Thus by these two flames, arising from the same fire, her most pure heart was as an immense furnace of divine love.

The Divine Son, moved with compassion by the excessive love of His most pure Mother, appeared to her with infinite goodness and said: "My beloved Mother, I have prepared for thee alone a solitary place, where thou mayest enjoy in peace the sight of My Divinity, without being prevented by thy state of viatrix [i.e., wayfarer]; there thou mayest freely take thy flight; there thou shalt find the infinite, which thy excessive love seeks to consume itself without measure; from thence thou mayest come to the succor of My Church, of which thou art the Mother; and being enriched with My treasures, thou mayest impart them to thy children." By this new favor all her faculties were purified by the fire of the sanctuary, and she felt new effects of the Divinity. From this moment her senses no longer received the impressions of sensible objects, except as far as was necessary for the exercise of charity.

She had received this favor at the moment of her conception, but after her triumph over Lucifer, she possessed it in an ineffable manner. As then in the Temple of Jerusalem they cut the throats of the victims which were to be sacrificed on the altar outside the sanctuary, where were offered only the holocausts, incense and perfumes, which were consumed by the sacred fire, so in the divine Mother, the true temple of the Incarnate Word, were offered in her exterior senses the victims of the virtues, cares and necessities of the Church, and in the sanctuary of the interior faculties, the perfume of her contemplation and the abstractive vision of the Divinity.

As the mirror represents to our bodily eyes all that is presented before it, so that all may clearly see the object without looking at it, so did she know in God all the necessities and trials of the children of the Church, and all that she was to do for them, according to the good pleasure of God. The Almighty excepted only those works which the divine Mother would do through obedience to St. Peter and St. John; she begged this herself of the Lord, that thus she might give an example of obedience from which those who should make profession of this vow might learn not to seek other means of knowing the will of God, when he who is superior and holds the place of God commands.

With regard to what did not concern obedience, in which Holy Communion was included, the knowledge of the Mother of God depended not on sensible creatures, or on the impressions received through the senses, but she was entirely free from everything and in utter solitude, enjoying the abstractive vision of the Divinity without interruption, whether asleep or awake, occupied or at leisure, at work or at rest. Moreover, she never discoursed interiorly, or made any effort to know that which was most sublime in perfection and most agreeable to the Lord. She knew the incomprehensible mystery of the Divinity in a more excellent manner than the Seraphim of Paradise, and she was thus nourished in her solitude by this bread of eternal life.

She knew, on one occasion, that a woman of Jerusalem, already baptized, had miserably apostatized from the Faith, having been deceived by the demon, who, for this purpose, had employed a magician, her relation. The great Queen, filled with zeal, was much afflicted and begged St. John to warn the unfortunate woman of her enormous sin; at the same time, this merciful Mother prayed the Lord with many tears to recall the strayed sheep into the fold; and, although conversion is always more difficult for those who have voluntarily departed from the right path than for those who are only entering on the way of eternal life, nevertheless, the power of her prayers obtained the remedy. The poor woman listened to St. John, obeyed him and abjured; she confessed with tears of true repentance; then the Holy Virgin exhorted her to persevere in resisting the demon, which she happily did.

To resume what we have said in the course of this holy history with regard to the time at which the great Queen was raised by the Lord to this sublime state, we may make the following supputation. When she went from Jerusalem to Ephesus, she was fifty-four years, six months and twenty-six days old, and this was on the 6th of January, the fortieth year after the birth of Christ. She remained in Ephesus two years and a half, and returned to Jerusalem in the year of Our Lord 42, on the 6th of July; she was then fifty-six years and ten months old. When she was elevated to this ineffable state she was fifty-eight years old. In it she remained for one thousand, two hundred and sixty days, as computed by St. John in the twelfth chapter of the *Apocalypse*.

Chapter 43

WHAT MARY DID WHILE THE HOLY GOSPELS WERE BEING WRITTEN.

When the august Mother for the last time descended from Heaven with the Church in her most pure hands, as described in the *Apocalypse*, under the figure of that holy, new and celestial city descending from Heaven, she learned from her Divine Son that it was becoming and necessary that the holy Gospels should be written, so that she might dispose of everything, as the Mistress of the Apostles; nevertheless, being the Queen of Humility, she obtained that it might be done by means of St. Peter, the chief of the Church.

In the first council, spoken of by St. Luke in the Acts of the Apostles, after they had solved the difficulties regarding circumcision and had determined many other rites, St. Peter, having first conferred with the holy Mother, announced that the holy Gospels should be written. They all invoked the Holy Spirit in order to know to whom this charge should be given. The Supper-room was filled with celestial light, and they heard a voice saying: "Let the Sovereign Pontiff, Head of the Church, name four persons to write the works and the doctrine of the Saviour of the world."

St. Peter, prostrate on the ground, returned thanks with all the others; the choice was made; he immediately arose and said: "Let Matthew, Mark, Luke and John, our dear brethren, write the Gospels, in the name of the Father, of the Son and of the Holy Ghost," and all answered, "Amen," to confirm the election.

Some days after the choice of which we have spoken, St. Matthew, who was in the Supper-room, retired into a private apartment, being resolved to enter on his office as evangelist. He prostrated himself on the earth to beg the Lord's assistance in the divine work, and immediately the most Holy Virgin appeared in his chamber on a throne of majesty.

St. Matthew prostrated himself upon the earth and begged the divine Mother to give her benediction and protection to his enterprise; after giving him her blessing, she bade him be seated and assured him of the divine assistance and her continual prayers. She warned him not to write anything about herself, except what would be necessary to make known the mysteries of the Incarnate Word; then having suggested to him the order in which he should write, she disappeared. The Evangelist began to write his sacred history in the Hebrew tongue, and finished it afterwards in another part of Judea.

Four years afterwards, that is to say, in the forty-sixth year of the birth of our Saviour, St. Mark, being in Palestine, resolving to begin his Gospel, begged his Angel Guardian to make known his determination to the divine Mistress, that she might obtain for him the light of Heaven; as he was in prayer, the great Queen appeared to him on a royal throne, attended by many Angels. He prostrated himself in her presence, and said: "Great Queen, I am unworthy of this favor." "The Most High," replied the divine Mother, "whom thou servest and lovest, hath sent me to assure thee that the divine Spirit will guide thee in writing the Gospel." She commanded him not to write anything that would serve to her praise; then the Holy Spirit, in the form of fire, descended on the Saint and surrounded him. Being thus filled with the Holy Ghost, he commenced his Gospel.

When St. Jerome says that St. Mark wrote his Gospel at Rome, at the request of the faithful, we must understand that as he had no copy of it with him, as is true, he wrote one in the Latin tongue.

Two years afterwards, St. Luke began to write his in Greek; the Holy Virgin appeared to him also, and having conferred with her, he afterwards happily finished his gospel in Achaia. St. John was the last to write the gospel, which he did in Greek, in Asia Minor, in the year 58, after the most Holy Virgin's death; for the demon, knowing that his enemy was no longer in the world, began to sow heresies and errors, which St. John was left to combat. The Saint was at that time in prayer, reflecting in what manner he could prove the divinity of Christ, when he saw the holy Virgin descending from Heaven with glory and ineffable majesty, accompanied by an infinite number of blessed spirits. She said to him: "John, my son, and servant of the Most High, this is the suitable time to make known to the world the divinity of my Son. As for the mysterious secrets which thou hast learned regarding myself, it is not opportune that they be now manifested to the world, through fear that Lucifer may take occasion from it to trouble those of the faithful who may be inclined to idolatry. The Holy Spirit will assist thee, and I wish that thou wouldst begin to write in my presence."

St. John venerated the great Queen of Heaven, and being filled with the Holy Ghost, began his Gospel, assisted by the divine Mother. She assured him of her continual protection, gave him her blessing and returned to Heaven. Thus the great Queen, as Mother of the Church, cooperated in the grand work of the Gospels, and the faithful should be ever grateful to her for so extraordinary a favor.

To continue, then, our history. As the Church continued to spread still more and more, so also was the solicitude of our holy Mother increased. Only St. James the Less and St. John remained at Jerusalem; the other Apostles being dispersed throughout the world; but the merciful Mother bore them all in her heart, compassionated their labors and sufferings, prayed to the Lord for them and shed continual tears for her dear children. But what we should particularly admire in the divine Mother is, that in the midst of her solicitude for the universal Church, she never lost her peace or tranquillity; she recommended her Angels to assist the Apostles in their necessities, to help them, and also to take care of the disciples. She wished, like a watchful Mother, to take charge of the clothing of the Apostles, desiring they should all conform to the example of her Divine Son; again, when their garments were worn out, she provided new ones for them. She was constantly occupied in spinning, weaving and making tunics; the Angels assisted her, and carried those garments to the Apostles wherever they were. She took care of all like a tender mother, so that it is impossible to describe, in particular, the thoughts, the solicitude and the activity of this merciful Mother, for she passed no day without thinking of her dear missionaries. She even frequently appeared to them in person, when they invoked her in any difficulty.

St. Peter had gone to Antioch to establish his see; in order to surmount the difficulties which surrounded him, the vicar of Christ found himself many times in great pain and affliction. Then he invoked the divine Mother, and she immediately and miraculously appeared to him on a resplendent throne. When St. Peter saw her so glorious with light, he prostrated himself, and thanking her for so great an honor, said: "Whence is this to me, a sinner, that the Mother of my Lord should come to console me?" The Queen of humility descended from her throne, and obscuring in some degree the refulgence of her splendor, knelt before the Head of the Church and, as viatrix [wayfarer on earth], begged his blessing. He gave it with great fear, and shed many tears at the sight of the great humility of the Mother of God, the sovereign Queen of the Universe. Then he consulted her on the most difficult affairs of that time, in particular on the celebration of the different feasts, the institution of divers rites and the dignities which should be established in the Church; the prince of the Apostles received great light and consolation from her.

The Virgin Mother was carried by Angels to her oratory in Jerusalem. When St. Peter went afterwards to Rome to transfer thither the apostolic see, as the Lord had commanded him, he again found himself in trouble, and the divine Mother appeared to him; it was then resolved to celebrate the feast of Our Lord's Nativity, Lent, the remembrance of the Passion and the institution of the divine Sacrament of the Altar.

On another occasion, while St. Peter was still at Rome, a terrible persecution was raised against the Christians, and the Roman Church was in affliction. The Apostle had recourse to the Mother of Piety, and sent his Angel Guardian to bear to her news of the tribulation. At this intelligence the Mother of Wisdom bade her Angels transport the Vicar of Christ to Jerusalem. They obeyed, and brought him into the presence of their Queen. It would be impossible to express the ardent affection of St. Peter and his many thanks to Mary for so singular a benefit. The Apostle, inflamed with love, knelt and kissed the ground which had been trodden by her sacred feet. The Mother of Humility begged him to arise; he did so, and she prostrated herself and begged his blessing, saying: "My Lord, give thy benediction as Vicar of my God, my Son, to thy servant." St. Peter obeyed, and thanked the Lord for all those celestial consolations.

Then the Apostle recounted the trials of the faithful in Rome. With great goodness she strengthened, consoled and enlightened him; gave him wise advice how to conduct himself on that occasion. She begged his benediction and ordered her Angels to reconduct him to Rome. The Holy Virgin remained on her knees, with her arms extended in the form of a cross, begging the Lord to assist St. Peter and give grace to the faithful in the persecution; therefore, at his return, St. Peter found all things in peace.

It is impossible to recount all that the divine Mother did for the Church during the years that she survived her Son.

Chapter 44

THE EXERCISES OF PIETY PERFORMED BY THE HOLY VIRGIN—HER PREPARATION FOR HOLY COMMUNION.

Among the privileges possessed by Mary from the first moment of her conception was that of never forgetting what she had once known, thus enjoying by privilege that which the Angels possess by nature. All the images and stages of the Passion remained as firmly and as vividly impressed upon her mind as when she had first received them. During the last years of her life, when she had received the grace of the continual abstractive vision, she enjoyed it miraculously, for she suffered from the remembrance of her Son's Passion and always desired to be crucified with Christ.

Sometimes she spent many hours in her oratory, meditating on her Divine Son's Passion; sometimes she visited the holy places where He had suffered, shedding sorrowful tears. She arranged with St. John that on each Friday of the year she would celebrate the death of her Son; therefore on this day she never left the oratory, and the Apostle remained in the Supper-room, to meet those pious and devout persons who came to visit her; when the Apostle was absent, one of the disciples supplied his place. The great Queen retired for this holy exercise on the eve of Friday, two hours before night, and remained in it until Sunday. If any pressing necessity called for her personal attention, she sent an Angel under her form, so careful and watchful was she in all that regarded the exercise of charity towards her dear faithful, whom she esteemed and loved as her beloved children. She always carried a cross with her, and during this time she extended herself on one much larger; thus while she lived she renewed in herself the Passion of her Son, and by her holy exercises obtained from the Lord great favors and graces for all those who would be devout to the divine Passion, and, as all-powerful Queen, she promised to grant them ineffable graces, through her desire to see this devotion perpetuated in the Church.

She celebrated the institution of the august Sacrament of the Eucharist and composed new canticles of praise and ardent acts of love and thanksgiving. She invited her Angels Guardian to accompany her in those acts, and, as she possessed in her most pure heart, Jesus, under the sacramental species, she excited the blessed spirits to admire this prodigy and render to the Lord praise, honor and glory. The Angels were overwhelmed with astonishment, and, as it were, stupefied at beholding in a mere creature such incomparable charity, such elevated sanctity, such profound humility. Their wonder was still further increased when they saw her preparing herself for the next Communion.

In the first place, she offered for this intention the weekly exercises of the Passion; after these exercises, when she had retired on the evening preceding the day of Communion, she commenced her pious exercises of prostrations and extended herself on the earth in the form of a cross. Then she arose and continued her genuflections to adore the immutable being of God, she begged the Lord to allow her to speak to Him, and prayed that notwithstanding her natural vileness, He would give her the Holy Communion. She offered Him the Passion and death of her Son; the Hypostatic Union and all the works and merits of Christ; the purity and sanctity of the angelic hierarchies; their works and those of all the faithful children of the Church, both present and future. She made acts of profound humility, considering that she was but dust and of a material nature, infinitely inferior to the Divine Being. In the consideration of what she was and what the God was whom she was to receive under the sacramental species, she excited affections so sublime that they surpassed those of all the Seraphim. But as she considered herself the last of all creatures, she, with profound humility, invited the Angels to beg the Lord to prepare and dispose her to receive Him worthily. The Angels obeyed her with admiration and joy; they accompanied her in her prayers, which she continued during the greater part of the night.

When the hour of Holy Communion arrived, she assisted, kneeling, and with incomparable modesty at the Mass celebrated by St. John, reciting during it hymns, psalms and other prayers, for the Epistles and Gospels had not then been written, but the Consecration has always been the same. At the end of Mass she prepared to communicate; she made three profound prostrations, and all burning and inflamed with love, received under the sacramental species that same Son to whom she had given the sacred humanity, in her virginal womb. Then she retired and continued her recollection and thanksgiving for three hours. St. John had the happiness of seeing her many times, at this moment, vested with splendor and more brilliant than the sun. Knowing, as the Mother of Wisdom, with what ineffable decorum the unbloody Sacrifice should be celebrated, she wove and made, with her own hands, the sacerdotal vestments and ornaments for the celebration of Mass, and she was the first to introduce the custom of celebrating with ornaments of divers colors. She received alms and gifts for this end, and when she worked at them, she sometimes knelt and sometimes stood. Those sacred vestments preserved a celestial perfume, which inflamed the hearts of the ministers.

From the provinces in which the Apostles had preached, there came a great number of distinguished converts who wished to see and venerate the divine Mother. After having beheld this model of all virtues, they offered her considerable sums for her own use, and the benefit of the poor, but the great Queen replied that she had made profession of poverty like to that of her Divine Son, and that all His disciples conformed to the example of their

Divine Master. They answered that she might distribute them among the poor, or employ them in the divine worship, and the merciful Mother, in order to console them, accepted some of the things so earnestly pressed on her, such as fine linen and ornaments, which she afterwards prepared to be used in divine worship, by the priests, or for the altars. The remainder she distributed among the poor and those houses provided for their accommodation, where she visited and served them herself. She distributed her alms on her knees, for in the poor she recognized the person of her Divine Son. Retiring into her oratory, she recommended them to the Lord. To all those benefactors she gave lights and counsels of eternal life, inflaming them with ardor to follow Jesus Christ.

Wonderful was the astonishment of strangers who beheld her for the first time; the faithful, the pagans, the Jews, all were ravished with admiration at the sight of her majesty, grace, humility and superhuman charity; being much moved, they cried out: "This is truly the Mother of God!" and they embraced the holy faith. In their relations with her, they felt that she was the true channel of divine grace. Her words, full of profound wisdom, carried conviction to every intellect and communicated to all the light of eternal life; in the same manner, by the infinite grace and ineffable beauty of her countenance and sweet majesty, she attracted all hearts and led them to a perfect life. At this sight, some were seized with astonishment, others shed tears, others spoke of it with admiration, all united to praise her, confessing Christ to be true God, because His Mother was so incomparably beautiful, amiable, humble and holy.

During the last years of her life the great Queen ate and slept very little, and even this she did in obedience to St. John, who begged her to retire at night for a little repose. She slept for only half an hour, or at most, an hour; even then she did not lose the sight of God; her heart watched continually, and she practiced fervent acts of humility, resignation and love. Her ordinary nourishment consisted of some morsels of bread, and sometimes, at the urgent entreaty of St. John, she added a little fish. The Saint was highly favored, because, as her son, he ate at the same table with her, and she prepared his food and served him as a mother does her son; moreover, she obeyed him as a priest, and as one who held the place of Christ. Although nourishment and sleep were not necessary to the life of the divine Mother, nevertheless she took them through obedience to the Apostle, and through humility, to pay in some manner the debt of human nature, for she was prudence itself. The remainder of her time was employed in exercises of charity towards God and her neighbor.

This was the forty-fifth year after the birth of Christ, and the Virgin Mother was sixty years, two months and some days old. Her life was drawing to its close; therefore, as the stone, by the movement which draws it to the center of the earth acquires greater rapidity the nearer it approaches it, so as the divine Mother drew near the term of her glorious life, did the ardor of her most pure spirit become more vehement and the amorous desires of her heart more impetuous to reach the center of her eternal repose.

From the first instant of her conception she had been as a river flowing from the immense ocean of the Divinity, in the understanding of Him by whom she had been formed from all eternity. She then came into the world with an incredible effusion of gifts, favors, graces, privileges, virtues, merits and sanctity, and she advanced in all to such a degree that the whole sphere of creation was not sufficient for her. Again, by the incomprehensible motion of her ineffable charity, she hastened to unite herself to that sea from which she had come, to re-enter in its bosom, and afterwards, by her maternal charity, to inundate the Church. During her last years, by the sweet violence of her love, she lived in a kind of continual martyrdom of charity.

Her most holy Son descended from Heaven to visit her; He was seated on a throne of ineffable light and environed by legions of Angels. Approaching His august Mother, He renewed and strengthened her in the languishing state to which her love had reduced her, saying: "My Mother and My Dove, come with Me to the heavenly country, where thy tears shall be changed into joy, and where thou shalt rest, delivered from all pain."

The Angels placed their Queen on a throne beside her Son and ascended with her on high, chanting celestial melodies. She adored the Most Holy Trinity; her Son kept her beside Him, to the great joy of the whole court of Heaven.

The Incarnate Word spoke thus to His Eternal Father: "My Father, Thou knowest that this is the Virgin, who gave Me human form in her most pure womb, who nourished Me with her milk, supported Me by her fatigues, accompanied Me in My labors and sufferings, who has always faithfully cooperated with Me in the Redemption of men, and has executed Thy holy will in all things. She is wholly pure and exempt from all stain of sin; by her holy works and heroic virtues she has attained to the most sublime sanctity. Besides the gifts communicated to her by Our infinite power, when she came to the recompense which she had merited, she could not freely enjoy it, but returned to instruct and govern the Church Militant, confiding in the justice of Our divine providence; it is time that she be rewarded as Queen of all created things." The Eternal Father replied: "My Divine Son, Chief of all the elect, all My treasures and all things are at Thy disposal; let Our Beloved participate in them, according to her dignity, and for Our glory." At these words the Divine Son announced in the presence of the heavenly court, and promised His Mother, that on each Sunday, after the holy exercises, she should be carried by Angels into Heaven, both body and soul, there to celebrate, in the presence of the Most High, the great mystery of the Resurrection.

The Lord also willed that, in the Holy Communion which she made each morning, the Holy Humanity should appear to her united with the Divinity, in the Divine Person, in a manner more admirable and sublime than had yet happened. Then He turned towards His dear Mother and said: "Beloved Mother, I will be always with thee during the time of thy mortal life, and in a particular manner, incomprehensible even to the Angels; thus I will be the recompense of thy exile."

In the midst of these ineffable favors, the Holy Virgin retired into the most profound depths of her nothingness; she blessed, praised and thanked the Omnipotent; concentrating herself in the lowest estimate of her nature, she humbled and abased herself at the time that she was exalted, and thus rendered herself more worthy. She was still more enlightened and renewed in her faculties, to prepare her for the clear intuitive vision. The veil was drawn, and she beheld the infinite essence of God, and possessed for some hours the glory and happiness of Heaven, in a degree greater than all the Saints. Drinking thus of the waters of life at their very source, she satiated her inflamed desires, and arriving then at her center, the violence of her love was appeased and she could return to communicate those graces to her children. After this ineffable prayer, she returned inexpressible thanksgivings to the Most Holy Trinity and interceded most earnestly for the Church.

Being carried back to her oratory, she there, according to custom, prostrated, and humbled herself in a manner which no other child of Adam has done or ever will do. From that time until the hour of her happy death she was raised into Heaven every Sunday; there her Divine Son advanced to meet

her, and the angelic choirs chanted the *Regina Cæli
lætare, Alleluia*—"O Queen of Heaven, rejoice,
alleluia!" She asked advice on the most difficult
affairs of the Church, interceded for all the faithful, but in particular for her dear Apostles and disciples, and returned to earth like the richly laden
vessels spoken of by Solomon. (*Prov. xxxi.*) This
special grace was granted to her because when she
had been conducted into Heaven at the Ascension
of her Divine Son, she had willingly deprived herself of the Beatific Vision in order to apply herself
to the government of the Church. In her solicitude, the violence of her love diminished her
strength, and it was therefore necessary that she
should be ravished into Heaven to receive additional strength for the government of the Church,
to enable her to bear the excess of her love; and
again, because when, each week, she commemorated
the Passion of her Son, she seemed, as it were, to
die with Him, therefore it was necessary that she
should rise again with Him.[1]

---

1. Here we would remind those who think this too extraordi-
    nary to meditate a little on the miracle of the Mass, which
    is said every day and in every place. After a short reflec-
    tion we shall see that what we believe Jesus has done and
    is doing every day for us is no less marvelous than what He
    has been pleased to do for His Mother, as we see in this
    "Mystical Life."

Chapter 45

FEASTS CELEBRATED BY THE
QUEEN OF ANGELS.

All the brilliant titles which the most Holy Virgin had in the Church such as Queen, Sovereign, Mother, Guide and Mistress did not remain fruitless in her, for she exercised those offices with superabundant grace. As Queen, she knew all her dignity; as Sovereign, the extent of her empire; as Mother, all the children and servants of her Church, even to the end of the world; as Guide, she knew those who walked with her; as Mistress, she was filled with sovereign wisdom and possessed the fullness of that science by which the holy Church should be governed and taught, by means of her intercession. She had then a perfect knowledge of all the Saints who had preceded, as well as those who were to come after her, with their actions, lives, death and recompense. She knew clearly all the rites, ceremonies and feasts that would be established by the Church in the course of time, together with the reasons, motives and necessity for each. This fullness of knowledge produced in her a holy desire to emulate the thanksgiving, worship, veneration and remembrance rendered by the Angels and Saints of the heavenly Jerusalem, and in order to introduce the same into the Church Militant, inasfar as it could imitate the Triumphant, she began the practice, and also inspired the Apostles to celebrate a great number of feasts. Although she had begun to celebrate many feasts from the time of the Incarnation of the Word, yet from the Ascension of her Son, during the last years of her life, she kept them with greater solemnity.

On the 8th of December of each year she celebrated her Immaculate Conception, for which she felt she could never return sufficient thanks to God. She began the celebration on the eve of the feast and passed the night in most admirable exercises, shedding tears of joy; she made prostrations, acts of veneration and canticles of praise to the Lord. She considered that she had been formed from the dust of the earth, as a descendant of Adam, according to the universal law of nature, but that nevertheless she alone had been elected, delivered and preserved from the common law, and thus exempted from the grave tribute of sin and conceived with the plenitude of grace and supernatural gifts.

She invited the Angels to aid her in returning thanks and sang with them canticles of praise. She also invited the other blessed spirits and Saints of Heaven and became so inflamed with love that it was necessary for her Divine Son to descend from Heaven to strengthen her. He conducted her with Him, and there she satisfied the ardor of her heart by humble thanksgivings. The three Divine Persons rejoiced at having preserved her from the common contagion of the children of Adam; they ratified and confirmed the possession of all she had received, and a voice issuing from the divine throne said: "Thy ways are beautiful, O daughter of the King, conceived without sin."

Then the choirs of Angels and Saints sang the words, "Mary conceived without Original Sin." The humble Queen responded to all those favors with acts of praise and thanksgiving, with a humility so profound that it surpassed even the intelligence of the Angels. Then she was elevated to the intuitive vision of God during several hours, and after descending from Heaven performed acts of most profound humility.

She celebrated the feast of her Nativity on the 8th of September, the day on which she was born, but as usual, began her exercises on the preceding evening. She thanked the Most High for having been born to the light of the world and having had the happiness of being carried into Heaven. She took a heroic resolution of employing all her life in the service of the Lord, and the accomplishment of His Will, and implored the aid of His grace that it might direct all her actions and make them tend to His greater glory. Her Divine Son descended into her oratory with many choirs of Angels, the ancient Patriarchs, the Prophets, and in particular, St. Joachim, St. Anne and St. Joseph, and they celebrated the nativity of the great Queen. She adored her Divine Son with profound respect and veneration and renewed her humble thanks; the Angels sang: *Nativitas tua, sancta Dei genitrix, Virgo*—"This

is thy nativity, O Virgin, holy Mother of God"—
and the Patriarchs and Prophets, with Adam and
Eve, sang canticles to the glory of the Reparatrix
of the world. The Divine Son raised His Mother
from the earth, on which she lay prostrate, placed
her at His right, and manifested new mysteries to
her. She was wholly transformed into her Divine
Son and filled with an ardent desire to labor.

St. John frequently participated in the joy of these
festivals by hearing the angelic harmonies. The holy
Evangelist came to celebrate Mass in her oratory,
and communicated the great Queen, who was seated
on the throne of her Divine Son, whom she received
under the sacramental species into her pure and
inflamed heart. The view of these mysteries caused
a new increase of joy to all the Saints, who assisted
at this Communion, the most worthy—after that of
Christ—that has ever been or ever shall be made
in the Church.

After the great Queen had received her Son
under the sacramental species, He caused her to
become like to Him in the adorable Sacrament, and
in this glorious and supernatural manner she
returned into Heaven. O hidden and admirable wonders of divine Omnipotence! If God shows Himself
so great and admirable in all His Saints, may we
not think that He is much more so in regard of His
holy Mother? Moreover, she celebrated with the
princes of Heaven the remembrance of the benefits she had received and invited them to aid her
in returning thanks for them. Recognizing such profound science in their Queen, they sang: "Let thy

Creator be eternally blessed and exalted, O Mary! Thou art the glory of the human race; thou art the marvel of the power of the Word of God, the lively image of all His perfections. Thou art the worthy Mistress of the Church Militant, the particular glory of the Church Triumphant, the honor of all creatures; Reparatrix of thy race, thou art worthy that all nations should acknowledge thy virtues and greatness and that all generations should praise and bless thee."

At the anniversary of her Presentation in the Temple, she retired into her oratory and passed the preceding night in holy exercises. She returned humble and profound acknowledgments to the Lord for having conducted her into His Temple at so tender an age and for having loaded her with benefits in that holy place. At this feast she felt a natural attraction for solitude, because it is retreat that unites the soul most intimately with God. The Lord, according to His custom, visited her and said: "My Mother and My Dove, behold thy God and thy Son; I wish to give thee a temple and a habitation the most elevated, sure and sublime, which is My own being; enter then, My Beloved, into thy true retreat." At these sweet words, she was placed at the right of her Son, and immediately felt that His Divinity penetrated her by a union incomprehensible, pure and divine. She called this solemnity the feast of the Being of God.

On the anniversaries of the deaths of St. Joachim and St. Anne she celebrated their feasts by acts of worship and veneration of the Lord and rendered

Him thanks for having given her parents so holy. She blessed the Most Holy Trinity for all the gifts, graces, and favors that had been conferred on them during their lives and for the ineffable glory with which they were crowned. Her blessed parents, vested with glory, descended from Heaven with the Divine Son to converse with their child. The Angels of each choir sang the praises of the Lord, each explaining some divine attribute, and their Queen, ravished into ecstasy and filled with incomparable joy, repeated their admirable canticles. Finally, having received her Son's benediction, she begged that of her parents, and after giving it, they returned to Heaven.

On the feast of St. Joseph she recalled to mind the faithful companionship of her most chaste spouse. He descended into her oratory, all glorious and resplendent, accompanied by numberless Angels, who sang hymns in his honor; the divine Mother of wisdom repeated them and composed others, by which she thanked God for the favors He had heaped upon her spouse. After several hours of thanksgiving, she entertained herself with St. Joseph and begged him to recommend her to the Most High and to thank Him for the favors that had been granted her. She recommended to him the necessities of the Church and begged him to obtain the divine assistance for the Apostles and disciples who were preaching the Gospel. Then she begged his benediction, and he returned to Heaven. We must not omit recording that on each of her feasts Mary prepared food for a great number of poor persons and served them on her knees; she also begged St. John to seek out the most necessitous and miserable. During the day, she visited the sick in their houses and in abandoned places; thus did the great Queen celebrate her festivals.

It is impossible to express with what recollection and acts of worship she solemnized the feasts of the Incarnation and Nativity of the Incarnate Word, for she considered the Incarnation as the first work of divine Omnipotence, operated in her womb. She comprehended the depth of this adorable mystery; she beheld the great designs of God, as also the ingratitude of man and his want of cooperation and, as chosen depositary of the divine Council, she understood that to her it belonged to correspond to this ineffable benefit and to compensate and supply for our ingratitude and cowardice. For this reason, she, in the name of the redeemed world, performed each day many prostrations, genuflections and acts of adoration of the Lord, saying interiorly to Him:

"Omnipotent God, prostrate in Thy presence, in my name and that of the whole human race, I praise, bless, glorify, exalt, confess and humbly adore Thee for the admirable benefit of Thy ineffable Incarnation, in the mystery of the Hypostatic Union of human nature with the divine Person of the Eternal Word. Although great numbers of men live in forgetfulness of this benefit, remember, O merciful Lord and Father, that they live in frail flesh, that they are full of ignorance and disorderly passions and cannot come to Thee, unless they be drawn and led by Thine infinite goodness. Pardon, O my God, their negligences, as being the effect of weak nature. I, who am Thy slave and a vile worm of the earth, thank Thee in my name and that of all creatures for so inestimable a benefit, and I unite myself to all the Angels and blessed souls in Paradise. And Thou, my Son and my Lord, I supplicate Thee to take into Thy hands the cause of men, Thy brethren, that through Thee they may obtain pardon from Thy Eternal Father. I implore mercy for Thy people and mine, for as Thou hast become man, we have all the same nature with Thee. Deign, then, not to reject us from Thee, and as God, give an infinite value to our works, that they may be worthy of Thee. Thou art our salvation, our good and our only hope."

These prayers and others were repeated by the great Queen from the evening of the 16th of March until the 25th, during which time she neither ate, drank, nor slept. The Evangelist alone approached her in order to administer the Holy Communion, and the Almighty renewed at that time all the graces and favors He had conferred on her in the nine days preceding the Incarnation.

The Eternal Word descended from Heaven with great glory and majesty, and attended by many Angels. The humble Virgin, prostrating herself on her face, adored her Son, true God; the Angels raised her from the ground and placed her at His right hand. She became wholly transformed and surrounded with glory, and in this sublime state, sang canticles of praise and thanksgiving. The Divine

Son said to the Eternal Father: "I confess and praise Thee, My Father, and offer Thee this creature worthy of being presented to Thee, as being chosen among all creatures to be My dear Mother, and the proof of Our infinite attributes. She alone has worthily and fully recognized and accepted with her whole heart the immense benefit conferred on men by My becoming incarnate and delivering them from eternal death; therefore We cannot reject the prayer of Our Beloved."

At the hour in which the ineffable mystery of the Incarnation had been accomplished, the Divinity was manifested to her in an intuitive manner. She then prayed for the conversion of the world, for the extension of the Church, for those engaged in the apostolate and for the souls in Purgatory. She sent her Angels to deliver them out of it, which she did with the authority of a queen, and commanded those souls to return thanks to the Most Holy Trinity for the mystery of the Incarnation.

The Nativity of her Divine Son she celebrated in a different manner, and on it also received new favors. On the eve of the feast she performed her usual preparatory exercises, and at the hour of His birth, Jesus descended from Heaven, accompanied by thousands of Angels, by St. Joachim, St. Anne, St. Joseph, St. Elizabeth and her son, John the Baptist, and by other Saints and patriarchs.

The Angels raised Mary to the throne of her adorable Son, and her humble oratory was transformed into a paradise. The heavenly choirs sang: *Gloria in excelsis Deo*—"Glory be to God on High"—

and other canticles composed by Mary in praise of God.

Having obtained the permission of her Divine Son, the humble Queen descended from the throne and prostrated herself before Him, to render thanks in the name of all mankind for the inestimable benefit of Redemption. She prayed fervently that all the children of the Church might obtain eternal life. This prayer was granted by the Lord, who allowed her to dispose of His mercy and merits, as being the absolute Mistress over them. She implored the Saints to thank the Lord for her; her Divine Son gave her His blessing, and returned to Heaven. Never shall men, nor even the Angels be able to comprehend what the world owes to the Divine Mother, for the benefits and mercies she obtained for the human race, particularly on those feasts which she celebrated, always rendering thanks for them to the Most High, in the name of all.

On the anniversary of the Circumcision, at which Jesus had shed the first drops of His Blood for our salvation, she retired to perform her accustomed preparatory exercises, and her Divine Son descended from Heaven with His cortége of Angels and Saints. The divine Mother elicited ineffable acts, in considering that, on that day, the Incarnate Word had subjected Himself to the law of sinners, as if He had been one of them. She humbled herself beneath the dust and felt a lively compassion for the Infant God, who had suffered so cruelly, at so tender an age.

She accepted this immense benefit for all the

children of Adam and wept tears of blood over the universal forgetfulness and ingratitude of men, who value so lightly the Precious Blood shed for them and correspond so feebly to such an incomprehensible benefit; and she was overwhelmed with confusion in presence of her Sovereign; for this reason, she offered to shed her blood and die in suffering, to make a return for such great love. She passed the day in holy entertainments with the Lord and added new inventions of her love in favor of mortals. She begged Him to pour out on all the living those graces and favors she had received from His omnipotent hand and infinite goodness, that all might be converted, and none be lost. She offered to the Eternal Father the Blood of her Son shed at the Circumcision and the humility with which He had offered Himself to that rite. She adored Him as true God and true man. Then her Divine Son, having blessed her, returned to Heaven. She celebrated the feast of the adoration of the Magi and made several days of preparation in order to dispose the gifts she wished to offer to the Incarnate Word. The principal offering she sought to prepare was gold, that is, the souls that she wished to lead back to grace. This she did by the ministry of her Angels, whom she begged to aid souls by strong and special inspirations to be converted to the Faith; and by her fervent prayers she obtained for many of the agonizing a true conversion and their salvation.

To this first gift she added that of myrrh, by innumerable prostrations on the earth in the form of a cross and other exercises of mortification. The third offering was the incense of ejaculatory prayers and the aspirations of ineffable love, with the sweet and pure affections of her virginal heart. On this day, her Son descended from Heaven with His ordinary cortège, and she invited the blessed spirits to come to her aid; she offered to Him with great respect and admirable veneration the gifts of which we have spoken, and she prayed for all men, offering them in their name. She was raised to the divine throne, and her Son, in order to give some repose to the transports of her ardent love, caused her to lean her head on His bosom, and while the Angels sang canticles of praises, the Lord filled her with celestial benedictions. After having loaded her with new favors, Jesus returned to Heaven, and prostrate on the earth, she rendered thanks for His infinite mercy.

She also made a commemoration of the Baptism of Our Lord, in order to return thanks for this inappreciable benefit. After many fervent prayers, she retired for forty days to celebrate the Redeemer's fast, which she kept in the same manner, retiring for all that time into her oratory and taking neither food nor drink. She saw only St. John, who came to administer the Holy Communion. During this time the Apostle remained in the Supper-room, and when the sick or poor came to visit the divine Mother, he consoled and comforted them and healed them by the application of some relic of the Mother of piety. When they led any demoniacs to her, the demons fled away before they reached the door of her dwelling.

If, during those forty days, the great Queen neither ate nor slept, who shall be able to describe her interior and exterior acts of worship and veneration, her prayers and genuflections inspired by the activity of her most pure soul! She applied them all to the good of the faithful, the exaltation of the Church and the justification of souls. She received many visits from her Divine Son; the Angels also brought her celestial nourishment, to strengthen her in the fasts and mortifications with which she afflicted her most pure body. At other times, the Lord Himself presented nourishment, exhorting her to repair her strength, and at the same time filling her with heavenly benedictions.

Amidst these favors, the Queen of virtues made heroic acts of humility, submission and respect, acknowledging herself unworthy of those favors and begging grace to serve God better in the future. After this fast, she celebrated the feast of her Purification and the Presentation of the Infant Jesus in the Temple, and she offered her Son to the Eternal Father. The Angels, on this day, adorned her in a divine manner, and being thus prepared, she made a long and fervent prayer to the Most Holy Trinity in which she interceded for the whole human race, and particularly for the Church. In recompense of her humility in subjecting herself to the law of purification, she received an increase of favors, graces and privileges, and also benefits for those for whom she had prayed. She celebrated the feast of the Ascension still more solemnly, knowing that in Paradise it is kept with extraordinary rejoicing: this celebration she began on the feast of the Resurrection.

During all this time she recalled to mind the benefits and favors she had received from her Divine Son on that occasion, and returned thanks by new canticles and holy exercises; and by new graces she was prepared to receive others more sublime. On the feast of the Ascension, Our Lord descended into her oratory, attended by a numerous cortège of Angels, patriarchs and Saints. She awaited this visit prostrate on the ground, confounded and annihilated in the depths of her being, but her heart was raised to the most sublime degree of love possible to a mere creature. The Lord ordered her to be placed on the throne at His right hand; then He asked her, with ineffable goodness, what it was that she most ardently desired. She immediately replied: "My Son and my God, I desire only that Thy holy Name may be known and glorified, and that all may acknowledge the great favor Thou hast conferred on us, by elevating to the right hand of the Eternal Father the dust of our humanity; and I pray that all may glorify Thy Divinity."

"My Mother and My Dove," responded the Son, "come to the heavenly country, where all thy desires shall be accomplished, and thou wilt enjoy the solemnity of this day among the inhabitants of Heaven." Immediately the immense procession turned towards Heaven and passed through the air. Arrived at the august throne of the Most Holy Trinity, she prostrated herself and composed an admirable canticle of praise and thanksgiving, which included all the mysteries of the Incarnation and Redemption, with the victories of her Son over death and Hell. The Most High took great complacency in it, the Saints answered it by other canticles and glorified the Most High in this creature, so admirable, and all felt new joy at the sight of their Queen. The Divine Essence was manifested to her intuitively, and the Lord gave her entire possession of that glorious kingdom which had been prepared for her from all eternity.

On each year she received these favors and was asked if she wished to remain there, but her charity for the faithful pressed her to return to this valley of tears. Each year the Blessed Trinity received anew this sacrifice of charity for her neighbor, to the great admiration of all the heavenly court. All her prayers and demands in behalf of the Church and her children were heard and granted, to be accomplished throughout all succeeding centuries. The protection of this powerful Advocate would be still greater, if the sins of men did not prevent it. Then the Angels bore their Queen, in a chariot of light, back into her oratory, where prostrate on the ground she made most fervent thanksgiving.

St. John witnessed these marvels and frequently beheld the divine Mother environed with light, and as Mary would prostrate herself at the feet of the Evangelist to ask permission for the most trifling things, the Saint had frequent occasion of beholding and admiring her, to the great joy of his spirit. She considered the effects and benefits of the great feast of the Ascension, in order that she might more

worthily celebrate the Descent of the Holy Ghost.
During the nine days preceding this feast, she
earnestly begged the Lord to renew in her the ineffable gifts of the Holy Ghost.

When that day, so happy for the Church, arrived,
her desires were accomplished by the divine power;
for, at the same hour in which the Holy Ghost had
descended on the Church, assembled in the Supper-room, He again descended each year on the
divine Mother, His living temple. In this ineffable
favor she was assisted by millions of Angels, who
chanted hymns to the Holy Spirit, who renewed
her by a superabundance of gifts and an increase of
those she already possessed. She humbly thanked
the Lord for having by this descent completed the
work of the Redemption and begged Him to continue through all succeeding ages the effusion of
His grace and power on the Church, without regard
to the sins of men, and her prayers were granted
by the Holy Spirit.

To these feasts Mary added two others, one in
honor of the Angels, the other, in honor of the
Saints. For the first she prepared by canticles in
which she celebrated the work of their creation,
particularly that of sanctifying grace, and of their
glorification, the mysteries of which she fully understood, being the Mother of Wisdom. On the feast
itself she invited them all to glorify the Most High;
thousands of glorious spirits from every hierarchy
descended into her oratory and, during the entire
day, sang alternately with the Blessed Virgin in
honor of the Supreme Creator, who had manifested

Himself by the works of the creation—above all, in having created a Mother so pure and so holy.

For the feast of All Saints she prepared by long prayers and her accustomed exercises of devotion. On the feast the holy Patriarchs, Prophets and other Saints descended into her oratory, and she chanted new canticles because the death and Redemption of her Son had been efficacious in regard to the blessed. She rejoiced to behold so many assured of their eternal beatitude, and she blessed the Father of mercies. This festival she celebrated as Mistress of the Church, by whom, she foresaw, it would be solemnized in future ages.

From the first moment of her conception the most holy Mary had been continually occupied, and even her sleep had been no obstacle to her continuous application; but in the last years of her holy life she was indefatigable and worked with more than angelic activity. She seemed like the flame of a great conflagration in its activity, yet all that she accomplished seemed little to her earnest love.

Chapter 46

THE ARCHANGEL GABRIEL ANNOUNCES TO THE BLESSED VIRGIN HER HAPPY DEATH—OTHER MARVELS.

The Holy Virgin had attained her sixty-seventh year, without having interrupted, even for one instant, the course of her admirable and heroic works, stayed the aspirations of her heart or diminished the ardor of her love; on the contrary, her love increased in every moment of her existence, and she was in a manner spiritualized and divinized, so that the flames of her burning heart allowed her no rest. The Eternal Father desired His beloved daughter; the Incarnate Word, His dear Mother, and the Holy Ghost, His most pure Spouse. The Angels and Saints earnestly longed for the presence of their Queen, and all the heavens demanded their Empress, that her presence might complete their happiness and fill them with glory and joy. The most Holy Trinity sent the Archangel Gabriel, accompanied by many blessed spirits, to announce to their Queen at what time and in what manner she should pass to eternal glory. Entering her oratory, he found the holy Mother prostrate in the form of a cross, weeping and imploring mercy for sinners, but as if awakened by the melody of the Angels she raised herself to a kneeling posture to hear the embassy of the Lord. All the Angels bore crowns and palms in their hands; they were of different kinds, signifying the divers merits and rewards of the great Queen.

The Archangel having saluted her by the *"Ave Maria,"* continued: "The Omnipotent and the Holy of holies sends us to thy Majesty, to announce the happy end of thy pilgrimage. Only three years still remain ere thou shalt enter for all eternity into the glory of the blessed, who all desire thy presence." She received this agreeable news with ineffable joy, and prostrating herself on the earth, replied as at the Annunciation: "I am the handmaid of the Lord, be it done to me according to thy word." She begged the Angels to aid her in rendering thanks for such agreeable news, and began a new canticle, to which they responded during two hours; then she bade them pray the Lord to prepare her for her passage. The Archangel answered that she should be obeyed, and taking leave of her, they returned to Heaven. She remained prostrate, shedding tears of humility and joy, and said these words: "O Earth! I render thee thanks that thou hast borne me, unworthy as I am, during sixty-seven years. As I have been created of thee and in thee, so in thee and by thee I shall arrive to my desired end, the view and possession of my Creator."

From that moment she multiplied her pious exercises, as if, in the past, she had something to repair. This she did, not from the fear of death or on account of sin, which she had never committed, but from the ardor of her love and her vehement desire of eternal life. She multiplied those actions, not that she might arrive the sooner, but that she might enter richer and happier into the enjoyment of the Lord. During those three years she frequently sent her Angels to the Apostles dispersed throughout the world, in order to animate them to heroic enterprises, and she showed greater demonstrations of love to the faithful in Jerusalem and addressed to them pressing exhortations to remain steadfast in the Faith. Although she did not communicate to them her secret, she acted like one who was about to go on a journey and wished to leave everyone overwhelmed with benefits.

With St. John she acted differently. Kneeling at his feet one day, she asked his permission to speak; having obtained it, she said: "My lord and my son, thou knowest that among all creatures, I am the most deeply indebted to the divine power. Know then that Infinite Mercy has deigned to reveal to me that the term of my mortal life and my passage to eternal life will soon arrive; three years only remain of my exile. Then I supplicate thee, my master, to aid me, during this short time, in applying myself to attend and correspond to the immense benefits I have received; pray then for me, I beg of thee."

These words grieved the loving heart of St. John; he answered with deep emotion: "My Mother and my Queen, since thou art all-merciful, deign to help thy son who will be left alone and deprived of thy precious company." Overcome by grief and tears, he could say no more; the merciful Mother consoled and encouraged him; nevertheless, from that day, the Apostle was overwhelmed with sadness and grew faint and languid, like the flowers which fade at sunset.

Mary promised that, as a tender Mother, she would ever assist him, and she frequently prayed her Son to strengthen him, that the violence of his sorrow might not shorten his life. St. John revealed the sorrowful tidings to St. James, and both Apostles became more assiduous in visiting their august Mistress.

In those three years, the Almighty so disposed events that all nature began to be affected and gave evidence of mourning for the approaching death of her whose life added beauty to all created things. The Apostles, although dispersed throughout the world, felt an ardent desire to behold their Mother and Queen, while the faithful who were near her had a presentiment that they were about to lose their glory and their treasure. The skies, the animals, the birds and all creatures were moved and troubled. During the six months which preceded her death, the sun, moon and stars gave fainter light than ordinary, yet men were ignorant of the cause. St. John alone accompanied these signs by his tears, from which the faithful came to understand the reason. They therefore hastened to the Supper-room to render homage to their Queen; they threw themselves at her feet, asked her blessing and kissed the ground upon which her feet had trod. The Mother of Mercy consoled them all, and though their loss was inevitable, she was moved at their grief, and by her prayers obtained that all the children of the Church should receive the graces and privileges they desired.[1]

It would be impossible to describe the immense concourse of people who thronged to see her or the wonderful miracles which she operated during that time. She converted many to the True Faith, brought numbers back to the state of grace, provided for or remedied the wants of the miserable, frequently supplying them miraculously. She confirmed all in the fear of God, in the Faith and in obedience to the Church, and, as treasurer of the divine graces, poured them out upon the children of the Church before departing from them. Moreover, she consoled them all and promised to do much more for them when she should have entered Heaven.

Her most pure mind was raised by inconceivable raptures, from the flames of her love to the sphere of the Divinity, without her being able to arrest the impetuosity of her inflamed heart. To give some relief to its violence, she retired into solitude and satiated her desires with the Lord, saying: "My sweet Love, my only Good, Treasure of my soul, draw me to Thee by the odor of Thy perfumes; burst these mortal bonds which still detain me. Heavenly Spir-

---

1. Are not these the exact words of St. Bernard in the *Memorare*, in which he says that it is unheard of that anyone has ever addressed Mary without obtaining relief?

its, tell your Lord and mine the cause of my sorrow; tell Him that to please Him, I embrace suffering for exile; this is my desire. I cannot live in myself, but in God alone; if then He wishes me to live, how can I exist separated from Him who is my life? On one side He gives me life; on the other, He deprives me of it, because there is no life without love; how then can I exist without the life which is He whom I love alone. In this sweet violence I languish."

By these and similar words did the Holy Virgin appease the fire of her vehement love, to the admiration of the Angels who assisted and served her. Her Divine Son strengthened her by His visits, which became more frequent. She reiterated her prayers for the Church and for all the ministers who, in future ages, would preach the Gospel.

Among the marvels which the Lord operated for His holy Mother in the latter years of her life was one which was known, not only to the Evangelist, but to many others who approached her. It was that each time that Mary received Holy Communion, she remained during several hours surrounded with such splendor and light that she seemed to be transfigured like her Divine Son on Mt. Thabor.

With St. John's permission she went to visit the holy places, accompanied by the thousand Angels of her guard, and with many tears bade them a last adieu. She remained a longer time at Mt. Calvary; there she prayed for her beloved faithful, both present and future, and considering the dolorous death of her Son, sacrificed for the human race, the flame of her ardent charity became so strong that she would have died had not her Divine Son come to her in person and said: "My Mother and My Dove, coadjutrix in the redemption of men, thy requests have already reached My Heart. I promise that I will be ever liberal to men, and will continually aid them, that by their free will they may attain to eternal glory, with the merits of My Blood, provided they do not despise it. In Heaven thou shalt be their Mediatrix and Advocate, and I will pour out My merits and infinite mercies on those who shall obtain thy protection."

Prostrate at His feet, Mary adored her Divine Son, and having kissed the ground consecrated by the death of the Incarnate God, she commanded her Angels ever to guard and defend that sacred spot.

She returned to her oratory, where, with deep and tender emotion, she made her last adieu to the Church, saying: "O Holy Catholic Church, which in future ages shall be called Roman, my Mother and my Queen, thou hast been my only consolation during the time of my exile, my refuge and strength in suffering. Thou art my stay and my joy; in thee have I dwelt a stranger far from my country; thou hast kept me, since in thee I received the life of grace from thy Head and mine, Jesus, my Son and my Lord. Thou art to the faithful, His children, a sure guide to conduct them to eternal glory. Thou dost fortify them in their dangerous pilgrimage. Thou hast adorned and enriched me with beautiful ornaments, that I may enter into the nuptial chamber of the Spouse. In thee does thy Head dwell in the adorable Sacrament. Happy Church Militant, my beloved, the time has come in which I must leave thee. Deign to pour out on me thy precious gifts; wash me in the Blood of the Divine Lamb, which has been confided to thee, and which is capable of sanctifying many worlds immersed in sin. Holy Church, my honor and my glory, I leave thee in the mortal life, but shall find thee in the life glorious and eternal. From thence I will ever watch over thee tenderly and pray for thy prosperity and progress."

After this farewell the great Queen resolved to make her last will and testament, for which she asked the permission of the Lord, who deigned to confirm it by His presence. The Most Holy Trinity, accompanied by thousands of blessed spirits, descended into her oratory; a voice proceeding from the throne said: "Our spouse and Our elected one, make thy will according to thy desires, for it shall be accomplished and confirmed by Our divine power."

"Almighty and powerful Lord, Eternal God," answered she, with profound humility, "I, a worm of the earth, acknowledge and adore thee from the depths of my soul. Father, Son and Holy Ghost, three distinct Persons in one indivisible and eternal nature. I declare and say that this is my last will: I have no temporal goods to leave, for I have never possessed anything but Thee, my Sovereign Good; I thank all creatures that have sustained me, without any merit on my part. To John, my son, I leave two tunics and one mantle, which have served to cover me, that he may dispose of them as he pleases.

"I beg the earth to receive my body; I commit my soul, freed at length from the body, into Thy hands, O my God, that she may love Thee eternally. I make the Church, my Mother, heir of the merits I have acquired by means of Thy grace, and my sufferings, that they may serve for the exaltation of Thy Holy Name.

"Secondly, I offer them for the holy Apostles, and also for the priests who live now or shall live in future ages, that they may be worthy ministers who may edify and sanctify souls.

"Thirdly, I apply them for the spiritual good of those devoted to me, who will serve, invoke and intercede with me, that they may receive Thy grace, and in the end, life everlasting.

"Fourthly, I desire and pray that on account of my sufferings and works Thou wouldst consider Thyself indebted, and obliged to cause the unhappy children of Adam to come forth from the miserable state of sin, and from this moment I desire and wish to intercede for them in Thy divine presence, as long as the world shall last.

"This, my Lord and my God, is my last will, always subject to Thy good pleasure."

This testament was confirmed by the Most Holy Trinity and approved by Christ, who engraved in the heart of His Mother these words: "It shall be done according to thy will and thy orders."

Prostrate on the ground she returned thanks and prayed that the Apostles might be present at her death, that in her last passage they might pray for her and assist her with their blessing, and her prayer was granted. The Holy Trinity ceased to be visible, and the Humanity of Jesus Christ returned to Heaven.

Chapter 47

HAPPY DEATH OF THE MOST HOLY VIRGIN, AND BURIAL OF HER MOST PURE BODY.

The day on which the true Ark of the Covenant was to be placed in the temple of the heavenly Jerusalem was approaching, and three days previous the Apostles and disciples were, by the ministry of Angels, reassembled in the Supper-room. The corporal strength of the great Queen was already yielding to the violence of divine love, because the nearer she approached to the Sovereign Good, the more did she participate in the quality of love which is God Himself. The great Queen came to the door of her oratory to receive St. Peter, the Vicar of Jesus Christ; falling on her knees, she begged his blessing and returned thanks to the Most High for giving her so great a consolation; she did the same in regard to the other Apostles. Then she retired into her oratory, and St. Peter delivered a discourse to the disciples. They entered into her oratory to assist her; they found her kneeling on the little bed on which she had been accustomed to take her short repose; she appeared all brilliant with beauty, vested with celestial splendor and surrounded by her thousand Angels, who assisted her in visible forms. The natural state and appearance of her most pure body was the same as when she was thirty-three years old. She had no wrinkles on her face or hands, neither was she weakened nor emaciated by age, as happened to all the children of Adam. This was a special privilege of the most Holy Virgin, corresponding to that of her holy soul; it seemed to be the effect of her being exempt from the fault of Adam, the consequences of which were never felt by her most holy body, as they had never had access to her pure soul.

St. Peter and St. John knelt by her bedside, the others all around, according to their rank.

Looking at them with her accustomed modesty, the great Queen said, "My dear children, permit your servant to speak." St. Peter answered that all would attend to her words, but that as Mistress and Queen, she should first seat herself; she immediately obeyed, having begged their blessing, which they gave through obedience, shedding at the same time many tears at seeing such profound humility, united to such exalted greatness.

She arose and knelt before St. Peter, saying: "My lord, I supplicate thee as universal Pastor, to give me in thy name and that of the Church of which thou art the chief, thy holy benediction, and to forgive thy servant for having served thee so badly during this life, which she is now about to leave for that which is eternal. I beg that thou wilt allow John to dispose of my garments, that is, my two tunics, and give them to two poor girls, who have sometimes served me through charity."

After these words she prostrated herself and kissed the feet of St. Peter. Kneeling before St. John, she said: "John, my son and my lord, pardon me for not having exercised in thy regard all the duties of a mother, as I should have done, according to the office entrusted to me by the Lord. I most humbly thank thee for the kindness with which thou hast assisted me as a son, and now I beg thee give me thy blessing, that I may attain to the possession of my God." She continued to take her leave of the other Apostles, the disciples, and the rest of the faithful. Rising from her knees, she thus spoke: "My dear children and my masters, I have kept you all within my heart, and have ever loved you with tender charity, as being commended to me by my most dear Son, whom I have always considered in you all. To accomplish His Holy Will, I leave you to go to the heavenly dwelling, where, as your Mother, I promise you shall all be present to me in the clear light of the Divinity. I recommend to you my Holy Mother the Church, the exaltation of the Holy Name of God, the propagation of the evangelical law, the love of the words of my most holy Son and the remembrance of His life, Passion and death. Love the holy Church, and also love one another with your whole hearts. To you, Peter, holy Pontiff, I recommend my son John, and all the others."

She ceased to speak; her words, like burning arrows, penetrated the hearts of those present; shedding torrents of tears, they threw themselves upon the ground, and by their sighs and groans moved the merciful Mother so deeply that she could not resist the loving complaints of her dear children. After some time, she engaged them to pray with her and for her.

In the midst of this silence, the Incarnate Word descended from Heaven, seated on a royal throne of ineffable glory and accompanied by all the Saints and an infinite number of Angels, and the Supper-room was filled with light. The holy Mother kissed His feet and adored Him; this was the last act of worship and humility exercised in her mortal life, by which she surpassed those of all mankind; recollecting herself, she abased herself beneath the dust, although she was the Mother of God.

The Divine Son blessed her and, in the presence of this assembly of Saints, said: "Dear Mother, it is for thee to enter for all eternity into Paradise, where a throne is prepared for thee at My right hand. As My Mother, I caused thee to enter into the world pure and exempt from all stain of sin, so in leaving it, death shall have no power to touch thee. If, then, thou dost not wish to pass by it into eternal life, come with Me, without dying, to participate in the glory which thou hast merited." The Mother, with joyful countenance and bowed head, replied: "My Son and my Lord, I beg Thee to allow Thy Mother and servant to enter into eternal life by the gate common to all the children of Adam, and to Thee also, the true God."

The Lord approved this humble sacrifice, and the Angels began their celestial canticles, which were heard by all; and not only the oratory, but the whole house was filled with admirable splendor, so that, on account of it, the streets were filled with crowds of people who hastened from the city, the Lord permitting this, that there might be many witnesses of His Mother's glory.

When the Angels began to sing the first verse, "Come, my dove," she extended herself upon the bed, and the tunic seemed as if glued to her sacred body; with her hands joined and her eyes fixed on her Divine Son, she seemed all inflamed with the fire of divine love. When the Angels chanted: *Surge, propera, amica mea*—"Arise, make haste, my love"—she said to her Divine Son the same words that He had pronounced upon the Cross: "Lord, into Thy hands I commend my spirit," and having gently closed her pure eyes, the Holy Virgin expired.

Thus her death was the effect of love, without any other cause, and no malady of any kind. It was operated thus: the divine power suspended the miraculous course, by which until then she had been preserved in her natural strength, without being consumed by the supernatural ardor and sensible fire of her divine love; but this miracle having ceased, the fire of love produced its effect in consuming the moisture of the heart, and thus the natural life of her body was terminated.[1]

---

1. Some writers think that the Holy Virgin died at Ephesus, but this opinion is not sustained by any judicious and enlightened critic. The testimony of the most illustrious Doctors of the Church and the most solid proofs are in favor of what is given in this book.

Surrounded with immense glory, the soul of the pure Virgin passed to the right hand of her Son. To their great astonishment, those who had assisted at the death of Mary began to hear the chants of the Angels, from a distance, as if receding in the upper regions of the air. The virginal body, which had been the temple of the Holy Ghost, remained brilliant with light and splendor and exhaled a delicious perfume, which caused interior joy to the assistants. The thousand attendant Angels of the great Queen remained to guard the inestimable treasure.

The Apostles and disciples were for some time ravished out of themselves, and shed tears of mingled joy and sorrow. They sang hymns and canticles in praise of the august Mother.

This glorious death occurred on Friday the 13th of August, three hours before sunset, the age of the Blessed Mother being seventy years, wanting twenty-six days. This precious death was signalized by many miracles; the sun was eclipsed for a few hours; many birds entered into the dwelling, and by their plaintive cries seemed to mourn the death of their Queen; so remarkable were the evidences of their grief that many were moved to tears. The whole city was filled with astonishment, and all confessed the power of the Almighty. Many of the sick were healed, and all the souls in Purgatory were delivered, that they might accompany their merciful Mother to Heaven. At the same instant in which the Virgin Mother expired, three persons who dwelt near her also died, but in the unhappy state of mortal sin. When they appeared before the tribunal of

Jesus Christ, the Holy Mother begged grace and mercy for them; they were allowed to return to life, and having done penance for their sins, happily persevered in grace and were saved.[2]

The Apostles and disciples thought of burying the holy body in the valley of Jehoshaphat, where there was a new sepulchre prepared by divine providence. As the body of her Divine Son had been embalmed, they prepared precious ointments, according to the custom of the Jews, to do the same in regard to the holy body of the divine Mother; this charge they entrusted to the two young girls who had received the tunics of the great Queen. As they entered into the oratory, carrying spices and new linen to envelop the sacred body, they were stopped and blinded by its great splendor, so that they could not approach or behold it. Trembling with fear, they returned to tell the Apostles, who understood that this most pure body, which had been the Sacred Ark of the New Testament, might not be touched or moved, even by the hands of virgins. St. Peter and St. John, entering, beheld the splendor of the holy body and heard the divine harmony of the Angels, who sang: "God hails thee, Mary, full of grace; the Lord is with thee"; and others responded: "Virgin before childbirth, Virgin in childbirth, and Virgin after childbirth."

---

2. St. Liguori relates a similar fact in *The Glories of Mary*. As to the deliverance of the souls in Purgatory, many revelations say that they were all delivered in the great jubilee of the year 1300. Could the death of the Blessed Virgin have been less efficacious than a jubilee?

The Apostles, ravished with astonishment at these marvels, knelt and heard a voice which said: "Let no one uncover or touch the sacred body." They prepared a coffin, and the celestial splendor being somewhat diminished, the two Apostles approached, and with great veneration fastened the tunic around the sacred feet, without, however, touching them. Then raising it, they placed it in the coffin in the same position as it had lain on the bed. They found it to be extremely light, scarcely more than the weight of her clothing.

After the virginal body had been placed in the coffin, its splendor visibly decreased, so as to allow all the faithful to gaze upon the more than angelic beauty of the face and hands of their Mother, the Lord permitting this for their consolation. The wax tapers placed around it, although they continued to burn for three days, remained unconsumed. The Almighty also willed that the burial of His Mother and the prodigies by which it was accompanied should be known to all; therefore, He touched the hearts of the people of Jerusalem, and following the impulse of grace, the Jews and Gentiles ran to the sacred spot. At the mere sight of the venerable body, the sick were cured, demoniacs delivered, the afflicted consoled, and all present filled with joy and consolation.

The Apostles bore on their shoulders the coffin containing the propitiatory of divine favors; issuing from the dwelling, they proceeded through the city to the valley of Jehoshaphat, followed by an immense concourse of people, who extolled aloud the rare virtues and qualities of the glorious deceased. This was the visible procession. Let us speak of another, more beautiful and brilliant, but not visible to all. In the first rank were the thousand Guardian Angels of the Queen, continuing the celestial melody which was heard by the Apostles, disciples, and many other faithful; this they continued for three days without interruption.

There also descended from Heaven many millions of Angels and legions of the most sublime spirits; also the ancient patriarchs and prophets; in particular St. Joachim, St. Anne, St. Joseph, St. Elizabeth, St. John the Baptist and other Saints, sent to assist at the grand ceremony.

This magnificent procession, both visible and invisible, composed of the inhabitants of earth and of Heaven, advanced slowly onwards. All hearts were moved, for on this day the treasury of Divine Mercy was open. Not only were all the sick people of Jerusalem healed, all demoniacs delivered, all in tribulation consoled and strengthened, but a still greater number of blind Gentiles and obstinate Jews were enlightened and confessed the truth of the evangelical faith; coming to the knowledge of Jesus Christ, they confessed aloud with many tears that He was the true God, the Redeemer of the world, and begged for Baptism. Still more, the Apostles, in carrying the most pure body, felt admirable effects of divine light and ineffable interior joy.

All those present were amazed at the fragrance which issued from the sacred body, at the angelic music they heard, at the miracles they saw operated before their eyes, and being greatly moved, struck their breasts with contrition, acknowledging Mary to be the true Mother of God, and God to be grand and omnipotent in this creature. At length they arrived at the blessed tomb, in the valley of Jehoshaphat, and while they sang hymns of praise, St. Peter and St. John laid the sacred deposit in the tomb; they covered it with fine linen, and reverently closed the sepulchre.

The Saints returned to Heaven, and the thousand Guardian Angels continued their celestial harmonies. All the people returned to the city; the Apostles and disciples re-entered the Supper-room, which venerable sanctuary retained an agreeable odor for an entire year. The Apostles agreed that in turns, by two and two, they would watch the holy sepulchre of their Mistress, during the time the celestial melodies should be continued, and that the others should apply themselves to catechize, instruct and baptize the converts. St. Peter and St. John never departed from the tomb, and the others returned to visit it both by day and night.

We cannot pass over in silence the concourse of irrational creatures which came to the holy spot. Birds sang on the tomb their plaintive melodies, and the beasts of the forest gave evidences of their sorrow for the great loss of the Mistress of the Universe.

Chapter 48

TRIUMPHANT ENTRY OF THE AUGUST
SOUL OF THE MOST HOLY VIRGIN INTO
HEAVEN—ASSUMPTION OF HER BODY—
HER CORONATION.

No sooner had the august and incomparable soul of the Holy Virgin been separated from the body than Jesus Christ placed it at His right hand on the throne, and the immense procession of Angels and Saints turned towards Heaven. The Redeemer entered with His Mother, all brilliant and glorious, without having subjected her to the particular judgment on the gifts and favors she had received on account of the promise made to her when she was exempted from Original Sin, as elected Queen, as a privileged one, having no share in the miseries of the children of Adam.

From the first instant of her conception she was a clear and resplendent aurora; surrounded by the rays of the Divine Son, she surpassed the brilliancy of the most ardent Seraphim; again by the union of the Word with the holy humanity she had been so elevated that, as it were, she touched the Divinity. It was therefore suitable and necessary that she should be His companion throughout all eternity, and that there should be the greatest possible resemblance between the Son and the Mother.

Under this august title, the Divine Redeemer presented her before the divine throne and said: "My Eternal Father, My dear Mother, Thy beloved Daughter, and the cherished Spouse of the Holy Spirit, comes to receive eternal possession of the crown and glory which We have prepared in recompense of her merits. Among the children of Adam she is as a rose among thorns, spotless, pure and beautiful, worthy of being received into Our hands. She is Our elected one, chosen and singular, to whom We have given grace and participation in Our perfections, beyond that of ordinary creatures. In her We have deposited the treasures of the Divinity; she has found grace in Our sight, and in her We have taken Our complacency. It is then just that she should receive the recompense and reward due to her as My Mother, and as during her life she has been as like to Me as is possible to a pure creature, so she ought to resemble Me in glory, and be placed on the throne of Our Majesty, so that where is Sanctity by Essence should also be she who has received the greatest participation in it."

The Eternal Father and the Holy Ghost immediately approved this decree of the Incarnate Word, and the soul of Mary was raised to the right hand of her Son, on the royal throne of the Most Holy Trinity. It is the most sublime excellence of our holy Queen to be thus placed on the very throne of the Divinity, and hold the rank and title of Sovereign

Empress, while all the other inhabitants of Heaven are the ministers and servants of the Most High.

It is impossible to express the intensity of the accession of joy which the Blessed received on this solemn day. They intoned canticles of praise to the Most High for the incomprehensible glory of His Daughter, Mother and Spouse, in whom they exalted the work of His all-powerful hand. Although the Lord could not receive new interior glory, since, from all eternity, it is infinite, yet, the exterior manifestations of His complacency in the happy accomplishment of His eternal decrees were greater on this day, for from the throne there proceeded a voice which said: "All Our desires and Our divine Will are accomplished in the glory of Our Beloved, and all has been done to the entire satisfaction of Our Complacency."

On the third day in which the most pure soul of the Virgin Mother enjoyed eternal glory, the Lord manifested to the heavenly court His Will that her great soul should return to the world and reassume its body, in order that she might be raised to the divine throne both in body and soul, without waiting for the General Resurrection. All applauded the divine decree; the Redeemer Himself descended from Heaven with the glorious soul of His Mother by His side, and accompanied by the Saints and blessed spirits.

Having arrived at the sepulchre, at the sight of the virginal temple of the Most High, the Lord thus spoke to the Saints: "My Mother was conceived without stain of sin, in order that of her pure virginal and immaculate substance I might assume the humanity with which I came into the world, already redeemed from the slavery to which it had been subjected. My Flesh is the flesh of My Mother, she also cooperated with Me in the work of the Redemption; therefore as I have arisen, I must raise her, and in the same moment in which I arose, for it is My will that she be like to Me in all things."

Amid the canticles chanted by the Saints for the new benefit, the holy soul of Mary, at the command of her Divine Son, re-entered into her most pure body, and it arose from the dead. In this resurrection her body was vested with the four glorious qualities of light, agility, subtility and impassibility, each of which corresponded to the glory of the soul from which they took their origin. The Holy Virgin with these qualities issued from the sepulchre both in body and soul, without removing the stone, leaving in the tomb only her clothes and the linen.

It is impossible to describe here the light, splendor and admirable beauty of her glory; it will suffice to consider that as the divine Mother gave to her most holy Son a human form in her virginal womb, and gave it most pure and spotless for the Redemption of the world, so, in return for this gift, the Lord gave her in this resurrection and new birth a glory and a beauty like to His own. In this mysterious and Divine correspondence, each gave as far as was possible, for the Virgin engendered Jesus Christ like to herself as far as possible, and Jesus Christ, in raising her, communicated to her His glory, as far as a pure creature is capable of receiving it.

The magnificent procession departed from the sepulchre chanting celestial melodies and ascended through the region of the air to the empyreal Heaven. This occurred on the Sunday after her death, at midnight, the same moment at which Christ had arisen; hence none of the Apostles were aware of the miracle, except those who were watching the tomb at the time. The Saints and Angels re-entered Heaven in the order in which they had descended on earth; after them came the glorious Redeemer, and at His right hand, the Queen Mother, whose garments were magnificently adorned with gold and precious ornaments; the Blessed were filled with wonder and astonishment at the sight of her admirable beauty, and broke forth into new canticles of admiration and joy. Then were heard those mysterious eulogiums of Solomon: "Go forth, O daughter of Sion, and see your Queen whom the stars of morning praise, and whom the children of the Most High bless. Who is that cometh up from the desert as a column of smoke, composed of every perfume? Who is this that seems like the aurora, more beautiful than the moon, bright as the sun, and terrible as an army in battle array? Who is this that cometh up from the desert, leaning on her Beloved, and overflowing with delights? Who is this in whom the Divinity itself has found greater complacency than in all other creatures, and whom He has raised above all to the throne of His inaccessible light and majesty? O marvel, never before beheld in Heaven! O prodigy of an omnipotent

God, who thus glorifies and exalts her!"

Vested with this wonderful glory, the Holy Virgin arrived at the throne of the Divinity, and the three Divine Persons received her into Their eternal and indissoluble embrace. She seemed as if absorbed within the three Divine Persons, and as if submerged in that infinite ocean of the abyss of the Divinity; the Saints heard these words of the Eternal Father: "Our Daughter Mary has been elected and chosen by Our eternal Will as the only and singular one among all creatures, and she is also the first in Our delights. She has never degenerated from her title of Daughter, which in the Divine Understanding has been given her from all eternity; therefore she has a right to Our eternal kingdom, of which she is to be acknowledged and crowned the legitimate Sovereign and Queen."

The Incarnate Word said: "To My true and natural Mother belong all the creatures that I have created and redeemed, and all that I possess as King, she must also possess as legitimate Queen."

The Holy Ghost said: "By the title of My only and elected Spouse, to which she has corresponded with perfect fidelity, the crown of Queen is also due to her for all eternity."

After these words the three Divine Persons placed on the august head of the most holy Virgin a crown of glory, which far exceeded any that ever has or ever shall be awarded to a creature. At the same instant a voice came from the throne, saying: "Our friend and Our chosen one among all other creatures, Our kingdom belongs to thee. Thou art the

Sovereign, the Queen and the Mistress of the Seraphim, the Angels Our ministers, and of the entire creation. Guard, then, command and reign happily over them. In Our supreme consistory we give thee empire, majesty and dominion, because although filled with grace above all creatures, thou hast humbled thyself in thy mind, and hast always placed thyself in the last place. Receive now the exalted rank which is thy due, and participate in the Sovereign dominion exercised by the Divinity over all of the earth, and by the power which We give thee, thou shalt hold Hell in subjection. All shall fear and obey thee, even in the infernal caverns. Thou shalt rule over the earth and the elements. We place in thy hands the virtues and effects of all natural causes and their preservation, so that thou mayest dispose of the influences of the heavens, and of the fruit of the earth, of all that exists or shall exist. Distribute them according to thy good pleasure, and Our Will shall ever be ready to accomplish thine. Of the Church Militant thou art the Empress, Queen, Mistress, Protectress, Advocate and Mother. Thou shalt be the friend, patroness and protectress of all Our friends, the just. Console them, fortify and fill them with every good, if by their devotion they render themselves worthy. Thou art the depository of all Our divine benefits, the treasury of all Our graces. Into thy hands We remit the help and favors of Our grace, so that thou mayest dispense them; for We will grant nothing to the world but what shall pass through thy hands, and We will refuse nothing which thou mayest desire to grant. Grace shall be spread abroad on thy lips, for all that thou shalt wish and ordain in Heaven and on earth; Angels and men shall obey thee in all places, because all that is Ours belongs to thee, as thou hast always belonged to Us, and thou shalt reign with Us for all eternity."

For the execution of this eternal decree, the Omnipotent ordered all the heavenly court to render obedience and homage to her as their Queen, and they promptly obeyed, acknowledging themselves her servants and vassals and venerating her with a worship, filial fear and respectful veneration like to that with which they adore the Lord. Thus they relatively paid the same respect to His august Mother; and the small number of the Saints who were in Heaven both in body and soul prostrated themselves and venerated their Queen by corporal homage. The Empress of the heavens was thus glorified and crowned amidst these magnificent demonstrations, which gave great glory to her, new joy to the Blessed, and a subject of complacency to the Most Holy Trinity. She added new glory to all the heavenly Jerusalem, particularly to St. Joseph, her chaste spouse, to her parents and relations, but above all to her thousand Guardian Angels. The Saints beheld in her most pure heart a little globe, as it were, of singular beauty and splendor, which caused and shall eternally cause them admiration and particular joy; this was the recompense and proof of her having worthily preserved in her breast the Incarnate Word under the sacramental species, and having received Him worthily with purity and sanctity without any defect or least shadow of imperfection, but with great devotion, love and worship. As to the other recompenses corresponding to her heroic and singular virtues, it is impossible for us to form any worthy conception of them. We will only say that this resurrection took place on the 15th of August, her most pure body having been in the sepulchre thirty-six hours, the same as that of her Divine Son.

The Apostles and disciples, particularly St. Peter and St. John, guarded the sepulchre both night and day, and remarking that the heavenly music could no longer be heard, they understood that the divine Mother was arisen and had been translated into Heaven, both in body and soul, like her Divine Son. They re-assembled the disciples and the faithful, opened the sepulchre and found it empty. St. Peter venerated the tunic and the linen, as did the others also.

Thus they were fully assured of the resurrection and Assumption of the Holy Virgin into Heaven. They celebrated this new wonder with tears of mingled joy and sorrow, and sang hymns and psalms to praise and glorify the Lord and His divine Mother. Divided between feelings of astonishment and tenderness, they gazed on the sepulchre as if unable to retire from it; then an Angel of the Lord, descending from Heaven, said: "Men of Galilee, why are you astonished? Your Queen and ours lives already both in body and soul, in Heaven, where she shall reign forever with Christ. She has sent me to you to confirm this truth and say to you on her part that she again recommends to you the Church, the conversion of souls and the propagation of the Gospel of Jesus Christ, to which ministry she wishes you to return immediately, as He has commanded you. From the highest Heaven she will watch over and protect you."

By these words the Apostles were reanimated, and in their apostolic career they frequently recognized the all-powerful protection of the Queen of Heaven, but particularly at the hour of their martyrdom, for she then appeared to each, assisted him as a merciful Mother and presented his soul to the Lord, as she will also do for all those who will serve her in life and invoke her in death.

If you have enjoyed this book, consider making your next selection from among the following . . .